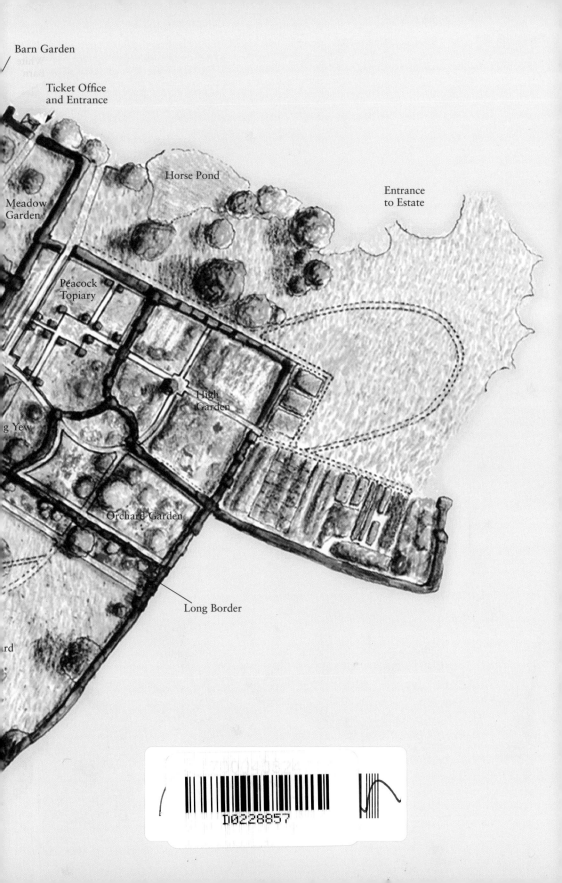

Barn Garden

Ticket Office
and Entrance

Meadow
Garden

Horse Pond

Entrance
to Estate

Peacock
Topiary

High
Garden

g Yew

Orchard Garden

Long Border

rd

Dear Friend
and Gardener

Dear Friend and Gardener

Letters on Life and Gardening

*Christopher Lloyd
and Beth Chatto*

F

FRANCES LINCOLN LIMITED
PUBLISHERS

Frances Lincoln Limited
www.franceslincoln.com

FOREWORD

From Beth Chatto
Christopher Lloyd and I first met about 20 years ago. It came
about through a difference of opinion. On first reading his book
The Well-Tempered Garden, I was entertained, amused, informed
again and again of things I had forgotten, or things I had never
known, tipped head-over-heels by controversial ideas, led on by
an opinionated style of writing – which far from being off-putting,
became addictive – but one thing troubled me. He didn't have any
time for bergenias, a group of plants I can't garden without! So I
wrote him a letter. He replied inviting me to lunch. This was the
beginning of our friendship, based on similar values and interests
but above all on our passion for plants. Our gardening has been
broadened, I think, by our enthusiasm for other forms of art,
including music and cooking – the whole activated by our need
for other people, their responses and input into what we do.

Yet we garden from almost opposite starting points.
Christopher's garden, historic Great Dixter, is splendid
architecturally, both itself and the fine old farm buildings now an
integral part of the garden design. Together with ramparts of yew
hedging, domes and archways to provide a framework, all are a
picture in themselves, timeless, unchanging. Within this framework
Christopher experiments with exciting, sometimes revolutionary
ideas which both enchant and shock. That is good. Every gardener
is an individual, borrowing or rejecting ideas as they fit their
character and situation.

I have been gardening for 54 years, influenced in particular
by my husband Andrew's life-long study of the natural homes of
plants. For the first 18 years of our married life we gardened in
the home of my late mother-in-law where I learnt to bring up our
two daughters, Diana and Mary, discovered which plants would

or would not put up with dry chalky boulder clay, and helped my husband run our fruit farm at Elmstead Market, seven miles away. Although I was not aware of it at the time, I was gaining valuable experience, attempting to handle myself and other people and master some of the problems in running a business – all needful when it came to starting my own nursery. I had no formal horticultural training, but on the whole I think that has not proved a handicap. Further inspiration and encouragement came from a 36-year-long friendship with the late artist-gardener Sir Cedric Morris, whose plant collection was legendary.

In 1960 my long-hoped-for dream was achieved when we moved into our newly built home on the farm. There was no traditional farmhouse, so we tucked a simple split-level house into the low gravel bank facing an overgrown hollow. Apart from a few ancient oaks there were no remarkable features. The site was wasteland, a wilderness lying between our farm and our neighbours. It consisted of a long spring-fed hollow where the soil lay black and waterlogged, surrounded by sun-baked gravel, situated in one of the driest parts of the country. But it was the extreme variation in growing conditions, from starved gravel to soggy bog, which intrigued us, the possibility lying before us of growing plants adapted to problem areas. Now, 36 years later, we have a series of contrasting yet harmonizing gardens, each based, after trial and error, on plants adapted by nature to different situations.

For me it has been a love affair and lifework to make a garden. During this time our family increased by six grandchildren and now includes my staff and students from around the world. A young Japanese girl, Yuko Tanabe, has been studying here over the past year. Unknown to me, or to Christo, she had been visiting Dixter as part of her training to be a garden designer. She expressed surprise that Christo and I were exchanging letters, and were indeed friends – 'because you are so different'. I replied that it was because we each painted our own canvas in our own individual way that our friendship had remained alive and invigorating. At that moment, looking up through the treetops blown bare now of autumn leaves, I noticed the young *Paulownia tomentosa*, planted about seven years ago, flaunting tip shoots crowded with beige-velvet buds against a pale blue sky. 'Look Yuko,' I said, 'this is the first year it has made flower buds.' She answered, 'Christopher is the magician, you are the mother.' I liked that.

Beth Chatto
Elmstead Market, 1998

From Christopher Lloyd

Unlike my correspondent, I did not have to wrest a garden from a wilderness, nor, for that matter, create a large nursery, with the attendant anxieties of a large staff, whom Beth cares about as though a part of her own family.

Great Dixter, where I was born in 1921, has always been my home. My parents bought the property in 1910. Edwin Lutyens (later Sir Edwin) restored the 15th-century manor house and supervised the additions, which have remained unchanged. He, too, designed the gardens, apart from the Sunk Garden, which was made after the First World War to my father's design. So the fabric was all instated before I appeared on the scene.

After the Second World War, I took a horticultural degree (B.Sc. Hort.) at Wye College, University of London, and continued there for another four years as an assistant lecturer. I then returned home with the idea of making a living from that base. A love of literature and of letter-writing, instilled by my mother, enabled me to start writing on gardening subjects. My first article (on *Lobelia cardinalis*) was published in 1952 and my first book, *The Mixed Border*, in 1957. I also started a small plant nursery, which I have deliberately kept small so as not to have the anxieties that size brings.

I should explain that I had four brothers and a sister, all of whom moved out of the parental home, though one brother remained on the estate at Little Dixter, and looked after the business side of opening the house and garden to the public, which gradually became of increasing importance. I am now the sole survivor of my generation, none of whom showed the slightest interest in gardening. I did from the start, and my mother was a passionate gardener. During the seven years when I was at Wye College (only 25 miles from Dixter), I would leave her weekly instructions on how to keep the garden going in my absences. She remained mobile to the last week of her 91-year life, dying in 1972. After that I was on my own, but I did not rattle around in a huge barn of a house, as some people supposed. I believed that it should entertain many friends and relations, especially young people, glad to get away from their parental homes but as yet without homes of their own.

With visitor numbers currently up to an annual figure of 35,000; myself writing weekly articles for *Country Life* magazine (since 1963) and *The Guardian*, as well as many others, and a book every other year or so; the nursery, thanks to Fergus Garrett's energy and organization, becoming much more productive without employing much more staff; that staff being helpful and positive in their attitudes – one way and another we are quite a healthy as well as happy enterprise.

Fergus, a friend since his student days, became my head gardener in 1994 and has made possible all sorts of changes in the garden, mainly in terms of planting rather than structure. All this has enabled the financing of major repairs to the house and outbuildings, for it is my main object in life (besides enjoying it!) to pass Dixter on to the next generation in good order.

So that's about the sum of it. I realize that I have been lucky and privileged, but I try to deserve my luck by taking my responsibilities seriously. Dixter is a lovely place to live in and for others it is an oasis.

Beth and I have been friends for many years, visiting and writing to or telephoning each other; in 1987, we went round the world together, taking in conferences in Melbourne and Toronto, so the writing of an organized series of letters has been no shock. Speaking for myself, I am most grateful to Frances Lincoln for undertaking the publication of this correspondence. There were tensions in the first months of Beth's and my writing to one another, in part because the publishers indicated that, as these letters would mainly appeal to a garden-minded section of the public, it should concentrate more on gardening and less on 'elitist' (as some might see it) matters such as visits to Glyndebourne Opera or my receiving an honorary doctorate. We (Beth and I) disagreed, feeling that a rounded picture of our lives would of necessity include much that is non-horticultural. This tension disturbed us for a while, but we soon settled down, receiving more encouraging reactions from the editors. May our current excellent relations with them long continue.

Christopher Lloyd
Great Dixter, 1998

– ❦ –

Addendum. In October of last year I was diagnosed as having Parkinsonism and some references are made to this in our letters. This was a mistaken diagnosis: my illness proved to be both more serious and more treatable, and a recent triple bypass operation has left me feeling better, temporarily weak, but optimistic.

INTRODUCTION
From Fergus Garrett

This is an extraordinary book, an exchange of letters between two great friends and two of the greatest gardeners of all time, Christopher Lloyd and Beth Chatto.

Christo (as he was known to his friends) was one of life's great characters, a true maverick with magic at his fingertips. He was born and gardened most of his life at Great Dixter, a medieval manor house restored and added to by Sir Edwin Lutyens. Lutyens also created the gardens – a masterpiece in design – a series of rooms compartmentalised in lines of yew and incorporating the old farm buildings into the frame. All this set in the rolling East Sussex countryside with woodlands and meadows lapping at its shores.

For over fifty years Great Dixter was Christo's experimental ground and inspiration for his countless books and articles. Never one to sit still, his gardening was laced with new discoveries, setting trends and often challenging conventions. He loved colour and put together exhilarating and unusual combinations, always pushing boundaries and sparking reaction from his public. Christo loved life and lived it to the full, his house constantly brimming with guests young and old. He collected and cultivated people, with good food and rich recipes from Jane Grigson, fresh fish from Hastings, and vegetables pulled from his garden gracing his table. Life at Dixter under Christo was lively, vibrant and entertaining.

Beth is arguably the most influential gardener of modern times. Inspired by her late husband Andrew's life-long research into the natural associations of plants in the wild, Beth was able to transform problem areas by choosing plants adapted by nature to thrive in challenging situations, too dry, too wet, or too shady. Her influence and inspiration is widespread. Turning a tangled wasteland, overgrown with blackthorn, brambles and willows around their split level home in Essex into a plantsman's paradise, she and Andrew masterfully overcame the extreme conditions of their site – transforming the dusty dry gravel beds and sodden bog into a garden. Beth's painterly eye has shaped the most intricate and sophisticated interlocking tapestries and contrasting textures of a community of a wide range of plants all living in harmony. With a love for good music, the arts and elegant cooking, and an interest in people, Beth's life shared a degree of common ground with Christo. But, their gardens and gardening styles were quite different and perhaps this was at the root of their successful friendship. As Beth rightly says, they were not standing in each other's light and so a deep and longstanding relationship developed.

Both Christo and Beth are great teachers. They are also acutely observant, have a great command of English, and find descriptive language incredibly easy. Their letters are conversational as well as educational bringing their respective worlds alive. It is clear that they have great respect for one another but don't always agree and the resulting discussion is always so interesting.

Christo passed away in 2006 and the horticultural world lost one of its great masters. Beth is now nearly ninety years old but still an inspiration for like-minded gardeners from all over the world. Both continue to enrich our lives through their words on paper, delving deep into the world of plants and life in and around their respective gardens.

Fergus Garrett,
Great Dixter, 2013

Part One

Sunday 14 January

Dear Beth,

I'm just getting over flu. Spent the whole of last night in front of my fire because I couldn't stop coughing, the night before, when lying down. That worked well.

I can think again. Luckily it's a no-visitors weekend.

Well, now, visitors, and my mind is on the question of watering in time of drought. I visited Sissinghurst, I should think late August or early September, before the rains had had their effect – September was our second wettest month, with nearly 127mm (5in) of rain. The lawns were brilliant green. One of their staff is employed for lawn care, so I suppose it would be unfair on him to allow it otherwise. Tony Lord, in his recently published book on Sissinghurst, gives laborious details on lawn care under difficult conditions, such as the Moat Walk, which everyone walks on.

I can understand the situation, and I also realize that the public expects perfection in lawns as their right. More than half the visitors are National Trust members and they feel they have a share in Sissinghurst's reputation. My lawns were dreadful at the time (I do practically nothing for them anyway) and I'm sure that in similar circumstances, Vita Sackville-West's were only a little better. But public numbers and public expectations are a great burden. What rather annoyed me, however, was that the borders were dry and parched and that there were very few nice plant groupings for that time of the year – only isolated incidents. Clearly, the lawns were considered more important. That seems to me to place good sense on its head. I'm sure there were hosepipe bans for private gardens, but they would not apply to a garden or nursery or potato field run for commercial profit.

In your area, I'm not sure that such restrictions were in operation, because I understand that, surprisingly, the Norfolk Water Board is so efficient that they have succeeded in providing water for everyone. I suppose if you start out with a particularly low rainfall, you know where you stand and act accordingly, whereas a county like Yorkshire, with an expectation of high rainfall, will be caught napping when surprised by a drought.

I know that your garden was suffering, in August, because you told me so, and you were about to relent when David (Ward) said, 'No Beth, not now that we have come so far.' I think David was wrong (though I know it was what you wanted to hear).

To what extent are we gardening for ourselves, for the public or for our plants? My own feeling is that principles can go too far. THEY GET IN THE WAY. Obviously I'm not such a moral person as you. But when I see plants suffering, it's like having a pet animal that you've neglected to feed. But the animal will touch your heart by mewing or whining. The poor plant cannot do that.

Your argument is that we must instruct by setting an example. You have been a teacher from an early age and so was I. There is nothing I like better than putting my precepts across, by example. But, but, but . . . Those unhappy plants. You can turn your eyes away from them; you can tell yourself, truly in many cases, that they will recover; you can tell the public that this is an exercise in what they too can achieve without water; you can also tell them that it is a lesson on which plants to grow if drought is your expectation. But none of that truly adds up to a happy situation, when, as happens more years than not, there is the stress of drought. I know you have done all you can to minimize its effects by giving the plants lovely water-holding goodies, such as mulches and manures, but I think that a point should come when one feels strong (not weak) enough to face the facts. It is your garden; they are your plants. When they are happy, you are happy.

Today has been beautiful and was made for me by finding the first two crocuses, not just there but open to the sun. They were self-made hybrids of *C. chrysanthus*. I love crocuses and tulips best of all the spring bulbs and for the same reason: that they respond so gladly to encouragement from sunshine. Gazanias and other South African daisies are similar, later on. There was also a wide open celandine, nestling against the circular steps.

Thank you so much for your last, sympathetic, letter. I couldn't smell the geranium leaf but am told that it was of lemon.

Do keep an eye on the evening sky (when there is one) during the next few months. Venus will be making a more glamorous appearance than it usually does; this happens perhaps once in eight years.

Much love, from Christo

– ❀ –

Friday 19 January

Dear Christo,

I am sorry about the flu. It must have been pretty bad to keep you up all night, but tell me how you beat it off so quickly and efficiently? Perhaps a drop or two of the pure malt beside your chair makes a good antibiotic.

January seems to get a lot of people down, in spirit, if not with sniffles. I have avoided those so far, and your letter has given me a real kick start – just what I needed, and doubtless just what you intended.

Concerning whether to irrigate or not, of course I do not disapprove of all watering. That would be hypocritical, since we must irrigate the nursery crops and do water parts of the garden, such as the Wood Garden, in very dry times. But my thinking on the subject is based on the assumption that water is our most precious commodity as the world population continues to explode, and modern demands for water are often in excess of actual need. Combine this with the likelihood of hotter and drier summers to come, then surely we must be prepared to reconsider some of our gardening practices.

Which brings me to the recently made Gravel Garden and subject of your letter. Last summer was our stiffest test so far. It was anguish for me during the last weeks of the drought, wondering how far I could go, watching my plants subjected to

17

oven-like wind and no rain for eight weeks. The contrast with how it looked in June (or with gardens sprinkled nightly) was painful. Not what you might expect from a garden open to the public. But for me it is not a public garden, but my private garden which I love to share with like-minded gardeners.

We put up a notice saying this part of the garden is an experiment without irrigation, to see which plants will survive without stress, hoping it may be helpful to those who have hosepipe bans.

Most of the plants were selected for endurance, but I expected we might lose some and was prepared to make changes. When temperatures ranged between 25 and 35°C (77 and 95°F) and no measurable rain fell, the Gravel Garden – compared to the burnt lawns and roadsides in the vicinity – remained furnished with interesting shapes, textures and tones of scented foliage. There were few flowers, I admit, but many seed heads and grasses, while the winding gravel pathways were the shining focal point, my dried-up river bed ebbing and flowing as the plants expanded or retreated.

'It looks and smells exactly like the Mediterranean,' said a 90-year-old botanist to one of my staff near by. I could have hugged him.

One man did write and ask for his money back. This seemed a little hard since visitors can pass through the Gravel Garden without paying, before they reach the main garden. Here, some borders were watered, but we didn't water grass walks anywhere, and on the higher dry land they did look like Ryvita.

On the day the rains came, Saturday 1 September, a coachload of ladies arrived at 11.00am, taken unawares by summer's hasty retreat. Unsuitably clad, they prinked around the nursery in thin shoes and thinner dresses, but soon left. The rain continued to fall steadily and gently all day, every cell in my body and the garden responding thankfully. A few days later an envelope dropped on my desk containing 53 tickets, and a letter requesting a refund from these ladies, since they had been disappointed by wet weather!

The talking point across the country for the next few days was how amazingly the grass had revived. Naturally people become concerned when it has looked stone-dead for weeks, but in my experience it always is the first to recover. For me there were more exciting resurrections in the Gravel Garden. The tiny fern-like leaves of *Leptinella squalida* had been reduced to grey fluff, while *Phuopsis stylosa* had left behind a network of strawy stems creeping among the gravel. Such gaps appearing in a stone mulch are not so unsightly as when plants disappear against bare soil.

Within days of the rain, both plants were completely restored, brand-new carpets flaunting spring green. Caryopteris, sedums and perovskia made waves of colour; the flowers were back.

Sorry I have spent over-long on drought and irrigation, but for me, it is a philosophy of gardening rather than a matter of morals or principles, and so may well run like a thread through our chain of letters.

Let me tell you quickly of my New Year decorations. The day after Twelfth Night, I picked branches of *Salix* 'Tortuosa' and put them into two large jugs on a low table lit by the window behind. I enjoy pruning these tangled shapes to make curious and satisfying silhouettes against the daylight, or at night when the pale curtains are pulled behind them. To anchor them to the jugs' rims I used pieces of *Magnolia grandiflora* which had been broken by heavy snowfall before Christmas. Low winter sunlight, when it deigns to appear from beneath the dustbin lid of cloud, transforms these simple groups, glistening along the polished stems of willow, warming the rusty backs of the magnolia leaves. Tiny green leaves are now breaking from pointed buds. As they twist and lengthen they will form a pale haze of green leaf before there is any sign of life on the bare branches outside.

Hope you are feeling much better.

Much love, Beth

— ❧ —

Saturday 20 January

Dear Beth,

Something I must get off my (wheezing) chest: is it any use
my keeping a seat warm for you at Glyndebourne next July?
It's Strauss's *Arabella* on Monday 22 July. A revival of a lovely
production which I've seen several times. Fergus is coming,
Pip Morrison (the landscape design student you met in August,
when he was volunteering here), and John and Johanna Watkins
(he let drop that Glyndebourne was somewhere he'd love to go).

My bug won't leave me. I've had a fever for 11 days, now, so
am at last turning to modern medicine and antibiotics (but why
aren't my own antibodies at work?).

Thank you for your letter. 'Modern demands for water are
often in excess of actual need', you write, and that is very true.
Phil Clayton's neighbour, near Guildford, left his sprinkler on all
night, last August, on the lawn, I think. But when you continue
about the likelihood of hotter and drier summers to come (I don't
think we really know much about that) and that surely we must be
prepared to reconsider some of our gardening practices, I wonder
just what is going on in the back of Beth's mind. More gravel and
xerophyte gardens, with an exemplar financed by the local water
authority? Little informative plaques telling the visitor that all this
has been done without turning to mains water supplies? A pat
of congratulation for the public-spirited initiator of this and that
water-conserving enterprise?

I confess to being unattracted to the concept of gardening with
a moral implication. It puts a dampener on going all out to garden
full-bloodedly in whatever way appeals to you most. You would,
or should need to be terribly disapproving of my old rose garden,
turned tropical. You're not; bless you. You enjoy it the way I do
and want you to. An expression of exuberance, but certainly heavy
on water. Still, if we're to have hotter summers, I am assembling
the right sort of plants to take advantage of it!

Perhaps, after all that talk, we're about to have another winter like 1947? That started just around now and today the temperature has dropped several degrees.

I had a long letter from Michael McCoy, from where he works near Melbourne. He asks after you.

Helen Dillon has been lecturing out there. Michael is an intellectual and starved for input and good conversation in which views can be aired and developed. He always seizes an opportunity:

'. . . but I upset her at the interval when I asked her to elaborate on her opinion that the misty, quiet light of Ireland restricted their use of bright colours, but that we should be able to use them lavishly in our bright clear light. She was immediately defensive and put up all the usual arguments that the colours look too gaudy etc. I suggested that the opposite view was also logical, i.e. if we live in a dark gloomy climate let's have as much bright lively colour as possible to cheer us up. I don't understand why she was so affronted, but when a famous rose writer came up and asked if she could top up Helen's coffee, she said she would go and do it herself.

' "But if I do it you can keep talking to Michael," said the rosarian.

' "This conversation is finished," said Helen with emphasis, then went to top up her coffee. I think Helen finds bright colours hard to handle herself, and looks for a boost from theory.'

Poor Michael. Yet he should have got a really stimulating conversation. I think he's dead right and so does Fergus. When he worked for Brighton Parks (before they were dismantled), his boss, Pete Skinner, said, 'Remember that we get a lot of grey days, here, so if you're doing any bedding, make sure there's plenty of good colour there.' Of course, it's not as simple as that. White can be quite a staring colour, standing forth under a grey canopy.

How are your painful shoulders, Beth? Are you sleeping in a more relaxed state of mind so that you don't wake up all twisted with pain? Is that nice young woman still coming in to massage you in the mornings?

I have some Xmas roses flowering, some you gave me last year. I hadn't grown them for decades and they quite took me by surprise.

Much love, from Christo

— ❧ —

Wednesday 24 January

Dear Christo

After phoning you, I'm relieved to hear you are feeling better, but please stop thinking you are wasting time. I know it feels like it, but if you don't behave sensibly now there may not be more time! These viruses are so devious, they lull you into thinking you are OK. But not so. About two winters ago I behaved like a fool, carrying on as normal too soon, but the bug came back. I was flattened; it took weeks to become myself again. You may well be made of tougher stock, but take notice of Fergus: do as little as you must.

I am thrilled to be invited again to Glyndebourne. Although we have seen *Arabella* together, it was such an exuberant colourful production, I would love to see it – to hear it once more, and to take in some of the bits I missed – unless you preferred to share something different. From 1 to 16 July I shall be staying with friends in Germany so I would be home to whizz round here and take in what has come and gone, before I set off for Dixter.

Although concerned to hear of your lingering fever, I could not help laughing at the picture you painted of institutionalized xerophytic gardening, ending with your concession that you are preparing for the End of Gardening as we know it, by assembling plants adapted to tropical conditions. What happens if, as you suggest, we are in for another winter like '47? (Certainly today it feels likely – the strong east wind is cruel and the temperature has been dropping rapidly throughout the day.) Will Beth be fretting about the fuel needed to conserve such plants in winter? No. She has enough to occupy her watching the Gravel Garden and seeing which plants survive in arctic conditions as well as the heat of last summer. Let's wait and see what comes with the rest of the country's gardeners.

I'm sorry to hear that Helen Dillon was upset by Michael McCoy. The last time I met him I thought him a very promising young horticulturist and a dear man, but possibly, at that moment, Helen was played out, if she had just given her talk, or edgy if she still had it to do.

I understand your frustration over too many monochromatic or analogous harmonies. They can all become just too much 'good taste', no zip or sting, no originality. But I remember us walking round Helen's garden: it was a bit like going round a picture gallery. There were many contrasting pictures, hidden surprises, each complete in themselves. Towards the end you drew my wandering attention to an almost Lloyd-like mixture of hot colours, admittedly on a small scale, but it has stayed in my mind as something I enjoyed.

If I am asked to pontificate about colour I always feel a bit stumped because I do not really set out with a colour scheme in mind. I am much more concerned with shapes, selecting first plants that are adapted to the conditions, with interesting foliage, which will furnish the scene for as long as possible. Then I pay attention to their flowers and add more ephemeral colour with bulbs, herbaceous plants, even half-hardies, to reinforce, or repeat colours. But after that, I am often excited by chance seedlings which may inject a colour I would not have thought of using, and providing it is not gross or overpowering (scale is as important with colour as with anything else), I may well find it an improvement on any of my considered planting.

Do you grow *Cornus sanguinea* 'Midwinter Fire'? It was new to me three or four years ago, but now I wish you could see this group of three little shrubs at the entrance to my Wood Garden. Against a background of bare black trees and shrubs shrouded in cold mist, they make an indefinite haze of warm colour, glowing like the remains of a bonfire. The colour is brightest in the heart of the bush, where the stems are pale yellow, while the terminal twigs and branches are vivid coral-red. They are underplanted with *Vinca minor* 'La Grave' for quick ground cover all year and posies of blue stars in spring, but now I've had another idea to emphasize the effect of the dogwood. I have planted *Luzula sylvatica* 'Aurea' in among the group to bring the yellow tints in the stems of the cornus down to ground level. This beautiful woodrush has broad grass-like yellow leaves forming low arched mounds. It looks bright in winter, if not browned by exceptionally hard weather.

With forecasts of more bad weather to come, I spent Monday morning in my vegetable garden. A stiff wind had blown aside the gloom for a few hours and flapped the laundry dry. I dug leeks and celeriac, with hot soup in mind, putting the remaining roots of celeriac, about a dozen, into a straw-filled box standing in one of my tunnels, covered with a bundle of Netlon for frost protection. There was not room for it in my outdoor cellar in which I store my organically grown carrots and beetroot. This simple idea I saw last year in Germany, and Keith, who deals with all my technical problems, soon made it for me. My 'cellar' is a slab-lined pit in a spare corner of the vegetable garden, filled with sand and fitted with a hinged lid for easy access. I put carrots in one half, beetroot in the other. A well-fitting lid covered with roofing felt keeps out the rain.

As I pulled the curtains at 5 o'clock on Monday, the sky was still sufficiently clear to let us see the thinnest sliver of new moon, and Venus sparkling just to the south. I picked up a pair of ancient opera glasses which have very good lenses and the sparkles became an irregular ball of yellow. It was exciting to see.

Do take care of yourself.

Much love, Beth

PS What extravagant notions you have of me! I don't have aroma therapy every morning, only once a fortnight to help relax my achey shoulders.

—❧—

Sunday 4 February

Dear Beth,

I'm sorry I can't challenge you with an opera new to you at Glyndebourne, but the only other one I want to see is Berg's *Lulu* (that's challenging all right) and you'll still be in Germany when I see that. It's sure to be revived, as this is a new production. They're only giving eight performances, which doesn't show great confidence in their public. Doubtless the users of the blocks of seats allocated to institutional sponsors would like *Figaro*, endlessly repeated, though only as third-best choice to Wimbledon or Lord's.

You are so organized about growing and storing your vegetables. I eat an enormous quantity of celeriac, and we protect that by covering the rows with a strip of hessian, in frosty weather. Generally, that works well, though I have to admit the last root Perry brought in was frosted at the top.

Another excellent root I'm growing this winter (although, like Jerusalem artichokes, I find it windy) is salsify. It was growing in a place we wanted to sterilize, so Perry moved and replanted it all. It doesn't seem to have noticed. There's a lovely Italian way of using it, which I must try on you when you come in March. You boil the roots – 15 minutes is long enough – and finish them by frying in butter. Then, add the grated rind of a lemon, chopped, plain-leaved parsley and a chopped small clove of garlic, a minute before serving.

Besides parsnips, my other roots that are still in the ground are carrots. What a mess they are in. First starved of rain in August, then stimulated to grow again in September, they are crazily cracked and full of slugs. Does that make them organic? I'm sure we used Bromophos in the rows when sowing, but the effect seems to wear off long before maturing, and there's plenty of carrot fly damage. I suppose you'd mush the remaining bits of root into a nourishing, raw purée?

I didn't know there was a bright-stemmed version of *Cornus sanguinea*, which is a pretty dull dogwood, as you see it on chalk soils in the wild. I couldn't find your 'Midwinter Fire' in Bean, even the supplement, but 'Winter Flame' is in Graham S. Thomas's shrub book, so I expect that's the same thing. He recommends it for dry soils, which yours mostly are. It sounds interesting. You gave me *Luzula sylvatica* 'Aurea' and it certainly is good now, early in the year. Fergus interplanted it with one of Elizabeth Strangman's blue-flowered pulmonarias, with a German name, 'Fruhlingshimmel' I think. They combine well, but are a bit lost in the garden as a whole. I mean, you have to make a point of going to look.

Jerry Harpur wanted to come for winter photographs, yesterday, as he's off to Argentina for ten days. I choked him off. There's still bits of snow lying around, ten days after it fell, 'waiting for more', as the old saying is. The winter crocuses will be far more numerous in two weeks' time and so will the snowdrops. Even *Galanthus* 'Atkinsii' is only half open, as yet.

I noticed that the snow melted first on lawns and meadow areas, last on cultivated ground, especially over mulch. Fergus was silent, when I pointed this out, but next time I saw him was voluble with a 'convincing' explanation. I was totally unconvinced. Given a *fait accompli*, a reasoned explanation is never hard to find.

The weather hasn't loosened up at all, but it has done us very little harm, I guess, and the fact that it is holding plant growth back must be good for the plants, even if not for me!

Olearia solandri is such a joy both to Fergus and to me – every time we walk past it, a great gust of heliotrope scent comes to meet us, interrupting whatever thoughts were running in our minds. I do think you'd like it, Beth, even though it needs a bit of shelter from cold winds (though an excellent coastal plant). Like so many New Zealanders, it makes a sort of heather honey impression, the stems and the undersides of its tiny leaves being a warm shade of (golden) brown. (The golden is a bit of an exaggeration, but if you love a plant you have to do your best for it.) It has an upswept habit to

2m (7ft) and is covered with tiny (insignificant) white flowers in August, even more strongly heliotrope-scented. Did your sense of taste and smell return fully to you after that nasty spell when illness deprived you of it?

It's getting dark and I must take the dogs out. Canna loves scooting round the garden. She's five months old, now. Not good with strangers, alas. She'll have to take to you – quickly. You mustn't make advances, but fondle her when she's near you and without appearing to be aware of what you're doing.

Much love, from Christo

– 🙢 –

Thursday 8 February

Dear Christo,

It will be great fun to see and hear *Arabella* again and to share with you the reactions of our young friends to an evening at Glyndebourne. I have marked the date, 22 July, on my calendar and a memo to think of something special for our picnic.

I shall just have returned from Germany and already I am trying to plan the vegetable garden so that peas and broad beans are not at their best while I am away. Last year they were, and we are enjoying them now, out of the freezer, but I prefer to plan a better succession. Last week I sowed broad beans, 'Express', and 'Hurst's Greenshaft' peas in pots. Putting out early potfuls means I have full rows, not ravaged by mice. Later I sow *in situ*.

I must confess, much as I love the decorative garden, the vegetable plot is, for me, both a place to relax and, occasionally, somewhere to hide. Yes, I admit, my vegetables are organically grown. I cannot see the point of going to all the trouble of growing them yourself, and then dowsing them with poisonous chemicals. Save yourself the bother and buy them from the supermarket, sprayed and scrubbed. I fear I shall rub salt into your wound when I tell you the carrots stored in my 'cellar' are free of any bugs this year! Sweet and tender to eat both raw and cooked, most of them are from a July sowing.

Most of the vegetable garden is laid out on the narrow bed system, 1.2m (4ft) wide beds with wooden sides to keep soil off the paths. I leave only about a handspan between the rows and, as soon as the carrots have been thinned, put a series of strong wire hoops across the bed. Over the hoops I fix fine fleece (easily obtained from horticultural suppliers), to make a tunnel, fixed at ground level with 'hairpins' made of stiff wire. If the drought is severe, like last summer, I do water the vegetables. But over the years we have transformed the orange sand and gravel into very presentable black soil by yearly applications of compost.

I shall be interested to sample your salsify recipe, since I only grow its cousin, scorzonera. It's an ugly thonged root when you bring it in on a winter's evening, but scrubbed and steamed it slides out of its black skin as white and slippery as a baby in the bath – and is delicious, lightly touched with olive oil and a scattering of sesame seeds.

This winter has been testing for salads; after several years so mild we thought it was easy. Up till Christmas I had lettuce and chicories under fleece outside, but temperatures of –8°C (18°F) have blackened them all. Inside my little tunnels I lost all the lettuce which have survived the last few mild winters and the pretty cabbage-shaped red chicory 'Alouette' looks very downcast, attacked recently by mildew (tho' I regularly take off affected leaves). It just is not tough enough to stand damp cold. But a narrow-leaved cos-lettuce-shaped variety 'Treviso' is splendid. I love the colour: deep purple-red with pale veins. Since Christmas it has continued to produce fresh leaves even more brightly stained with purple. Shredded, they look very well among green leaves of rocket, American land cress, and my last remaining pale green 'Sugar Loaf' chicory. I have sown more lettuce in pans to plant out in the tunnels by March, I hope, to provide early salad before we need the tunnels for tomatoes and peppers.

Incidentally, it was kind of you to remember my loss of taste and smell after that bad bout of flu. It was a sore deprivation for about six months. The senses may not be quite as keen as before – I think I miss perfumes like *Skimmia japonica* floating on the breeze – but thankfully I can enjoy the fine flavours of your cooking (and mine) once more.

We have had the odd hour of sunshine just recently. Suddenly, everyone has a smiling face even though it is still perishing cold. Low sunlight spotlights colour inside and outside the house where all seemed drab and drear before. The grass looks wonderful from a distance, shining emerald green. Close to, I worry about it: patchy in places, covered in worm casts. The worms are doing a good job of aeration I suppose, but we are also thinking of hiring a good spiking machine to penetrate the close-textured silty soil where most of our grass is laid. There is a lot of compaction caused by the passage of many feet.

But such worries diminish when the sun shines. Already there is a different feeling in the garden, an excitement that spring is near, just beneath the soil, just breaking the surface.

Beneath the Big Oak some double snowdrops are opening, including *Galanthus* 'Lady Beatrix Stanley'. We shall be swapping names of snowdrops for weeks to come, no doubt. There are so many which extend the season from late autumn to late spring. I'm very fond of *Galanthus caucasicus* var. *hiemalis*. This sturdy snowdrop with broad blue-grey leaves is always in flower for Christmas and has only just gone over. *G. caucasicus* itself, still with tight upturned buds, reminds me, curiously perhaps, of penguins huddled together against the Antarctic blasts, their bills pointing skywards. Do go and look. I think you will see what I mean.

On 20 January among frost and snow, I found the first aconite in flower. Since I was a small child, I look for them as the first sign of spring. The battered fronds of ferns have been cleared away to expose them in drifts between the shrubs. Sometimes we forget to cut the ferns in time and then it is a pity to find the green-ruffed yellow cups misshapen on leggy stems. We also cut away the old leaves of epimediums in late winter, or else we find we are too late to see their small columbine-like flowers, buried among last year's stems.

It hasn't been easy to find small things to pick this winter, has it? (No long lists of flowers in bloom on New Year's Day.) Most longlasting and effective, I find, are mixed collections of leaves and coloured twigs. For almost a month in the office we had a little pewter jug holding *Lonicera* x *purpusii* set off by a mixture of leaves: pale autumn tip shoots of *Gaultheria shallon*, flushed pink; a very narrow ruffled form of hart's tongue fern I found years ago in Germany; and black strap leaves of *Ophiopogon planiscapus* 'Nigrescens'. The bushy honeysuckle *Lonicera* x *purpusii* would be ignored in the summer garden, but in winter I often go to look at its bare twiggy branches thickly set with large pale green buds and sniff the heavenly scent of its small cream flowers.

Your *Olearia solandri* (from New Zealand) sounds tempting. I shall certainly come and consider it, but this morning, finding tender things like coronilla, *Salvia microphylla* and *Senecio viravira* all damaged on a west-facing wall makes me wonder. If the conditions do not worsen considerably, I will expect all three to break again, but we do have lower temperatures here, I think, than you so close to the south coast. At the risk of tedious repetition there is little between us and the Ural Mountains when the wind is in the east. They say that is what makes East Anglians so obstinate.

On the kitchen window-sill I have a small vase with two or three flowers of our earliest daffodil, *Narcissus* 'Cedric Morris'. The late Sir Cedric, my old friend, brought it home from Spain more than 40 years ago. It seemed to have been a one-off there in the wild, he could find no others around, and now the site has been blasted away to make a motorway. We always look, and find buds, if not open flowers, by Christmas, while established clumps continue to flower well into March. It is neither miniature (weedy), nor dwarf (stunted), but stands in perfect scale, about 25cm (10in) tall. I love the green stain on the back of its perfect little lemon-yellow flowers; the way its twisting petals curve gracefully round the frilly-edged trumpet. When picked, it lasts longer in a warm room than snowdrops.

This morning Andrew and I watched from the window a heron taking slow determined steps through the bed along the far side of the ice-covered house pond. He stood motionless for a while, fluffing out his pale grey feathers, facing the sun, for warmth perhaps. I picked up my binoculars to see him more clearly and saw, close beside his stick-like legs, a round knobbly 'knee' of the swamp cypress (*Taxodium distichum*) we planted about 30 years ago. Sometime last year I counted eight of these curious brown lumps, which are largely hidden when the marginal plants reappear. These are the tree's breathing roots – in the wild, the south-east United States, it grows in swamps and shallow water.

There is probably still plenty of food about the garden for birds, especially among the thick layers of fallen leaves, which I see blackbirds energetically scattering over the grass path, but I love to encourage the smaller birds close to the house. We watch them at meal times bouncing like clockwork toys across the paved terrace searching for seeds I have scattered. Bigger and bolder, the blackbird and robin dominate the food table, while tits of all persuasions perform acrobatics among the branches of the magnolia tree, waiting their turn at the nut basket.

It's time for tea – almost by daylight.

Much love, Beth

– ❀ –

Friday 16 February

Dear Beth,

Today was straight out of my idea of heaven – the first such day this year and the first time that all the winter crocuses have opened wide, in appreciation. Armed with my kneeling mat, I dropped to my knees to savour the honey scent of *C. chrysanthus* 'Snow Bunting'. Rosemary Alexander, who spends more and more time at Stoneacre (the National Trust property near Maidstone, which she rents), expressed doubts on whether it wouldn't be better to concentrate on snowdrops, seeing that crocuses spend so much of their time in an obstinately closed state, loudly proclaiming 'this isn't good enough for me'. I can see her point, of course. If you're in London for much of the week and it happens to be chilly when you weekend near your garden, it is rather disappointing to be confronted with mutinously sulky crocuses, and no comfort to be told, later, that no sooner had you returned to the Wen, than they had opened wide for nobody's particular enjoyment. In the circumstances, snowdrops might be preferable.

But it is the very obstinacy of crocuses, only overcome by weather which we, ourselves, can soak up with similar appreciation, that I find so appealing. However, I'm nearly always here. Snowdrops, in any case, do open wide and need to where the doubles are in question, so that you can lift their chins and admire the convoluted intricacies of their beautifully arranged centres. I don't know your 'Lady Beatrix Stanley', but I relish 'Hippolyta', which I know you also grow (I may have given it to you). There are an awful lot of different, named, snowdrops and the Galanthophiles are so excited about small differences that I become a little cynical when I see them priced at £10 per bulb. I remember standing next to our late, mutual friend, John Codrington, in front of a snowdrop exhibit in the Royal Horticultural Society New Hall, and him saying, 'I think I like my snowdrops straight'. I don't agree, and, like it or not, I do accumulate a range of different snowdrops without really meaning to, but I could see his point.

If you find yourself in a snowdrop wood at the right moment, with thousands of them all around you, the thrill is totally divorced from whether some of them are slightly different from others. My music teacher at Rugby, Kenneth Stubbs, a great family friend, used to drive me to a small wood at Southam, some ten miles from

Rugby, at snowdrop time, and I shall always remember the sense of wading, almost swimming, among them. Curiously, they were all doubles, and I still wonder how they managed to make such a thorough spread without being able to set seed. Who can have started them off?

After what you wrote, I rushed out to catch my *Galanthus caucasicus* looking like penguins with upturned beaks, and indeed they did. Some of them still do; they open in succession. You gave them me, now I remember. And *hiemalis*, too. (Incidentally, if someone is in Colchester, could you bring me a canister of that hair shampoo I like?)

When I tease you about your claim of there being nothing between you and the Urals, Beth, it is simply for this reason. Right close to you is the North Sea. East winds from Russia pick up moisture there and dump it on you as snow or fog, which is tiresome, but it is a large body of unfrozen water and materially moderates the original bitterness of the wind.

We have ordered that fleece, you wrote of, to protect our carrots from fly. I know we should have used that years ago. I do grow vegetables on quite a large scale, as I have so many resident visitors, so we can't always give the special or intensive treatments that make your vegetable plot ideal. Hence the drought afflicting my carrots and the cracks in them caused by the subsequent rains starting them into growth again, when their skins had hardened. I hardly know if you were addressing me or some invisible class when you wrote about 'going to all the trouble of growing them (vegetables) yourself, and then dowsing them with poisonous chemicals'. We take great trouble about applying no more chemical than is needed (and wearing the prescribed clothing for the purpose). We follow the instructions and, of course, do not eat any part of the affected plants until all residual poison has been nullified. It is a pity that organic gardeners cannot state their case without needing to vent blanket disapproval on all those who are not converts.

Currently, I am still eating delicious little Brussels sprouts from the garden. From the time they were sown, last spring, they have been through the hoop of aphids, cabbage root fly, white fly and caterpillars. We will have defended them against some or all of these, as necessary. Their flavour is excellent and all the vegetables I grow are far superior in that respect to the usual commercial product. Sometimes that would not be the case and I then don't bother – with onions, for instance. Differences in flavour are sometimes a question of variety grown, those best suited to mass production not having flavour high on their list of priorities.

It was Fergus's 30th birthday, yesterday. He was touched on receiving a birthday card from your Moira. It must be six or more years since he worked for you. What a memory. I know that your birthday is in June but I couldn't hazard which day. Fergus is off for a week to visit his (Turkish) mother in Turkey. He worked like fury ahead of leaving. In fact, we were working in the same area today and I had three hours of it, which is really good for me. One becomes so physically slack, in winter.

Much love, from Christo

– ✿ –

Tuesday 20 February

Dear Christo,

What a good thing you enjoyed your crocuses when you had the chance! Today we are blanketed in snow once more, with a wild north wind hurling stinging dry snow horizontally past the windows. Your way of having crocuses (and many other bulbs) naturalized in short grass is a far more effective way of growing them than in conventional borders. Left to seed themselves in little knots and ribbons of colour they appear like embroidery across a carpet before something else takes over the design. We are having a miserable season for them this late winter, either overcast or snowing.

We have been obliged to spend a lot of time under cover since Christmas. The men usually have winter jobs saved up for bad weather, repairing tools and machinery, overhauling all the barrows and trolleys. This winter we have had extra heating, night storage heaters, put into the potting and propagating area of our building where the women work all winter, standing on duckboards to keep their feet off the concrete floor.

To conserve some of the heat (not easy in outbuildings as you know) Keith and David Plummer have insulated the ceilings with fibre-glass and sheets of hardboard. They are high ceilings, so when the job was completed they painted them white, standing on scaffolding boards. Then, my three propagating girls were left to spring-clean their area, painting the walls, organizing better shelving for all their record books, reference books and the tools of their trade. It was fun to see them work under Keith's supervision, sanding down the benches, sawing great pieces of hardboard to make new work surfaces. When it was all finished to their satisfaction they placed a big jar of hazel catkins to welcome hardy visitors. Fudge, the stray cat who has adopted us, looked out from her igloo beneath one of the benches. For the very cold nights she has a big covered box, with a heating pad inside her basket.

The stock control girls in the adjoining room have been cleaning pots all winter, waiting for the new packing season to begin. Each day they load trolleys with trays of potted plants taken from outside and push them along gangways of the propagating house to be certain of having thawed pots for the next day. There should not be weeds in pots grown from commercial compost but always some appear – and of course some are blown in during the summer. By sorting through them in winter we start the spring sales with clean plants, while pots full of deads, perhaps rotted or frozen, are not left to take up space. When, in summer, visitors sometimes tell us how lucky we are to have such a lovely job, I think of my staff coping with the kind of conditions we have had this winter.

David Ward took advantage of a particularly horrid blizzard to closet himself in our wood-working shed, to make a nesting box for owls. Earlier Keith had received a windfall, a load of off-cuts of planed wood. In it David found good thick planks – just what was needed to make a long, narrow box which, apparently, owls like. It will be attached to an oak, to appear like a hollow branch. I hear a tawny owl most nights now, scanning the ploughed fields around us. I would be thrilled if a pair eventually adopt our box for their home.

After admiring the box, I negotiated the frozen puddles in the yard to find comfort in the big polycarbonate propagating house, breathing in the warm green smell of growing plants. Actually very little spatial heat is used here, apart from the heated benches. A thermostatically controlled blower is used only on very cold nights to unfreeze the pots brought in by the girls to clean next day. The rigid double-skin plastic absorbs and retains heat amazingly well.

I love to browse along the benches at this time of year to see what is happening. The central benches are full with trays of root-cuttings, an on-going job for the propagating team throughout winter. Early cuttings of oriental poppies and the pretty little pink dandelion, *Crepis incana*, already show healthy tufts of green leaves. Any day now tiny shoots will appear in trays of eryngiums, symphytum and crambe.

The side benches are full to bursting with cuttings already rooted and waiting to be potted. In a corner I found pans containing well-rooted cuttings of *Cobaea scandens* f. *alba*. There was no viable seed last autumn so for the first time we tried cuttings, and the plant being a perennial, albeit not hardy, the cuttings took. I'm so glad. It will save the trouble of ordering new seed.

Another delight was finding 'Hurst's Greenshaft' peas just pushing through. They will have to be sheltered in a single-skin tunnel to harden them off while this weather lasts.

The vegetable garden looks dejected compared with recent mild winters. Root veg and Brussels sprouts are OK, but most saladings outside have had it. The little vegetable tunnels full of chicories and rocket keep us going. The hardiest red chicory, I find, is the cos-shaped 'Treviso'. I cut a few leaves most days, and it has continued to grow, despite the cold and dark. 'Alouette' is the pretty cabbage-shaped one, but her delicate leaves are prone to botrytis.

Walking back to the house thro' the Gravel Garden I stopped to look at a garden of snow 'flowers', little parcels of snow held in the stiff stems and flat heads of plants not yet cut down, plants like *Caryopteris* 'Heavenly Blue', various forms of origanum, the tall *Verbena bonariensis* and many sedums. I remembered your little 'hedges' of *Aster lateriflorus* var. *horizontalis* in the Peacock Garden, crowded with dry papery bracts, sparkling with hoar frost.

Peeping into my little heated greenhouse I found something called tibouchina still in flower. It was given me last summer by Mrs Maubach, daughter of Georg Arends, in Wuppertal; she had a huge plant in a tub by her outdoor sitting area. It has softly furry oval leaves and terminal shoots carrying a succession of fat buds, which open to large, light purple flowers – very handsome. I think you would like it in the Exotic Garden. From Brazil, it seems to flower continuously. It has done so ever since I brought it home last July. Sometimes I bring it indoors, hoping to enjoy it more comfortably, but the lack of light causes the large petals to drop quickly. Now a last word, for the time being, on organic v. inorganic gardening. Of course, everyone is free to make that choice. As you know, I am not 100 per cent vegetarian, neither am I 100 per cent an organic gardener. If I see a hefty infestation of greenfly on *Euphorbia wulfenii* (which they adore), I reach for the Tumblebug. Similarly, I can't abide seeing my fuchsias and phygelius ruined with capsid bug. But overall, like many gardeners including yourself no doubt, we try not to use materials which will harm predators as well as pests. In the vegetable garden I prefer not to use weedkillers or systemic chemicals at all!

I have on my desk a little bunch of *Iris unguicularis* and frozen *Hamamelis mollis* I would have liked to write about – but they must wait till I see you.

Love, Beth

– ✣ –

Sunday 10 March

Dear Christo,

I so enjoyed my few days with you last week, despite the gloomy overcast weather with never a gleam of sun to coax open the tightly folded crocuses. This Sunday morning is glorious, sunlight falling warmly on to my hands as I write. I can see through the big window a bright patch of *Crocus tommasinianus*, opening in all shades from palest lilac to deep purple, in the place where, later, *Romneya coulteri*, the tree poppy, will bloom against the house wall. I can imagine those pallid little ghosts opening wide and flooding the Dixter meadows with soft colour, so unlike the riotous purple and gold of Dutch cultivated crocuses, which admittedly make a fine show on roundabouts.

As always, I much enjoyed the company of your young friends, feeling part of an extended family. You might have become a crusty old bachelor rattling around in your medieval halls like a pill in a box, but you are such a wonderfully generous host to many of us who look upon Dixter both as an inspiration and retreat from our own worlds. It is, I think, your great love for Dixter and the need to share all that it means to you which still gives you the creative energy to keep up such a demanding schedule of writing – not to mention the small matter of cooking for a houseful of guests and planning the garden with Fergus.

The discipline which has you sitting, immediately after breakfast, at your laptop computer, composing your weekly articles, is something I envy. To start with, I have never learnt to type. Rosie, my secretary, patiently transfers my handwriting on to the word processor, once I have stopped feeling obliged to do a dozen other jobs and settled down to write.

This morning one of the jobs was checking the caravan where my students who come here for work experience live. Fortunately, it is a large caravan with plenty of room – I love to see their faces when they first step inside, having imagined a tiny space where you eat, sleep and cook all in one room!

Hanna, an Austrian girl, is coming today for the Easter recess. She is taking a degree in landscape design at Sheffield University. I think it is useful for garden designers to have the chance to work in various gardens not only to get the feel of planting, but also to take part in the production of plants, to experience all the phases from seed, cuttings and divisions to strongly independent plants. So much is involved before the plants arrive where they are meant to grow. Will they have the attention they deserve before they have had time to put down roots? I often say our pots hold living creatures – they are not cans of beans to be dumped anywhere until someone finds time to deal with them.

I wish you could see the Wood Garden this minute. After spending three or four years dividing and spreading snowdrops, they now begin to make a picture, waves and ripples of white appearing in the leaf litter between the bare boles of the oak trees. It is not the same as an old established snowdrop wood (like the one I always look out for on the way to my daughter in Suffolk), since we use many different snowdrops as well as leaving space for other bulbs and plants to follow. Snowdrops themselves, I agree, are wonderful now for filling bare spaces. Later, the scene will be transformed – as is the case in your border where, at the moment, the large flowers of *Galanthus* 'Atkinsii' shiver on wire-thin petioles, but will subsequently be overwhelmed with a magnificent grouping of *Euphorbia sikkimensis* and *Rodgersia pinnata* 'Superba'.

I didn't plan to collect snowdrops, certainly don't feel I must have every named variation, but over the years we have built up a stock of those we find distinctive. *Galanthus caucasicus* tends to be a favourite. It doesn't seed, unfortunately, but makes up well, and is very handsome, with large flowers freely produced on tall stems, and beautiful grey foliage. After seeing your patch of G. 'Tiny' under the bay tree, I looked up the planting you gave me several years ago. It is doing well. Hanna and I will, I hope, be spreading it further in the next week or so. I like to wait until I have enough stock to plant three to five bulbs together. Last spring I did this with some Greatorex doubles (Mr Greatorex was, I believe, a snowdrop enthusiast from Norfolk – do you know anything about him?), and already they flower well and make a good effect. David also increases newly acquired bulbs (when perhaps we have only one) by chipping, after the leaves have died down. He cuts the bulb into maybe eight sections, puts them into a bag of damp vermiculite with fungicides and magic incantations, and by September we may have eight tiny pearl-sized bulbs clinging to the withered bulb scales. These take about three years more to flower.

Andrew was relieved to see me arrive home safely. He was, with good reason, concerned for my first long trip in the new car. I thought I had familiarized myself with all the new knobs and dials, but not so. About an hour from home, rattling happily along the A12 dual carriageway, I suddenly lost power and came to a halt with great towering container lorries hooting angrily as they roared around me, a horrid deep drop into clinker (no hard shoulder), on my left side. What could be wrong? Turning the engine again and peering more closely at the unfamiliar dials, I was mortified to see I had misread two that are almost identical, and one of them registered empty! I had run out of petrol.

I managed to shudder the car further on out of the traffic on to the narrow grass verge. A sign just behind me indicated a telephone two miles ahead. With its emergency lights blinking, I deserted my poor little car and started to walk, but after about ten minutes of walking through discarded rubbish with the traffic almost brushing my shoulder, I looked through the blackened roadside hedge, climbed over a wooden rail fence, and found myself facing a vast field of young corn, with a few houses on the skyline. Here I felt much less vulnerable. Walking in a tractor tread I reached another gap and dropped down into a small country road which lead to a small village complete with pub. What a relief! By telephoning enquiries, I made contact with the RAC where a friendly voice said someone would arrive within the hour.

On the dot of 2 o'clock a van arrived driven by a jolly fellow used to dealing with silly women, who, as he said, made him a living. Calling at a garage we filled a can of petrol, and found my car, still blinking and intact. Soon I was on my way again. But it had been a useful experience, so much worse if it had been night-time. And I had learnt how to read the right gauge and how to summon help. Now we must do something, not just talk about putting a phone into the car.

Part of my mind takes longer to return home from Dixter than the rest of me. Something I love specially is the familiar smell when I first walk into the house. Could it partly be the vast amount of old wood? Another pleasure is the sense of space, space above and all around us. Few today have the luxury of a large kitchen where people can work without falling over one another. I am happy in your kitchen, knowing where most things belong, making salad with Dahlia pressing hard on my toes to persuade me to drop a few pieces for her insatiable appetite.

Now I must take my leave of you and Dixter to go out and soak up the sunshine we have sorely missed this winter.

With love, from Beth

— ❧ —

Monday 1 April

Dear Beth,

I am using a 'new' laptop word processor. New very much in inverted commas. It belonged to Chris Lloyd, my great nephew, but he is about three models on from it by now. All the same, it is more up to date than my old one, which had developed black-outs lasting up to half a minute each, when in a bad mood, though perfectly behaved at other times. How human.

It is Chris's birthday, today, and of course he was mercilessly ribbed, when young. I was easily gulled, though deeply suspicious, when my father told me to ask the cook for some pigeon's milk.

What a horrible experience for you, when you ran out of petrol. I think you coped with the situation admirably. Well, I can't imagine you just lying down and dying! But you must have been exhausted by the time you reached home.

I thoroughly enjoyed your visit, as always. Quite apart from your company, you always get on so well with my young friends. And you're such a help to me in the kitchen.

I was properly confined to the kitchen over the weekend, when there were nine mouths to feed. Fergus organized a group of friends and students to tidy up the garden ahead of our opening to the public for the season, tomorrow. Actually, it took three of them more than a day to tidy the terrace, which isn't even open to the public, but which we need to look nice so that we can enjoy our pre-lunch drinks there, in congenial surroundings. But a lot more than that was accomplished and Fergus reckoned that it had saved one man ten days' work. Not bad, seeing that they were volunteers. Still, I did them proud, in the way of food and drink.

A lad and lass, students from Hadlow College of Horticulture (and Agriculture), applied themselves really well, whereas one from Wye College spent a large part of the time 'just looking', as we say in the shops. He is a dear man, but has always been indulged at home, I suspect. However, the difference does also reflect, I fancy, on the quality of those who are studying horticulture and the quality of the teaching at the two establishments. When I was at Wye, we learned a lot of practical know-how – sowing, pricking out, taking cuttings, grafting, planting, hoeing, etc. That is now looked down on as not being degree material. If you want to learn anything about handling plants, you must seek elsewhere – at Hadlow, for instance. John Watkins, whom you know, was working under Ray Waite in the glasshouse department at Wisley, when I first knew him. He teaches at Hadlow, now, and is first-rate, as is my neighbour, Kemal Mehdi, once a Wye student himself, but right into practical matters. John was one of our helpers.

Fergus and I decided to take a day out, last week, and we visited the gardens at Wye, which include those at what was once a private property, at Withersdane Hall. I spent many hours working in them, years ago. They are now a disgrace. Pruning, for instance, is of the worst municipal kind, chopping every shrub to have an even surface, preferably at the same level as the hedge behind, and paying absolutely no regard to the needs of the shrub, retention of young wood and elimination of old – that sort of thing. Any students who look at them at all could only learn how not to treat plants.

You can't blame the gardener, who is paid the lowest basic wage and has received no instruction himself. Small wonder if horticultural students look elsewhere.

Before going there, we visited an old haunt of mine, when I was a student and used to cycle and walk all around; the wild chalkland flora is so fascinating. We were just right for the flowering of huge boskages of *Daphne laureola*; such a handsome evergreen shrub. Albeit green, the flowers are most attractive, strongly reminiscent of *D. pontica*; lacking that species' delicious lemony night scent. However, I picked a sprig *of D. laureola* (wasn't there a play of that name in which Edith Evans starred?) and it developed a distinct and pleasant fragrance in the evening.

In the morning, we had visited Tim Ingram's nursery, on the outskirts of Faversham. He is one of those keen plantsmen who give one confidence that there will always be room for small, specialist nurseries, able to make a living by offering plants that garden centres would never hear of and wouldn't be interested in, anyway. Tim has a particular interest in umbellifers. At the midsummer RHS show, held at Wisley, these days, in 1994 he laid on an excellent exhibit devoted entirely to *Umbelliferae*. That's a family generally underrated. We spent a good two hours there. He has a largish garden as well as a nursery. Although there was a bitter east wind and grey skies (as so often this year), the winter damage was minimal. Last summer, before an open day in aid of a charity, he decided to liven up one border by planting some oleanders into it from the greenhouse. They were left and are still green and untouched by weather. Life is full of surprises.

Do you know that *Galanthus caucasicus*, of which we were writing two months ago, has only just faded? It certainly is a stayer. *C. ikariae* Latifolius Group is still in flower – I like its shiny, green leaves – and a very glaucous-leaved, tall hybrid, which Chris Brickell said is a *C. elwesii* hybrid. Its long stems make it good for picking. We should be spreading the snowdrops around, now, as we had planned to do, but there seem to be so many other, more urgent jobs demanding attention. The old story.

At the last RHS show, snowdrops were much in evidence; at least one firm was showing nothing else. I know that the propagation of snowdrops to work up stocks of some rarity is slow and exacting, as you described David's work on them in your last letter, but even then, I found some prices pretty steep. 'Atkinsii' for instance, which makes up so fast, at £3 a bulb. It has been around for years and years, too.

The prettiest effect in the garden, right now, is of the blue *Scilla bifolia* (I think I prefer it to the better known *S. siberica*) mixed into the yellow-green young shoots of *Valeriana phu* 'Aurea'. Dog's tooth violets, *Erythronium dens-canis*, are lovely in rough grass on the bank overlooking the Horse Pond and I like it when they are near to the tiny, trumpet daffodil, *Narcissus minor*. The pinky-mauve of the one and the yellow of the other seem right together, especially at this time of the year, when we have been starved of colour (and warmth!) for so long. All day, today, the thermometer (my old-fashioned Fahrenheit one, which hasn't brought itself up to date) has been well below 40 degrees (4°C).

Although they are very good and quiet, I must give the dogs their tea. Perhaps they're not impatient because they haven't twigged that the clocks have gone forward.

With love from Christo

– ❀ –

Friday 26 April

Dear Beth,

As an example of spring at its best, one could hardly improve on today. I hope your commitments allowed you to do things in the garden. I received a characteristic letter from Frank Ronan. 'I wish everyone would stop whingeing about the spring being late. It may well be that it is late (funny old year) but that's no reason not to enjoy it once it's here. The whole point about the joys of spring should be that the experience is so overwhelming that the last thing you'd think of is fishing out a calendar and making comparative measurements. Cherry-blossom time in London is a bit of a stunning experience. Not long now until the chestnut flowers, which really get me going.'

Me too. A white chestnut in bloom makes such a vast mountain of blossom. All you do is gape and wonder. And its newly expanded leaves are such a joy.

While with Fergus in front of the house this morning, I saw my first holly blue in three years. There was a spate of them, then nothing; such a fresh, light shade of blue. It intrigues me that in folklore, the holly and the ivy have always been closely associated, and there we have the holly blue larvae, in their first brood feeding on young holly leaves and flowers; in their second, in the autumn, feeding on newly flowered ivy.

At 10.00am, I had undertaken, as I do each year, to show a party of second-year Wye College students round the garden. It could hardly have been a duller experience. None of them seemed interested in gardening or plants, at all. It used not to be so and I have made a number of good and lasting friendships following a first meeting similar to this. Fergus was the most notable example.

Tomorrow, he will drive me to Brighton and support me on the occasion of my being conferred an Honorary Doctorship (is that the word?) – no, Doctorate – by the Open University. I am to be presented this by a lady who has already visited me here and has been a great help in explaining just what the OU does. In fact, she has sent me a prospectus for the course in ecology, which seems eminently sensible. Then I am to reply, for not more than two to three minutes! After that, a great number of graduands will receive their degrees, for which most of them have worked in their spare time from a job. Often, the whole course lasts for upwards of ten years, so it is quite an uphill struggle and one can only admire their ambition to improve themselves in this way.

A young photographer, Jonathan Buckley, was here all yesterday. He picks up on what the visiting public are commenting. Looking at *Euphorbia rigida*, whose flowering stems snake around at ground level, a visitor suggested that it needed staking! Can you imagine the writhing monster trussed, like Joan of Arc, to a stake? The weather was kind to Jonathan. First it was sunny (photographers seem to dread unadulterated sunshine); then clouds appeared and it became almost overcast (good for blues, like forget-me-nots), then more sunshine.

As we (the Wye students) stood by the Horse Pond, this morning, and I was pointing out how snakeshead fritillaries (and other small, early flowering things) can make a living around the gunnera crowns before these have expanded their enormous leaves, one student (evidently with an eye for such things) spotted the scarlet of a lily beetle, feeding on a frit. This beetle is fast becoming a curse, having arrived here only quite recently. Fergus says he has killed some 16 of them today. Both the adults and their larvae feed on the lilies and near relations, leaving little foliage. I do hope it won't arrive in Essex too soon. Its original centre, from which it has been spreading, seems to have been suspiciously near to the Royal Horticultural Society garden at Wisley.

I was at Wisley, yesterday, with my trials-judging committee. One trial, under glass, is of pelargoniums with scented leaves and a principal criterion for excellence is, naturally, the quality and power of each variety's scent. The snag is that by the time you have sampled a couple of them, one with each hand, the scents of the rest all become confused with what you already have on your fingers. Fergus suggested that someone on the Wisley staff should grab a leaf and hold it to the nose of each committee member in turn. Being half Turkish, I suppose he does not appreciate the embarrassment this would cause by placing one's nose close to a stranger's hand. Such familiarity. Anyway, this course of action was not recommended by anyone on our committee.

On Easter Tuesday, Pip and I set off on a six-day gardens and nurseries trip, westwards, ending up in Monmouthshire, where his parental home (a most hideous modern building, which he loathes) is.

As we were a little early for our first date – lunch with Mary Keen – at Pip's instigation we turned off the M4 to seek one of the most prolific native habitats of our native snakeshead fritillary (*Fritillaria meleagris*). He knew the parish in which it grows, some six miles south of Reading. As we crossed a hump-backed bridge, there was a flat water meadow to our right, and I suggested that that would be the sort of place for it. We went on to the village, which appeared, superficially, to be deserted, and I set about enquiring. The first property – a chaotic mess in its 'garden' – was currently uninhabited. At the second, which was semi-semi-detached, there was no knocker or door bell, so I tapped on the door. A small dog barked within. Then a cross-looking, elderly lady opened a nearby window. I explained our mission and, on realizing I wasn't trying to sell her something, her face softened. She knew about the frits, all right; we had to go back along the road we'd come, and just before a humpbacked bridge, on the left . . . etc. Actually, it wasn't that field but the next one to it and Pip was the first to find them – not yet out by some 10 or 14 days, but there they were, in quantity, the stems still curled up at ground level and the buds looking very like a snake's head.

We spent the first two nights with Rosemary Verey, and she was kindness itself, planning a packed itinerary. She took us to Highgrove the next morning, and that was most interesting. It is all, apparently, aimed to look its best in spring and early summer (HRH is in Scotland, after that), so was looking pretty good, mainly with bulbs, right now. The cedar close to the house is truly magnificent, with its splendid tiers of horizontal branches. I wasn't too happy about the bird feeders, hung about it. I'll tell you more, when we meet.

From there to a fascinating house and garden, Rodmarton Manor, owned by Simon Biddulph and his family, who only moved in five years ago, on his mother's death. The very long, curved house was built in stages by his grandparents in the second and third decades of the century, and a little beyond that – all with local labour, who also made the specially designed furniture. I could have gone on examining that for a long while but the garden was the thing and Simon has become totally engrossed by this, since their arrival. As far as I can make out, he and the gardener, Ken, who is now in his early fifties I imagine, but came straight from school, do the whole thing. And it is a large garden. The walled kitchen area is enormous and Ken is a natural on training wall fruit and rambling roses against the walls.

A lot of yew hedging and topiary. The yews are clipped between June and August – phenomenally early, in fact – and the first to be clipped do make a little secondary growth, later in the season. There are two beautiful old weeping birches – quite tall and with their silvered trunks showing at the top, before the branches start their downwards cascade. An excellent weeping ash, too.

In Pip's village he took me for a country walk to show me his favourite lifetime's haunts and we saw wild daffodils in patches alongside an alder-lined stream. They were just at their best. He also showed me a ruined stone house, which yet had firm remains, since it had been well built; he called it his house – the place where he would, in imagination, have loved to live. It was good to see these things through his eyes.

I must be off to bed, to be fresh for tomorrow. I have even had a new suit made for me! My terminal suit.

Oh! we've had an embarrassment in the nursery. A customer, to whom we sold 20 of the elegant bamboo *Himalayacalamus* (*Arundinaria*) *falconeri*, last autumn, rang (he was very nice about it) to say they were coming into flower! If that is not actually the end of them, they will look unacceptably hideous for a number of years. We can't replace with the same bamboo, obviously, as ours are coming into flower, too.

Much love, Christo

– ❦ –

Monday 29 April

Dear Christo,

As I feared, weeks have gone by without my finding time, or energy when I had time to write to you, which is a pity because much has happened. As is often the case I have written vivid descriptions for you in my head but never within reach of a pen. It is too late now to master the typewriter, let alone a word processor, much as I admire your flexibility in mastering the latter so efficiently. But you must know by now I have certain blocks: most machinery I happily leave to others, the kitchen excepted. But even there I could not tolerate a bread-making machine.

Before I get going I must moan:

O God make it rain

Loose the soft passion of the rain!

Send swiftly from above

This clear token of thy love,

Make it rain!

Something seems to have gone very wrong between God and this bit of the country. I first read this poem by Herbert E. Palmer when I was a schoolgirl and its strong imagery and liquid sounds have haunted me to this day. With good reason, since once more we are in a state of serious drought, having had only 10mm (½in) of rain in the past nine weeks.

This week the ceiling of grey rumpled cloud has been so low and pregnant, you felt it must give birth any minute. Two times a little patter of spots appeared on the paving – and then, nothing. Visitors arrive to tell us they have driven through torrential rain only a few miles away – ugh! Where are the sunshine and showers of April, blue skies between tears, cool, damp air for all the tender flowers of spring? Last weekend it was 23°C (73°F) in the house for heaven's sake! The lovely American erythroniums, *E.* 'Pagoda' and *E.* 'White Beauty', which originated in the foothills of the Rocky Mountains, emerging just below the snow melt, were visibly shrinking as they attempted to open. Mercifully, Monday was cold and dull (imagine being relieved by grey skies yet again!) but the relief turned into disbelief as the capricious weather moved off into the North Sea.

I can feel you itching to tell me off, but there is no need. We have already, so early in the year, been irrigating; for example in the Wood Garden which, apart from being decorative, is also a source of shade-loving plants needed for propagation.

For much needed relief, I sat and watched the television presentation of your Exotic Garden. Although I have seen the real thing several times, I was enchanted. It was a totally new experience, seen through the eye of the camera, sometimes poised overhead, or dipping between contrasting shapes and colours. Some of the combinations of flower and foliage caught in a frame made me think of William Robinson designs, flowing and exotic.

You will not have forgotten the occasion when you gave the 'Lecture of the Year' for Northern Ireland, organized by a group of dedicated nurserymen, led by Billy Douglas, a man vast in size and personality. Sadly he died last spring. I had been invited back to give the memorial lecture. Billy was a hard act to follow, but he had chosen his team with care – people who enjoy working together as friends, not rivals, each contributing something special. As a result, the facilities and ambience are the finest I have met anywhere. Greatest relief for a speaker and audience is a projector which focuses automatically, throwing a strong beam over the heads of a 600-strong audience on to a huge screen which descends from the ceiling. Behind me, on the stage, was a garden, designed and constructed by these busy nurserymen, as a compliment they hoped to my style of gardening. What a compliment! This high standard has evolved over the past 15 years, during which this event, drawing people from all over Ireland, has been taking place. There is no doubt this extraordinary event will be carried into the future 'to encourage a greater knowledge, understanding and love of horticulture' – that is their theme.

Not surprising that Billy's absence was palpable that evening. I missed him too. He had been a kind and entertaining host, with his wife Rita, on my first visit. But a natural leader has emerged from the group: Mike Snowden, the head gardener of Rowallane, he of the spun silken beard reaching down to his waistcoat button. I stayed with him and his wife June, so had the opportunity to look round an enduring garden.

It might appear dour at this time of year with no 'colour' at all, but I found it very peaceful to walk among stately conifers providing substance in winter among a wide variety of deciduous trees, both in turn providing a setting for the vast rhododendrons, the reason for most visitors making a pilgrimage to Rowallane. Thank God for those who planted (and plant) trees, knee-high saplings to give something inexpressibly precious to future generations. And thank God all those who care for them.

Soon after that I was away again, first to Guildford University, to talk to the Southern Counties group of the Hardy Plant Society, and then I drove down to Weston-Super-Mare, the only misadventure this time being a long delay (three hours' extra journey time) due to roadworks. Here, I met another young, but very successful group. Launched only three years ago, and quite independent, they filled the Winter Gardens with a lively audience, passionate, as they said, about plants.

After that, it was good to be home and know I had some time to work in my own garden, which suddenly had been transformed in one week from penny-plain to twopence-coloured. Despite no rain for weeks it is beautiful. In the Gravel Garden the bergenias have completely obliterated their winter-tired leaves, packed now with thick rhubarb-red stems crowded with flower. They make big swirls of pink, all shades, from pale rose to vivid carmine, against the gravel paths. We have never had such a show of them, as so often the flowers are reduced to brown mush by late frosts. (The blackthorn is only just opening its snow-white blossom on the roadside hedges so we could still have more frosts.) Marvellous contrast for all these pinks, including a great sunburst shape of the double-flowered *Prunus triloba* and the dark purple grape-like clusters of *Fritillaria* 'Adiyaman', are the luminous heads of *Euphorbia wulfenii*. These plants, with that magnetic shade of yellowy-green, will hold centre stage for months, well into June.

I wanted to tell you about the Wood Garden, how David and I have been doing a lot more planting there, how thrilling it is to see how previous years' plantings are making up. The Wood Garden is essentially a spring and early summer garden. But all that must wait.

Re-reading your letter before last, I telephoned my twin brother whose interest is in books and theatre. He immediately had the answer to your query. Edith Evans did appear in *Daphne Laureola*, a play by James Bridie, produced sometime in the '30s he thought. Now I will have breakfast. I have taken a leaf from your book and try to get up early, the only time there seems to be to write.

Love, Beth

—❧—

Tuesday 30 April

Dear Beth,

Your letter arrived this morning. Yes, it is dry. I don't think we've had more rain than you – only 10mm (½in) this month.

While Pip and I were in Herefordshire, we had a day of solid rain all through, getting heavier as the day progressed. But there was only about 4mm (¼in) at home. Still, these aggravations occur every year and it's useless to get worked up about them. I like your quote from Herbert Palmer, but speaking as an atheist, I find myself unable to believe that praying for rain will be of any use. Someone else will be praying for it to stay dry. And just think: our lack of rain during the past winter has been compensated for by abundant rains in the Portuguese Algarve and south Spain – the first for six years. Our loss has been their gain; you can't grudge them that. I daresay nature will compensate with a horribly wet and blowy autumn.

Meantime it's spring, and nothing seems to have suffered to date. Fergus drove me to Brighton on Saturday morning, with the sun behind us, and we returned in the evening with the sun behind us again. The light was wonderful. He was (as I am) especially entranced by the chalk escarpments that we passed near Lewes and we stopped in a bay, close to one such, to stare without being hustled. The patches of yellow on the cliff face were formed by wallflowers. He wanted to scramble up to them, there and then.

The poor fellow must have had a pretty dull time through the prolonged ceremony watching while over 300 graduands walked up to the podium, to be individually congratulated. The chairs we sat in, incidentally, were made by Rupert Williamson, whose workshop is at Milton Keynes, where the Open University is centred. They have encouraged local talent. You've admired his work at Dixter, and thank you for that cutting about the exhibition of modern furnishings that is being shown at Belsay Hall, Northumberland, this summer. So right to make the point that modern furniture doesn't need to be in modern buildings. The OU degree-endorsing congregations take place in 16 different locations – 15 in Great Britain, one in Paris – and all the furniture and equipment they own, including Rupert's chairs, follow them around.

I was sitting next to the Vice Chancellor, Sir John Daniel, and had an excellent view of the procession. Many graduands were quite middle-aged or elderly, wanting to make something extra out of their lives after being freed from earlier responsibilities – family, in most cases. There were three to four times as many women as men. And, as you might expect, the sciences attracted more of the younger students than the humanities. The expression and manner of each, as he or she approached Sir John, was a study in itself. Most had friends and relations in the audience – there were some 1,300 to 1,500 people assembled in this vast conference centre – and a cheer went up at the critical moment, from little groups scattered through the auditorium. The graduands themselves behaved in every possible manner, some extrovert, waving to their friends before holding out a hand well before arriving at the Vice Chancellor, some entirely introverted or shy. A pretty young woman might have little to say for herself, while one that you might have called ugly turned out to be the *jolie laide*, dynamic and fascinating as a personality. Sir John was marvellous, chatting to each of them. Their eyes creased into smiles, and you could tell by the crows' feet behind their eyes how used they were to smiling.

In four cases, there were wheelchair graduands, and the Vice Chancellor then stepped off the stage and went down to them. Others were deaf and, throughout the proceedings, a young woman stood to one side of the stage and conveyed what was being spoken to the congregation in sign language. I felt quite caught up in the proceedings. My own little speech was well received. That was early on.

I'm so glad that the gardening Lecture of the Year event will continue to flourish, following Billy Douglas's death. I'm not surprised. That band of small nurserymen has an excellent organization, and they pull together. I do think that, by and large, nurserymen and gardeners are a good bunch. There is more competition than ever, these days, but it doesn't seem to sour relationships.

Much love, Christo

∗⚘∗

Saturday 25 May

Dear Christo,

Weeks pass like days this time of year. No sooner do we start a new week than it is Friday! Where has the time gone? What have I done? As it is with you no doubt, all kinds of things influence my week – the weather, visitors, administration, planning, planting – and even more adverse weather!

Today at last a beautiful mild sunny day. I am almost exploding with things to tell you but first I must discipline myself and answer your letter. When it came, I wanted to sit down and reply right away. I did make a struggling start but ended up in bed with a hot water bottle, needing 24 hours down my 'deep dark hole', to retreat from all the pressures of the garden and business. (It was a perishing cold day.)

Many congratulations on your Honorary Doctorate. I am particularly pleased it is for the Open University. It seems to me a big compliment both to you and the other graduates who have been thoroughly motivated to pursue their courses and thus enjoy a new world opening up for them. Having been inspired yourself early in life you have in your writing, and by example at Dixter, spent a lifetime motivating people of all ages. No one is too old if they have a passion to learn. To absorb new ideas is to live anew, to see the world (and our gardens) with fresh eyes.

I am sometimes saddened (more truthfully irritated) when meeting young horticultural students in the garden, who all too rarely exhibit a real hunger for the subject. Perhaps I malign them, maybe they are too shy to express it. They all seem to be studying landscape design; yet when I ask a few elementary questions I find they are astonishingly ignorant about plants. What motivates them I wonder? Surely some passion (a lot, I would say) is required to fuel the energies, mental and physical, to pursue a career in horticulture? Many students seem to have chosen this career without ever having put together a few plants and then watched their performance for a few weeks, or months, let alone two or three seasons.

Are horticultural establishments too much occupied with principles, economics, government regulations and the latest fads and fashions of hard landscaping, leaving the students to discover for themselves the vocabulary of garden design? A day out to visit a well-known garden can be just a spree, a welcome break from the classroom, but without there being some knowledge and experience of plants and planting, I think much of it will be passed by, not seen. We can look, but we will not take it in, without knowledge. We take in what we recognize. As our plant vocabulary grows, this is reversed: we almost pass over plants familiar to us to reach out for something we do not recognize.

The subject is endless. We say ourselves one lifetime is not half enough. Creative gardening is such a vast canvas, and there are constantly new introductions to dazzle or confuse. Fortunately, I meet people of all ages (and I know you do too) who have this commitment. Sharing our love of plants with them is one of the prime pleasures of life.

Which reminds me, I owe you another big thank you for three blissful days at Dixter at the beginning of this month. In all the years I have been coming, about 20 years I think, I have never been in tulip time. It was, as ever, a lesson for me. Somehow I have never got on with tulip cultivars. Too often they have succumbed to disease, or else their sheer size and flamboyance has frightened me off. But like so much good planting, everything depends on the setting. At the porch I was welcomed by a potful of huge cream tulips, feathered with scarlet, lolling against a screen of the little South American nasturtium, *Tropaeolum tricolorum*, also scarlet, grown up a framework of hazel twigs. Who could resist that?

Then, in the Long Border, a colony of guardsman's red tulips, which you reassuringly said had been there over 20 years, all varying in height and size of flower, with a yellow-leaved elm and purple hazel for background. Other flame-, almost orange-red, tulips had pinkish-purple shadows on their satin-finished backs, combining all colours of the sunset. Then there were more feathered types, some in discreet blends of pink, purple and white, while another group, strangely subdued in bud (a marbling of brownish-red with flecks of yellow), flared open into a fairground mixture of hot red on yellow. It was exhilarating.

Then I turned away from the house and border to take in the distant view: the gently rolling farmland, sheep grazing, oast houses in a fold of the land, the valley bottom filled with woodland just showing a haze of new green, a solitary Lombardy poplar in the foreground. I know this so-called natural beauty is also man-maintained, yet because it appears changeless and effortless, we are entranced by it. Long may it remain so.

Nearer to hand, or rather to foot, lay your meadow garden, all passion spent, since the daffodils were finished, but to my eye no less beautiful with many grasses coming into flower with romantic names such as meadow foxtail, sweet vernal grass, timothy grass and crested dog's tail – while dark violet purple spikes of the green-winged orchid were threaded among them.

This early morning I wish I could have snatched you up in a helicopter to share the garden here with me. Such mornings are rare, when everything seems right. You have to make time, to stop and stare. In the Wood Garden, sunshine and shadows falling across the pathways accentuate the dominant colour now, a thousand variations of luminous yellowy-green seeping thro' the entire garden. Brightest of all are *Euphorbia robbiae* and *Smyrnium perfoliatum*, with the yellow-leaved *Symphytum ibericum* 'All Gold' making bold contrast of shape. The golden-leaved raspberry, *Rubus idaeus* 'Aureus', threads its bright path through a green carpet of *Omphalodes verna* where big clusters of juicy green colchicum leaves promise a good show of flower in the autumn. The yellow-leaved creeping jenny sprawls across the path like spilt sunlight. It also makes good ground cover for drifts of the black fritillary, *Fritillaria camschatcensis*.

Having envied yours for long enough I am now thrilled to see my *Exochorda* x *macrantha* 'The Bride' dripping with clusters of white flower, undamaged by bullfinches at last. There seems to be a sharp decline in these handsome but maddening birds. Could it be sparrowhawks, or magpies that are decimating them? Whatever it is, our flowering shrubs are at last being allowed to bloom.

Solomon's seal and the sweet lemon-scented smilacina are just opening, standing in carpets of sweet woodruff, spangled now with tiny white flowers. These plants remind me of staging my Chelsea exhibits. I loved doing that, but often wished then I had more time to be creative in the garden. Now eight years later, the Wood Garden and Gravel Garden (both made since then) have given me the chance to experiment with many more plant groupings, and to see them develop into mature associations.

This spring we have been doing more replanting in the older parts of the garden. Of course all these new areas look spotty and dotty at first, even though we plant in drifts where we can. The plantings need two or three years to gain character, for some things to seed around, for the plants to sort themselves out. I feel we just give the plants a start, then they take over. Sometimes something unintended produces a spectacular effect, but I could not tolerate this morning a huge and handsome plant of onopordum (the Scotch thistle) in among the woodland plants; it really was a cuckoo in my nest, much more at home in the Gravel Garden.

I am still reminded of the damaging frosts earlier in the month which burnt off new growth on astilbes, hostas, and the beautiful bronze leaves of young rodgersias. It even blackened young leaves on our native ash. Yet seedlings of the tall Indian balsam, such transparently delicate-looking things, were untouched. How strange! I particularly like the white form, *Impatiens glandulifera* 'Candida', and make sure it is tucked in open places in the Wood Garden, together with teasels to make features late in the year when there is not much else.

By holding everything back, the beastly cold winds throughout April and May have been frustrating for us in the nursery and garden, but have resulted in the most beautiful spring I can remember. Everything has come so slowly, the tender green foliage warmed here and there by bronze and amber shades are still with us.

The ancient oaks which form such an important role all round my garden are only now spreading tiny transparent yellow leaves, picking up the incredible colour of the euphorbias throughout the garden. *E. robbiae* in the shade, *E. palustris* by the waterside, *E. wulfenii* and *E. polychroma* dominating the Gravel Garden. Against tantalizing skies, heavy with French grey-navy blue clouds, these plants positively give off light. I can see them from my north-facing kitchen window as I prepare our evening meal and am enthralled by them. They lead my eye into the distant scene, blossoming trees, layers of new leaves, a dark pool of water rimmed with big yellow kingcups.

Sharing the garden with us, filling it with song from dawn to dusk, are nesting birds. By 4.00am the chorus is under way: thrushes, blackbirds, willow warblers, chaffinches and robins, with woodpeckers drumming a beat in the distance. Suddenly they all stop to get breakfast for their young, except the great tit who monotonously rings his bell all day. From my stove I can watch flycatchers and blue tits when I should be stirring the pot. Is it any wonder I am all behind with letter-writing?

Love, Beth.

PS While rain has washed out village fetes and cricket matches during the Bank Holiday period, we measured 5mm (¼in) for this past week, 40mm (1½in) in the past three months.

Monday 27 May

Dear Beth,

Here I am in front of a good fire, in the solar, just as it was six months ago. It took me ages to get installed (feet up on the sofa, both dogs alongside my right leg). First I realized that Canna wasn't with me; she is so absent-minded. I went back for her; she was still in the bathroom. Then, having returned, I found I'd left my specs in the bathroom. Back again. This time I counted my paces in yards; it was 73 yards (over 66m) each way. So the double journey, what with picking up my laptop from the parlour, was a good 300 yards (over 270m).

We're at the end of the Bank Holiday weekend and were satisfactorily busy. More than half our visitors are foreigners. The weather has been sullen on the whole. Of course we are glad to have a bit of rain, but the wind that accompanies these depressions is far from welcome. Anyway, I think one may now say that it is good growing weather and everything is looking lush (including weeds, of course). The bananas (*Musa basjoo*) have at last been unwrapped from their fern coats and are alive and well.

I had two young people (she's 23, he's 35 and they've known each other since last September) for the first time, yesterday and today, and that was really good. Fergus joined us for dinner. We met them at the dinner we attended at the Turkish ambassador's residence, some six weeks ago. Mike Reed has been working in Turkey, on behalf of Fauna and Flora International, organizing the propagation and growing of *Galanthus elwesii* and *Eranthis hiemalis* Cilicica Group, so that they are properly marketed to Britain, instead of being sent, for a pittance (the exporters received less than 1 per cent of the final retail price), straight from the wild (millions of them), to Europe via Holland. This has brought the local populace more than twice as much money as the other method, and there was a celebration, this month, at the harvest. Great rejoicings, in fact. Everyone has been affected, one way or another, in this small community, south of the Taurus mountains.

The extra cash means that greater health care can be afforded, or longer education for children beyond the official lowest limit of 11 years. Mike was really proud to have been the instigator and organizer of this project.

It is only a start, as you may imagine, and the same drain of bulbs as has been going on in Turkey has now shifted to Georgia, where the situation is currently so chaotic that organization is pretty impossible – except that the Dutch seem to get what they want (five million bulbs of *Galanthus ikariae* last year, it is estimated, and even more this year) from native habitats, for a minimal payment that will undercut the new trade in Turkey. Quite a horror story in its way.

Mike and his partner, Judy Tanner, are non-meat-eating and he, additionally, cannot eat dairy products without suffering (Pip Morrison is another such), so I have been cooking lots of fish and substituting olive oil for butter. Today, since we currently have a lot of purple-sprouting broccoli, I made an excellent dish taken from *Jane Grigson's Vegetable Book*. You cook the broccoli, then add a tin of chopped anchovies (or at least I did), olive oil, wine, seasoning and de-stoned black olives; warm it up and there you are. Eaten with my brown bread (made on Saturday).

I have guided three parties of Americans round the garden, in the past week, and it was raining (and blowing) on each occasion! I have another tomorrow. I hope there won't be a repeat. Fergus guides those who don't want to pay my fee and he is anyway very popular. Edward Flint stood in for him, when there were two parties in one day; he was so popular as to collect £40 by way of tips. I do have some lively young people around me.

Andrew, our business manager, got himself organized to open the shop, down in Perry's cottage below the nursery, last Tuesday. There had been a lot of preparation. Trade was very quiet, the first day, but has been building up steadily. I was brought in, beforehand, to sample biscuits, cakes, ice creams, sorbets, jams, chutneys, etc. – this at my request, because I'm anxious that we should sell stuff of good quality. It's the same with the books (all horticultural), garden tools and other hard-ware. Andrew has been tremendously energetic, over all this.

Well, that's it for now, dear Beth. One of the dogs is fidgeting disastrously – too hot under its rug, I daresay. I do hope you're coping with this excessively busy time of year.

One more thing, I received a message for you on a card from Roz Greenwood in Hamilton, Victoria, in respect of her companion Ann's sudden death: 'I had a wonderful message from Beth and if you speak to her please tell her that what she wrote was deeply comforting and that I will treasure her words.'

Much love, from Christo

– ❧ –

Saturday 8 June

Dear Christo,

It was sheer heaven this morning to walk through puddles on the nursery after a desiccating dust-dry week. Still no rain. But last evening the sky closed in, flat and menacing, the air heavy and still.

The temperature was over 25°C (77°F) in our shady, wood-ceilinged living-room. Thunder storms were forecast, but we don't believe it; maybe – but more likely not. I went to bed with only a sheet, too tense to sleep. By 11.00pm distant lightning flickered feebly round my room, but there was no sound – the drama was too far away.

Slowly, slowly, the storm crept closer with vivid sheet lightning and reverberating thunder sounding like piles of heavy furniture being tumbled above in the attics of the universe. A slight and silent pause – and then a drumming of heavy raindrops on my window-sill, on the magnolia leaves and on the table and terrace below. It was all we've waited for, a release, after so much anxiety and tension. I got up to walk about the house and watch from all the windows as lightning lit up the garden. It lasted about 20 minutes. I went back to bed and slept.

This morning I measured 8mm (1/3in), and was thankful even though it is little enough. But we had been spared golf-ball-sized hailstones which visitors later told me had fallen near Cambridge, smashing glass in greenhouses and denting cars. The garden felt invigoratingly fresh at 20°C (68°F). Yesterday it must have been nearer 30°C (86°F) in the Gravel Garden, which, in spite of the long drought, looks magnificent: the drought-tolerant plants, alliums, foxtail lilies, helianthemums, tall woolly verbascums, honey-scented clouds of crambe, soft blue catmint, and still weaving thro' it all, the electric green of euphorbias. I try to make time to walk round it every day, to enjoy every individual player as well as the combinations which contribute to the overall landscape effect.

I keep reading disturbing articles prophesying the climate in 50 years time; that East Anglia and the south of England will support only vast prairies of maize or sunflowers, with dust-bowl summers and winters increasingly cold. That the north will be like Provence, growing vines. Who knows? If it be so, my little experiment in the Gravel Garden will be a pathetic effort in the face of such extremes.

It may not greatly affect gardening in our lifetime; I am concerned for my grandchildren, but for now, we can only accept each season as it comes. I face the coming months with some optimism since this present moment of glory throughout the country has come despite last summer's ordeal, but also with caution and not a little anxiety.

I much enjoyed your last letter. It arrived the day after I had posted one to you. It is not nearly such a long walk for me when I've left my reading glasses in the office at the far end of the house, but today, finding myself having to trot back and forth from house to vegetable garden, I counted my steps: 100 each way, and that is a bore when I've forgotten either labels, scissors, string or my notebook.

Although I try to keep them organized in a little basket you can bet I then forget my knee pads, or, more important, my gloves. I hate wearing these but since I became allergic to most plants in my mid-40s, a mild attack, as I have now, of itching little watery blisters should be enough to warn me. It is especially likely in this very warm weather.

I was very interested to read of the good work done by Mike Reed in stemming the wholesale digging and exporting of bulbs from Turkey. Since the fever for plants – any plants in the wild – is accelerating all the time, the future could see the extermination of many, even common species. It is no consolation to think they would be preserved in gardens. Nothing takes the place of plants, animals, insects, et al., left undisturbed in their native homes.

Today I have spent in the vegetable garden. It is my most private place, apart from some of the nursery areas. Although I need the stimulation of the decorative garden and all that is involved in planning and maintaining it, here, among the neat rows of vegetables, where visitors cannot find me, and staff, considerately, rarely disturb me, I feel at peace. It is a source of so much satisfaction throughout the year, from seed sowing to the moment of carrying squeaky fresh vegetables and salads to the table. With such unreliable springs as we usually have, I cheat a bit by sowing most early things in pots and pans, keeping them in an unheated tunnel, ready to transplant as soon as conditions are suitable. Sowing things like peas, broad beans and onions is a cheerful way of spending an otherwise dreary day in February. Now my 'Hurst's Greenshaft' peas and broad beans are shoulder high, in full flower, just beginning to pod. There are basketsful of salad: 'Little Gem' lettuces, heavy with tightly packed heart; rocket rushing up to flower (succession crops on the way!). Whether it be an old wives' tale or not, I always pour a kettle of boiling water along the drills before I sow parsley. I recently read the seed should be sown then, immediately, but in April, when I sowed mine, I let the soil cool a bit, and now have well-germinated rows of both flat and curly types. Summer savory and sweet basil are both flourishing in this heat.

My soil is not very good for blanched celery although I manage celeriac. Today I planted out something called cutting celery. It makes thin green stems; a little patch is handy for flavouring.

Although I think the vegetable garden looks attractive now, its narrow wood-edged beds rapidly filling with all shapes, shades and textures of foliage, you might think it looks like a farmyard, since I mulch some of the crops with straw to conserve moisture and carpet the paths also with straw to prevent weeds germinating. As we do irrigate the vegetable garden, the paths would otherwise become green overnight and, naturally, spraying to kill weeds is verboten here, although I confess it is practised on paths elsewhere.

The overwintered vegetables benefited by the tediously cold spring; purple-sprouting broccoli, and that marvellous winter kale, 'Pentland Brig', have fed us for weeks. Next season's brassicas are waiting to go out, growing on now in largish pots. Since my soil is infected with club-root, I have to take the usual precautions, liming the soil and rotating crops, but also I find that pot-grown plants usually get away without undue infection. Calabrese is looking very healthy, just making its first flowering shoots, but still I keep my fingers crossed.

My small asparagus bed must be about five years old now. This year has been the best, with stems fat as cigars. The small vegetable tunnels are full of tomatoes, peppers and cucumbers with a few special runner beans, a form called 'Musica' already reaching to the top of their canes. It can also be grown out-of-doors. The beans are very long, wide and flat, stringless and crisp. Delicious. To keep pests away from the tunnels I plant an enchanting little marigold, *Tagetes* 'Golden Gem'. It grows and flowers non-stop throughout the summer. Charming anywhere, including little vases.

Now a final bit of showing off. This evening for supper we have eaten young carrots, sweet as honey, pulled from a corner of one of the tunnels where I sowed them last Christmas; and new potatoes the size of bantam eggs, grown for an experiment in a bucket. There were 35. And the tops taken from the broad bean plants. All served with salmon, topped with crème fraîche flavoured with grated lemon peel and chopped parsley. Such energy after 8mm ($\frac{1}{3}$in) of rain.

A little story to finish. Blue tits have nested again in the central tunnel of the hose-reel outside the potting shed. Every day the girls are using this hose to water trolley-loads of plants, but the parents are not the least perturbed. This morning Ulrike, my German summer student, noticed a baby teetering at the entrance, so she put out her hand and the little one hopped on to it, looked around and flew away. She waited and another one followed. What a delight!

Much love, Beth

— 🎕 —

From Germany, 6–10 July

Dear Christo,

Once more I am sitting at a table in the window of my room overlooking the courtyard of the Meierhof, the home of my old friend Helen von Stein Zeppelin. Ten years ago I wrote in my garden notebook of the wonderful party attended by about 100 people, nurserymen and their wives, who came to celebrate her 80th birthday.

Last summer, with Susanne Weber (her companion and invaluable right hand for almost 50 years), I stood by her bedside and we made our last farewells. She died the next day. Her daughter, Aglaja, is now manager of the nursery and a party has been organized for recent past students and their families. The courtyard is alive with young parents and about 25 small children dashing about, including tiny babies in prams, all creating a very moving thread of continuity. The old house, with its great sheltering roofs (reminding me of Dixter), seems alive with past, present and future.

When I first started my nursery, about 25 years ago, Alan
Bloom was in my garden one day, and said, 'You should go to
Germany and meet a great plantswoman.' So, about 20 years
ago, with his encouragement, I came for the first time and over
the years have learnt much and made good friends. Like other
inexperienced English gardeners perhaps, I did not then realize
what a rich collection of herbaceous plants were to be found in
European nurseries. In our insular way we tend to think they
are mostly a British invention but immediately I stepped into the
nursery at Laufen, I felt at home. As I walked beneath a narrow
archway tangled with old roses, stepping over clouds of alchemilla
and cranesbills, I felt welcomed by many familiar plants and
excited by many more I did not then recognize. In recent times the
introduction of new plants from all round the temperate world
is accelerating at a bewildering pace, the choice now is almost
too much.

Over the past ten years or so I have had students from several
countries, all seeking gardening experience in England. The
exchange of ideas and methods has been valuable for us as well
as for them. Of them all, from Japan, USA, Australia, Germany,
I have perhaps the softest spot for my German students, and this
week I have been welcomed and entertained by no less than five
of them, including the first, Mechthild, now a mother of three sons.

The day after I arrived, Thomas and Andrea, who were with
me last summer, carried me off to spend the day in their beloved
Black Forest mountains. We walked and climbed three hours up,
three hours down, through woods and meadows and along steep
rocky slopes. Only halfway did I suddenly remember my dodgy
knee of last year! 'Heavens,' I thought, 'I must not be careless and
end up on a stretcher!' Fortunately, all was well. Perhaps plenty of
practice walking daily round the nursery and garden enabled me
to enjoy once more the thrill of climbing into the sky, viewing the
vast landscape, the valley of the Rhine with the Vosges beyond,
all spread below like a map. Of course, I was delighted my young

friends were as glad as I was to make stops, and finally sit down at the top.

After writing this I went down to join the party in the courtyard and was welcomed by my students to sit in their group under the open-sided shelter where in olden times the horse carriages stood, and now hung with green curtains of *Parthenocissus quinquefolia*. Here were tables filled with great bowls of salads, all kinds of soft cheeses mixed with herbs, crusty round loaves of farmer's bread, and tender steaks of grilled lamb. Two wooden casks provided red or white wine. Huge fruit flans, cherry, raspberry, apple and apricot with bowls of thick cream went well with good coffee. It was a bubbly occasion; everyone had so much to say to their neighbours, all old friends from the days when they were students here.

Later in the evening slides were shown from days past. Especially interesting for me was to see the nursery at work throughout the year and to see it having fun too, on a particularly hot day, the staff hurling buckets of water at each other. There were hard times too, one especially in July 1983. The aftermath of a tremendous rainstorm found half the nursery washed away. Those plants not torn out of their pots or the earth were smothered in layers of clay washed down from the vineyards above. In the village, road surfaces were ripped open, walls dislodged, a large tractor half buried in rocks and stones. It was a sudden disaster and took months to recover. But as Thomas, one of my last year's students said, it was man-made. All kinds of measures are now being taken to protect the village, including grassing down the vineyards instead of leaving the soil bare after hoeing.

Sunday 7 July
This morning I walked with Suse Weber to the small neighbouring village, St Ilgen, to join in a big open-air lunch organized to provide funds for the church. Sitting at long, bare tables we could have sausage, grilled steak, potatoes and pickled gherkins, with wine or beer to drink. Need I say, it rained! Fortunately, we found

a place under shelter, and suddenly huge white umbrellas appeared from nowhere for those stoical enough to sit outside. Small boys dashed about clearing away empty dishes and glasses. Everyone seemed to know everyone else, warm greetings all around. When the rain had eased we looked into the simple Protestant church, admired the newly restored frescoes, then walked home.

The landscape around Laufen is framed by forest-clad mountains with high open meadows in the clearings. Below them, gentler slopes are ribbed with vines trained on horizontal wires. The owners do not live in scattered farmhouses, but in small red-roofed villages tucked into the creases of the valley which looks to me like a crumpled eiderdown. The vineyards and scattered fruit trees, plum, apple, cherry and walnut, line the small winding roads, which are fringed with flowering plants and grasses. Sometimes I am startled by an unorthodox viniculturist or perhaps his wife, who has planted lavender, roses, santolina, day lilies, even gypsophila to drip down over a stone wall built to prevent the clay soil washing down into the road. Almost every householder in the village owns a section of vines, driving out to work each day in small green tractors designed to fit the narrow rows. Almost all of the houses are large, combining ample living space with barns for storage. Solid wood for building is abundant and used everywhere for doors, window frames, shutters, balconies and wide overhanging eaves where hay is stored. Many have big arched doorways to let thro' the trailers piled high in autumn with the grape harvest.

It really rains here. All night it clattered on the fig tree beneath my window, splattered against the gravel-floored courtyard. I was obliged to get up and close the windows to deaden the sound. I can't remember doing that at home. Now I sit watching the rain run along the gutter where it joins the vast roof of the opposite wing of the house. In olden times this part of the building housed the cattle. The great expanse of chestnut-coloured tiles is broken by long, narrow 'eyelids' sheltering dormer windows, without glass, just wood-framed openings, letting air into this huge roof space, where once all the washing of the household was hauled up three dangerously narrow staircases. These roof spaces were also used to store grain, and sometimes horticultural chemicals needed by the rest of the village.

To cheer ourselves up after a solidly wet afternoon Aglaja took me yesterday evening to Mullheim, a little town not far away, to a Beethoven concert. The music was the Violin Concerto Op. 61 and the Pastoral Symphony. The soloist, Thomas Goldschmidt, was born in Freiburg, so is very popular here as he is also well-known throughout Europe and the US. He also paints, makes clay models and has eight children, so is very creative, like J.S. Bach. His youngest children, a twin boy and girl, sat with their mother just in front of us. Susanne tells me that Goldschmidt's mother was a famous singer, and when they were wondering why she was not present to sing in Bach's St Matthew Passion, the message came to say she had been occupied giving birth, also to twins.

I was very moved by the music; by being in Germany and hearing Beethoven brought to life by his own countrymen and women. Throughout the concerto the audience was rigid with anticipation, while the familiar storm from the Pastoral was electrifying. Listening and watching the sound leap from one instrument to another, and then the whole orchestra reverberating as one with thunderous sound, was a new and exhilarating experience.

Monday 8 July

This morning after breakfast I walked in teeming rain to the nursery and found Thomas and two girl students bailing water out of a long frame filled with drought-tolerant plants! They had been completely submerged until these young people set to work with hose and buckets to get the water away. Most of the nursery is on a slope and cannot be flooded except where the torrent meets a barrier, but everywhere is sodden, making work dirty and difficult.

Wednesday 10 July

Now I have moved to Endingen about 30 miles from Laufen. I am staying with Maria and Christoff Gurlitt. Christoff teaches mathematics in Freiburg, Maria translates English gardening books into German. Among her authors are Richard Bisgrove (she translated his book on Gertrude Jekyll), Rosemary Verey and Patrick Taylor. Maria is a perfectionist. Sometimes trying to find the exact word she needs reminds me of trying to solve crossword puzzles with Andrew. But I can also appreciate her frustration when faced with elaborate over-writing (this time an American author).

Maria's sister, Hilde, also a teacher, was a student with me for three summers. I think she came to know almost every plant in the garden and still remembers where they grow. Loving plants so much herself, she wants to pass this on to the small children with whom she identifies. I went to the kindergarten to see what they had made. Surrounding the low school building is a pleasant grassy area, and around the perimeter Hilde and her children, aged between three and six, have made a long curving border. Although the overall effect is uninterrupted, it is divided into sections, two children tending each plot. In spring, in groups of four, they shopped for seeds, choosing the prettiest packets. They sowed them, tended them, and each morning they look to see 'who has woken and who still sleeps'. The effect of mixed annuals backed with great sunflowers was astonishing. Hopefully, something of this living experience will remain for some of them, throughout their lives.

Saturday was spent in Freiburg with Hilde, who has the topmost flat in a large old building. I love this beautiful old town. In the centre is the elegant Munster, or cathedral, with its delicately carved spires, sitting like a jewel in the great open space of the market-place. All around is a facade of beautiful medieval buildings with their hightiled roofs, crow-stepped gable ends, overhanging oriel windows, painted shutters and flower-filled balconies, like something from a child's story-book, or the setting for an opera, while the forest-covered slopes appear at the end of almost every street.

Freiburg is a famous centre for music schools. There are often little groups playing in the market-place, thronged with people, shopping for the rich variety of fruit, flowers and vegetables. We had two unexpected treats. First three musicians from the Far East, perhaps Chinese, perhaps from Tibet, three men, two young, one middle-aged and plump, his deep bass voice harmonizing with the light voices of the young men and their curiously carved instruments. They wore national costumes: tall black hats, wide-sleeved brocade jackets and long embroidered boots with upturned pointed toes.

Later we thought we heard an organ, such a fine sound, where could it come from? Pressing through the shoppers (who also interested me – such a medley of styles, shapes and sizes), we found it was from an accordion, but such as we had never heard before, played by a young man with sensitive features, hair tied back in a long, dark ponytail, eyes closed. He was playing the famous Toccata and Fugue in D minor by J.S. Bach. He played with such passion, his legs alternately lifted off the ground as he swayed with the heavy instrument – and then with sweet precision, picking out the quiet passages. We could not leave until it was ended.

It must be 30 years since I sat on a bicycle! Tante Hermine, aged 77 years, said I could use hers so timidity was out of the question. A practice evening cycling through fields of maize, little orchards of cherry, apples, pears and plums with huge walnut trees everywhere along the roadsides, prepared me for something more adventurous.

On Sunday morning we set off to visit a specially pretty village, Burkheim, perched on a hillside overlooking vineyards and wooded mountain slopes. In this region the woodland is predominantly deciduous, with oak, beech, birch and willow. I noticed a lot of robinia, but introduced many years ago, it has become a weed tree. Although attractive, it seeds everywhere, smothering out native species.

Entering the forest, it was a delight after the heat outside to feel the air fresh and cool, shadows and sunlight making patterns across the damp path. Eventually we found a picnic place by a large pool, fringed with willow and birch trees, laid a cloth beneath the canopy of a huge oak, and smelt the strong scent of ground ivy bruised by our feet. Blue and red demoiselles skimmed the green water, fluff from the willows drifted through shafts of sunlight, little frogs plopped among the reeds and grasses.

When I was in Endingen last year, I bought Andrew a textbook on the geology and flora of this region, known as the 'Kaiser Stuhl' (King's Seat), to help with his research into the homes of some of our garden plants. The area is rich in wild plants as well as cultivated crops because of its structure. Over thousands of years volcanic mountains have been worn down, depositing rich, fertile clay soil into the lowlands. There are also seams of hard limestone which have been terraced since Roman times to grow the vines which still cover these slopes today. Among the wild plants which have caught my eye have been *Genista tinctoria*, *Dictamnus alba*, *Digitalis ambigua* and the silk-tasselled grass, *Stipa pennata*. Botanizing in the mountains reminds me of walking holidays in the High Alps and Dolomites with Andrew many years ago. Seeing familiar plants in their native settings is a bit like looking through old snapshot albums.

Finally, I must tell you I may have to throw out my clothes in order to be able to carry home the new plants I have collected for the nursery and garden. Just outside Freiburg, a brother and sister, Ewald and Heidi Hugin (both so blond they make a perfect Hansel and Gretel), are running a nursery of unusual hardy plants. I first met Ewald many years ago when he was head gardener to the Grafin von Stein Zeppelin at Laufen. It seems Ewald has connections all round the temperate world. You might think I had enough plants to care for, but I can't help feeling like a child in a sweetshop when faced with the temptation of new plants. Now I must stop as I have to carefully pack these treasures ready for my flight home.

And then I must think what I shall do for our picnic at Glyndebourne, less than a week away.

What a lot we shall have to talk about.

Much love, Beth

− ✿ −

Monday 8 July

Dear Beth,

It is 9.45pm and I have just been dozing in my bath – nice long baths for stretching out in, as you know – and I must hope that will enable me to keep awake for long enough to write to you. Perhaps that doesn't sound very flattering – of course, I should keep awake – but you know how liable I am to drop off. Often, when writing an article, I have to stop to close my eyes and be wafted away, for a few minutes, before resuming.

Today, I have written for *The Guardian* on the use of annuals in mixed plantings, rather than in beds on their own; and have finished off an article started yesterday, for *Practical Gardening*, on dahlias. (Tomorrow, I will write my weekly piece for *Country Life*.)

Then, this afternoon, I was visited by a party of six professional horticulturists, who really knew what they were looking at (not everything, but a lot). Klaus Jellito, who concentrates on seeds of hardy perennials for the wholesale trade, was one of them. He wondered how I should know about him (what modesty!). I mentioned you, among others. He is keen to have seed of *Allium cristophii* in quantity, so I might do something about that, if it's not too difficult to collect. He was also impressed by *Viola cornuta* 'Alba' and by its absolute whiteness, in contrast to any viola with heartease (*Viola tricolor*) in its blood. I could send him a bit of seed of that, but need most of what we can collect, which has to be done a little today, and a little more tomorrow and the next day, for ourselves. Like many white-flowered plants, it has light green leaves – a characteristic that I find appealing.

For the most part, they were Americans, Kurt Bluemel one by adoption, but still close to his Bavarian relations. He is such an interesting and knowledgeable man. Not easy to work for, I daresay, but then I don't have to. He was glad to see I grow some ornamental grasses: his forte, of course.

Leading and organizing the party was my close friend, Allen Bush, who has given up his hardy perennials nursery in North Carolina and moved, on remarrying, to Louisville, in Kentucky, his new wife's home area, and I visited them there last autumn, and he organized the lecture that I most enjoyed. Such a responsive audience and plenty of them. They sold a lot of my books, too.

I have two youngish (30s) Americans staying with me now, my kind hosts when I was in Philadelphia, last fall. They've not visited Europe before. A cheap fare to England is available but they are not flush for money and feared the expense of living in hotels, in England, not to mention the cost of food, which is noticeably higher than in the States. So I am able to provide a base.

We visited Sissinghurst, yesterday, which I'd not been to since last year. The season being late, their once-flowering roses were still flowering freely and making a great show. But I find it hard to understand how old-rose enthusiasts can turn a blind eye to the fact that when a bloom dies, its petals are not shed but turn brown and soggy (given present weather) in the truss. So later blooms in pristine condition have to be seen in this shabby setting.

Parts of the garden were really good and stimulating, best of all being the cottage garden, planted in shades of red, orange and yellow. The white garden was also at its peak, with the central rose arbour at full blast. Later, when it has finished, one wishes it weren't such a central and inescapable feature. 'Iceberg' roses were in full fig – how effective and yet how boring, with seeing them everywhere. The shrub has no style.

Also excellent was the herb garden – the best I know, although so full of admirers that it was hard to dodge them to see the plants. Everywhere I admired the high skill of upkeep, though some areas still seem to coast along in the wake of the high spots. There is still little sense of adventure at Sissinghurst, which is inevitable in the face of tradition. Really, it is amazing how much change is achieved by stealth. If the public could see it as it was in Vita's day, they would be both amazed and shocked.

I shall have my sandwich and a bowl of raspberries – the first, this being a late season. I'm in the Yeoman's Hall with the dogs by my side – not with the door into the garden open, as I should like, but with a gas heater on. Such has been the season. On a chilly day when I had let the dogs out to do their duties, Canna, as usual, wouldn't concentrate but was chasing bay leaves in the wind. Along comes Fergus: There's no chance, Christo. You'll be here a couple of hours. Shall I bring you a chair out? He so enjoyed his unpremeditated visit to you that Sunday morning, while I was in Scotland. Said it was so relaxed and became more and more so. He needs that. After three solid weeks of work, including weekends, his eyelids were fluttering involuntarily – a sign of strain and overwork. Now, he has had two relaxing days in London, and feels totally restored. But then he will get himself into the next climax of overwork.

He spent hours in London Zoo, where his girlfriend Amanda works, and was so impressed by the dedication of the staff to the animals they look after. I'm sure the Zoo doesn't get sufficient recognition for the work of conservation that they do, saving many creatures in endangered habitats, from extinction. All the time, they have the hope of being able to re-introduce their charges to the habitats from which they come, but so much depends on whether those habitats still exist to the extent of making this possible.

Amanda, who is in the birds department, is currently looking after a rare species of hornbill chick. The male is generally entirely responsible for feeding the young, but in this case unaccountably died. Amanda took over. The chick has to be fed every two hours, so she takes it home with her at nights. Other keepers are just as dedicated. Yet funds are being cut, all the time. How much is the public aware of all this, rather than being fashionably encouraged to exclaim 'poor caged creatures'?

10.30pm. Sandwich finished. Actually, it was a one-sided sandwich, being the crust of my own loaf.

We had a most destructive hailstorm, on Saturday, two days ago. The hailstones were large and didn't melt for a good half hour after falling. There was a lot of soft foliage for them to pepper, as though a shot gun had been fired at them. It was the day of our local flower show. Even with the rain during the run-up, a class for roses which had eight entries only mustered one exhibitor, in the event. Had the hail fallen a day earlier, the show would have been wiped out, apart from the photography, domestic and children's work (work done at school) sections.

It is horrid to write letters in a vacuum. Here are some points that I feel like taking up from your letter. I flaunted my Honorary Doctorate in your face, but I quite forgot to recognize (and you were too modest to mention) that you had received one such, a number of years ago, now, from Essex University.

Most landscape architects, designers or whatever they like to call themselves, are out for the money, of course, and it is a tiny minority who are truly committed and who embrace a love of plants. Hold on to them.

Our meadow areas are still wonderful, to my eyes, though the last of the many orchids are now running to seed. Late, this year, which will delay our mowing activities – probably till the end of August. The seed pods on *Camassia quamash* are still quite green, I noticed this evening. Late highlights are being provided by meadow cranesbills, common bent (a rosy haze) and tufted vetch, *Vicia cracca* – a great favourite with me. I saved some seed, last year. We shall pot the seedlings, individually, and plant them out in areas we should like them to colonize, in the autumn.

Early morning, as you describe it, is very precious. All is quiet and fresh. As we are sited near the top of a hill, the one view that I permit myself over the countryside (the rest being blotted out for the sake of shelter against wind, which is most gardeners' primary concern) is often filled with mist in its hollow. Trees in front of it are sharply etched, as a consequence. The early morning quietness seems to close the garden intimately around me, so that when I speak, to one of the dogs, it is as though we were in the privacy of a well-furnished room. Up to this morning, I have been turning the two sprinklers on soon after 5.00am. I then retire to bed again, for an hour, with the dogs, and we snooze. When thoughts concerning life at Dixter have stopped whizzing through my brain, I usually subside into a contented state of torpor. We finally rise around 6.30am. Fergus comes in at 8.00am. That is always a freshly renewed joy. Sometimes he is in such a rush that he immediately wants to visit each member of staff, to set them off on the day's tasks. At other times, he is ready to talk. Something interesting to discuss has nearly always occurred to one or other of us.

You write of willow warblers in the dawn chorus. I haven't heard them, or chiff-chaffs, here for years, now; nor whitethroats, nor lesser whitethroats – all taken for granted at one time. Butterflies, like silver-washed fritillaries and ringlets, have vanished. But I have been heartened by the huge influx of painted ladies from abroad, this year. I noted that there were masses of them, agile on the wind, on 10 June and they seemed to go to a wide range of flowers for nectar, anchusas being especially popular, but moon daisies by no means despised. Friends from as far distant as Monmouthshire tell the same story and I saw quite a few, as well as a red admiral, in Scotland. So maybe there'll be a plentiful home-raised brood, later on. I also saw a clouded yellow, on 10 June, but that was a lone example. Back in the 1940s, we had great clouded yellow years, when they were everywhere. No longer. Maybe changed farming practices will bring them back.

Yesterday, I picked 199 broad bean tops for my two American friends and myself. Pods are forming, but not so plentifully that I feel like sparing them to cook them whole. The peas will be ready in quantity next week, so I hope I shall have some willing slaves staying, to enable me to prepare them for the freezer. Those and broad beans are the most successful for putting down. If you buy them frozen, the beans are hard and the peas ostentatiously taste of added sugar, which should be quite unnecessary.

Can I remember, you ask, the countryside and gardens everywhere so sumptuous with blossom? That is surely on account of last year's hot, ripening summer, much as we revile it for putting many plants under stress. Even in Scotland, the results are evident. In Fife, at Balkaskie, for instance, the *Cordyline australis* on their vast terrace, were about to flower, although it was evident, from their largely undivided stems, that flowering is rare. There were, apart from the cordylines, amazing plants surviving there. A huge *Magnolia delavayi*, large old common myrtles, a loquat, some 25 years old, crinodendron, a double white Banksian rose (shy flowering, however), two species of *Hoheria*. A vast white *Clematis montana* rose from the terrace up three flights of a stone stairway. Such an overwhelming vanilla scent.

I was staying with Ruth and Robin Crawford at Balcarres at the time, and he got permission for us to visit. Ruth was her usual dynamic self and she has worked wonders on her new pond garden. Like you, she loves to take on new enterprises. How she manages with just Donald Lamb and one other beats me. They have a strenuous battle with sticky willy, as she calls goose grass, or cleavers. We too, but it is nearer to getting the upper hand at Balcarres. She is such a gifted gardener, and has given me the subjects for at least two articles.

This laptop is making my legs ache, so I will say goodnight, now. It is nearly 11.00pm anyway.

Tuesday 9 July

Canna greeted me effusively, when I called the dogs, early this morning. That is ominous. She usually lies in bed. Sure enough, she had left me a 'present'. After I had rubbed her nose in it, she knew that that was over, and was effusively affectionate.

I wrote my *Country Life* piece on roses and on how Ruth mitigates their bony habit by spacing the bushes (Hybrid Teas) quite widely apart and interplanting with all kinds of perennials, which act as suitable companions.

Before I forget, I must tell you what a success the 15 plants of calabrese you brought me in early May have been. At first, unused to the big, wide world, they sulked and their leaves turned purplish. Then they settled down and have been producing a huge crop. Twice, I presented them in an Italian way given by Jane Grigson, mixing them when cooked with some white wine, black olives (stoned) and chopped-up anchovies. But the crop was such that I froze quite a large batch.

Fergus, Justine (our intern) and Steve Brooke are working on the Long Border, refurbishing. Fergus reckons it is a reward for them, after doing a series of mundane jobs of no particular interest. The foxgloves have been pulled out and the oriental poppies cut back, leaving quite a lot of space for more planting. Our favourite photographer, Jonathan Buckley, is here. He spends the whole day. There was veiled sunshine, this morning, but it has turned glum.

A highlight, just now, is the floor of the Sunk Garden, where areas of paving are matted over with the pink burrs of *Acaena novae-zelandiae*, intermingled with self-appointed bird's-foot trefoil, *Lotus corniculatus*, which is yellow. Above them rear clumps of self-sown spotted orchids, *Dactylorhiza fuchsii*, now going over, and the fresh lime-green of biennial *Euphorbia stricta*, which you also mention. Fergus and I broke off for a mug of tea on the sunnier of the stone seats there, and were entranced by the effect of low sunshine illuminating the euphorbias from behind.

This tapestry looks wholly uncontrived, but takes quite a lot of upkeep, preventing undesirables from taking over.

In the Barn Garden above, the dragon arums, *Dracunculus vulgaris*, are opening a great surge of their handsome purple blooms and Fergus has discreetly supported them. They have pedate leaves resembling those of *Helleborus foetidus*. The arum smells a lot more foetid than that – of rotten meat, and there is a buzz of blow flies around newly opened blooms. Well, you can stand back.

I must tell a bit more about my two weeks in Scotland. Good luck with the weather: I never had to get out my rainwear, though it was chilly at times. Alan Roger was amazingly active; they have diagnosed diabetes, which is far easier to control, at his age (87), than a stroke.

Colin Hamilton's garden at Frenich (beautiful sunsets over Loch Tummel) was full of all kinds of poppies. Pip Morrison and Ruth Crawford came over for lunch, the day I arrived. It was Pip's first visit – he spent the night, in fact, and thoroughly enjoyed himself. After visiting Ruth and Robin at Balcarres, I went on to Edinburgh, where Pip has just finished his second year as a landscape design student. He enjoys the course a lot and can add to it his love of plants and visits to the Botanics, where he took me. I noted some fine trees, but most are unavailable in commerce.

Next morning, we fitted in a visit I was keen to make. I have for many years sold a moderately unusual range of plants to Holyroodhouse, whose head gardener, placing the orders, is Mr Muir. I thought it would be nice to meet the voice I have spoken to on the telephone. It seemed impossible to phone him, so we just called on the off-chance and were lucky. He is much younger than I had expected – early 50s, at a guess – and is really interested in the job, which also includes the wild grassland of Arthur's Seat and the Salisbury Crags. He drove me past them and one could see *Geranium sanguineum* and *Helianthemum nummularium* flowering beside the road. There are considerable constraints on

the efficient running of his gardens, but he is certainly not one
to moan and it is only a pity that there are not many with the
opportunity to enjoy the results of his work. They are anyway not
designed to have the public tramping through them.

After that we did some shopping before taking off, for the
weekend, for a large cottage on the west coast, overlooking
the Sound of Mull, with Mull itself, pretty forbidding in most
weathers, near enough to stretch your arm out to touch. The
cottage belongs to Sarah Raven, who is married to Adam
Nicolson, Vita Sackville-West's grandson, who live near here
and whom I got to know at the time that Pip was a volunteer
in the garden, last August. So he got to know them too and
was offered the use of the cottage. Sarah is keen on plants
and gardens, and intends doing some volunteer work here
quite soon. I knew her father, John Raven, who was a classics
don at King's, Cambridge, but also a gifted field naturalist
and gardener. He co-authored *Mountain Flowers*, in the New
Naturalist series that Collins later ditched. But I use that book
whenever I'm in the west Highlands.

Pip is gregarious, and had assembled nine of us to visit the
cottage from Friday evening to Monday morning. I thought it
sensible to make myself useful in the best way I can, so we shopped
for food on the basis of my planning the evening meals. In a
delightful Pakistani family's greengrocery, I was able to buy nine
dead-ripe avocados, to eat the same evening, and they also had
ripe mangos – so ripe as to look rather revolting, but I have never
tasted better. After starting the meal with them, we had two large
chickens done in two casseroles with masses of whole cloves of
garlic. You cook for three-quarters of an hour in a hot oven, and
this mellows the garlic wonderfully.

Next evening it was kedgeree with smoked haddock, followed
by a large, steamed chocolate pudding – my mother's recipe.
Steaming this was a bit tricky, as there wasn't a purpose-made
steamer, and with quite a bit of steam escaping, it took longer

than usual. Third evening, Delia Smith's Spanish Pork with Olives, the best casserole stew I know. That was followed by my mother's so-called Danish pudding, which is served cold: a layer of apple (already stewed, if the apples are hard, but they were soft), a layer of chopped dates, a layer of marzipan, made with ground almonds, sugar and egg yolks. That is cooked for 15 minutes in a slow oven. The pudding is then covered with stiffly beaten egg whites (difficult, without an egg whisk, to get them really stiff) and granulated sugar turned into them and baked for a further half hour. When cold, you cover with whipped cream and a scatter of toasted, flaked almonds (if you have them). This is always popular and the recipe was taken down by more than one.

We were five females and four males, incidentally. One couple got into trouble the first day, when Pip and I and two others were out in my car. Despite his warning not to, they decided to cross the Sound, each in a canoe, propelled by a double-ended paddle. But the Sound is treacherous, with wavelets whipped up by quite moderate winds.

On the return journey, Simon, a large young man overturned. Alice, his girlfriend, put up the alarm signal and a nearby yacht came over to the rescue. Simon's body temperature went down to 35°C (95°F) and he had to have medical attention, and the police came into it. Naturally they wanted to know whose the canoes were and Pip was nervous as being involuntarily responsible. However, all ended well and Simon soon recovered. The canoes were landed at some distance, and had to be fetched on the top of the second (estate) car.

On the Sunday, Pip and I went out on our own to a hill that I knew to have been John Raven's favourite, though he didn't mention it by name in his book. It is not very high – less than 2,000ft (600m) – but quite a long way to reach on foot, so we did some 12 miles (19km) that day and I was rather proud of myself being fit enough to accomplish it. It was good weather and a good day.

Pip drove my car and he is a good driver but may have the occasional lapse (he is only 20; I have more lapses than he does). On one straight stretch, along the return to Edinburgh, we had three cars in front of us tagging meekly along behind a heavy vehicle. Pip decided to overtake. But there are many selfish drivers on the road who, while not prepared to overtake themselves, won't allow anyone else to, unless they can pass the whole train of vehicles in one go. Pip found that he couldn't quite do this. He wasn't allowed to edge his way between the second and the third cars, so he came to a halt on the wrong side of the road as also did the approaching car. 'Smile,' I said to him. It's the best you can do in the circumstances.

I'll be seeing you here, soon. We'll be eight, including Pip, who is currently spending three weeks on his own in Corsica.

Love, Christo

— ✻ —

Saturday 3 August

Dear Christo,

It is already 12 days since I came home from my weekend with you (just two days after flying home from Germany), and our special evening at Glyndebourne. During these days my mood has been useless for writing, the days too crowded with incidents, good and bad, leaving me so tired that even small problems became dark trees in my forest of worries. But 10mm (½in) of rain this week and much lower temperatures than last summer finds the garden looking colourful and lively and finds me with energy to spare, so it is a pleasure to write and tell you what has been happening.

Before I begin I want to thank you again for such good company and good eating at our high-summer weekend at Dixter. You are so good at combining old friends, of all ages. It was a lovely surprise to find Raymond Treasure and Gordon Fenn sitting sipping sparkling wine with you on the terrace after a tediously hot journey (I used up a whole pile of tissues – never again do I make the journey on a Saturday). As Raymond and Gordon are both devoted to farming and gardening we can share so much with them. As farming and BSE in particular are such controversial topics now, it was fascinating to hear Raymond talking not only of present difficulties but also how farming practices have changed since the days of his great-grandparents. And as good food lovers all, I shall never forget the gourmet meal they made for us when we visited John Treasure, Raymond's cousin, with Fergus, only a few months before John died.

Inviting a party of three young couples to share *Arabella* with us made the occasion especially enjoyable. Although it was the second time I have seen the opera with you, it was a fresh and magical evening, made more so by sharing the reactions of the young people coming to Glyndebourne for the first time. It is not just the prestige of the place. It is the whole atmosphere, the sense that everyone involved gives their best.

For us, the event really begins with planning the picnic, prepared this year by Fergus and Amanda who made Turkish stuffed tomatoes. Weren't you intrigued by those tiny sweet dried currants which Fergus brings back from Turkey?

When you led us, in the mid-afternoon heat, to park ourselves in the empty centre of the large lawn at the back of the fine old house at Glyndebourne, I felt suddenly concerned for all our chilled provisions, but luckily the cold boxes did not let us down. The chilled champagne before the opening tasted wonderful and prepared us for an evening of sparkling fun. The whole production achieved such a high standard – the voices, characterization, costumes and scenery all fitted the music admirably. It matters not that the story might be farcical. There are times when one could wish for more such enchanting escapes from reality.

I have to tell you, I almost forgot we had used my car as well as yours to take our party to Glyndebourne, adding two hours to our total journey. Only just in time on the way home did I remember my last dilemma and managed to scrape to a filling station with the meter hovering on empty. What an escape!

I think I told you of my being bitten by a tick, probably when picnicking in damp grass in a forest by the Rhine? On arriving home from Dixter, and going through a folder of accumulated papers, I found a newspaper cutting brought in by one of my staff. It was written by a doctor who had been attacked by one of these creatures, and subsequently suffered, a month later, a swollen limb and fever.

Fortunately this subsided without treatment but he listed the more serious results of infection caused occasionally by these bloodsucking beasts involving neurological complications and worse! Although I had seen a doctor on my return home my ability to concentrate was somewhat diminished after reading this. My doctor's advice had been to do nothing until symptoms developed. To ease my mind if nothing else I resorted to my own remedies: Echinaforce, derived from the American purple cone flower, *Echinacea purpurea*, considered to boost one's resistance to infection, and tea tree oil for an antiseptic. (Do you remember us being shown small-leaved twiggy bushes of the tea tree growing beside a dried-up river bed when we were lecturing in New Zealand, about five years ago?) It is now about three weeks since I discovered this horrid creature clinging to my arm. The swelling has subsided considerably so I hope all will be well. Essex is one of the most heavily infected soils for tetanus. Everyone working on the nursery is regularly vaccinated but doubtless many people are not. The chances of becoming infected, by either ticks or tetanus, may be rare, but the chance is not worth taking.

I was very sorry to see the effect of the hailstorm in your garden, especially the damage on some of the large-leaved plants in the Exotic Garden. In spite of it I thought the planting there even better than last year, possibly more restrained, dare I say? Perhaps it had not yet burgeoned into the fullness of late summer and autumn. Every month brings change, adding or taking away as the seasons progress.

Wasn't it a joy to sit with our friends on the seat at the far end of the Long Border and watch the evening sun backlighting the ebb and flow of plants and shrubs spilling on to the paved walk; pin-pointing a scarlet rose; making transparent the plum-coloured leaves of the smoke-bush; outlining slender, tapering spires of the mountain spinach orache, so usefully grey-purple against creamy plumes of *Artemisia lactiflora* or bright yellow verbascum? Through a gap in the castellated yew hedge, we spied clematis and roses held high against the sky where they scrambled through trees and shrub. A conflagration of colour to warm the senses.

I needed this comforting memory to offset one of my bad days. It began with a horrid letter of complaint. Although fortunately we have few (we work hard to avoid them), they always hurt. I spent a considerable time with members of staff assessing the nature of the complaint and checking to see if arrangements made for the comfort of our visitors were adequate. Sensible suggestions for improvement we welcome, and act on them when we are able to do so, but we cannot please everyone, it seems.

Tired by the rest of the morning's problems, I was just nodding off to sleep when Rosie came to tell me the barley field alongside the garden and stock beds was on fire. Rushing to the scene we heard a loud roaring sound and were appalled to see a great wall of flame, well above our heads, rushing towards us. I trembled with fear that our precious boundary oaks, hundreds of years old, might be destroyed, and what about my nursery stock? We all fled back as the heat raced towards us, but suddenly there was quiet; the flames stopped by a wide mown headland (combined with the efforts of the fire brigade which had by then arrived).

Still shaking, I retired to the vegetable garden for relief, deciding to thin the young carrots I had sown just before going on holiday. As I knelt quietly doing this satisfying job, one of the lenses dropped out of my spectacles. Walking back to the office I laid all the pieces on Rosie's desk with the note, 'I shall be glad when it's bedtime!' thinking she might take them into town next day to be repaired. Soon she reappeared with the mended spectacles: she had been able to fix back the lens, her sharp eyes detecting the tiny screw. I was so grateful.

I much enjoyed your long July letter. (No, not a bit too long.) I saved it up for tea-time. I'm glad you met Kurt Bluemel, since I was disappointed to be away in Germany when he came looking for new seeds here. It made me smile to think of us all chasing round the world for new plant introductions. I was doing the same in Germany. Don't you find that whatever you hope may be a 'first' in your new catalogue will already be listed in the *Plant Finder*! It is astonishing the current enthusiasm for plants, and the speed with which new introductions can be circulated. Not all, I might say, stand the test of garden worthiness, nor, having some slight deviation, merit a new name.

To pick 199 broad bean tops and count them must be a record! It made me laugh because I always count them too. I wonder why we do that? I don't count sweet peas, or sprigs of parsley. Now the beans and early peas are pulled up, and I've replanted the site with winter chicories. Not the Belgian 'Witloof', but my favourite 'Crystal Head' and two kinds of red chicory; one makes a round cabbage shape, the other has long, narrow leaves. All of these and the curly endive I start in pots, to make sure of full rows, if the conditions are not favourable for sowing seed straight into the soil.

Alas pride goes before a fall! My second crop of 'Hurst's Greenshaft' peas were looking as splendid as the ones I left behind, most of which June has put in the freezer. I was looking forward to eating them fresh and honey-sweet, but I have just found they have mildew suddenly. Some pods may fatten up, but I fear the crop will be damaged.

Alpine strawberries, on the other hand, are a delight, protected under a layer of green netting supported by wire hoops. When I lift the netting the strong strawberry scent rushes out making my mouth water. This variety, 'Baron Solemacher', I brought home from Balcarres when we last stayed with Ruth Crawford. I marvelled at her energy and pioneering spirit, reclaiming yet more acres of wilderness with frighteningly little assistance, and imaginatively planting them with stout ground-cover plants.

I wonder if *Origanum vulgare* 'Compactum' would help cover the soil in her rose beds? I think you might like it, too, perhaps to replace *Persicaria vacciniifolia* beneath your hedges of *Aster lateriflorus* var. *horizontalis*. Or use it anywhere where a fairly formal edging would catch the eye. It makes dense round buns, about 15cm (6in) high, smothered just now with clusters of tiny pink flowers, saved from being nondescript by dark maroon-tipped calyces which add a spiciness. I think in certain situations where box is conventionally used, this compact attractive plant would be preferable as an edging and much less bother. This morning it is alive with bumblebees and painted lady butterflies, as are also the tall screens of *Verbena bonariensis*.

For days now the whole Gravel Garden has been aflutter with insects, including a moth I don't remember noticing before in such quantities. It's a sturdy-looking thing, triangular shaped, mousey-brown in colour, distinguished by a dark brown band, edged white, on its underwings. Not good news, my friend Janet the potter tells me. Could be an immigrant producing evil grubs (like vine weevil), to make trouble next year. Do you know anything about it?

Andrew and I enjoyed having Pip spend a day with us. It is good to meet someone so young who, from an early age, has wanted to be a gardener, and so already has a wide vocabulary of plants. He was a joy to me since plant names now often drop through the holes in my memory. I was pleased he could see how well the waterlilies have done since last summer when he plunged into your Horse Pond to dredge them out for me.

After a tour of the garden and nursery we joined Andrew for tea, sitting under the magnolia tree on the little sheltered terrace. (His emphysema means he cannot walk very far now in the garden without becoming breathless.) But he was very interested in Pip's course on landscape design in Edinburgh, and hoped he might eventually become involved in working with native plants, to preserve and enhance the environment.

Andrew always entertains with his general knowledge. We were talking about our local town, Colchester. It was originally founded by the Romans and called Camulodunum. One of the last governors of the British-Roman community, when at the same time Saxons were beginning to invade the east coast, was, we believe, called Arturius. Although the tales of King Arthur and Camelot are based in the West Country, Andrew wonders whether Arturius and Camulodunum might have been the origin of the legend – who would know?

There are so many nice things going on this time of year: drying herbs hanging up all around the place; spare beds filling the house with the scent of lavender and bergamot; fresh mushrooms springing up over the mown car park after 15mm (½in) of rain. (We had 48mm (2in) in July, better than last year.) Less nice things include big decisions to be made: we need to install a larger pipe to bring mains water to the property, more loos for visitors, more tunnels for propagation, not necessarily for more plants but better facilities to maintain good quality.

But now, Sunday after lunch, I shall put my sunbed in the shade of the magnolia and take a little nap, knowing you will be snoozing with the dogs beside the Horse Pond.

Much love, Beth

— ❧ —

Monday 12 August

Dear Beth,

10.15pm and Canna has just been sick in the darkest recesses of the room. She had the grace to jump off the sofa, first. I shall investigate in the morning. If it was her dinner, she will have returned to her vomit.

That fire must have been terrifying, but I think the oaks saved you as much as the headland or the fire brigade. When I was in Australia, the second time (without you), I kept hearing about the terrible bush fires, but one property was saved by the oaks that had been planted around the house. The usual gum trees accumulate inflammable dead material around them for years. It simply doesn't rot, so it is there, full of oils, to go up in flames when the moment arrives. Oaks, however, remain cool and green and accumulate virtually nothing, so they act as a barrier.

Keith's predicament with the wasps, which you told me about on the phone, reminds me that we have a nest in the roof which Fergus and Andrew intend to deal with. If you call in a professional wasp nest exterminator, it costs £50 at least, probably more by now. I know, because when I was away in September, about three years ago, Quentin, who never had qualms about spending my money, called in the pros to deal with a nest in the barn. Last year, we had a nest in the wall of the Yeoman's Hall, where I'm sitting. Fergus and Perry dealt with it with absolute success, using derris soon after dark (and after fortification in the pub), and when the wasps were all at home.

Today, it really rained. Thunder rain, but you could hardly call it thunderstorms. It was too polite for that. From 7.30am, the thunder was rumbling around for three hours, but never with loud claps that made you jump. The rain was ideal, falling steadily without wind. Then, in the afternoon, we had two really heavy showers (more thunder), with the rain coming down like the proverbial stair rods. A bit of hail, but nothing serious. It'll be interesting to measure how much fell, tomorrow morning.

You once asked whether I had changed everything to metric. No. My kitchen scales are the same as before the fashion changed and still measure in pounds and ounces. I don't see why they should be changed. They do their job perfectly well. It's the same with the maximum and minimum thermometers in the porch. They still work perfectly but happen to keep on registering Fahrenheit.

Really, one should train oneself to be equally at home both in metric and imperial. To an extent, I am, but not wholly. Young people can't think in imperial at all.

Thank you for being so kind to Pip when he visited you. He is coming back tomorrow. I am so glad. In the year I have known him, he has come to mean a lot to me (and vice versa, I believe). He can drive me to lunch at Scotney Castle the next day. An invitation from Betty Hussey, now 89, is tantamount to a command. I admire her so much and, despite the infirmities of old age, she is always such a lot of fun. With glee she related how a young official of the National Trust (who now own Scotney and will open the house, as well as the garden, as now, in due course), wrote in a report: 'When Mrs Hussey is no longer in residence . . .'

Pip will also, I hope, drive me to Wisley where I have a meeting on the Trial Ground – of tender and hardy salvias and gazanias from seed and from cuttings, among other things – this week. Being forced to look at plants really carefully, instead of taking them for granted as a part of the general scene, is very instructive, I find.

Pip will also help me with the apricot crop, some of which now demands attention, but he covered it with netting when last here. As the crop doesn't all ripen together, the net will need removing, or partially removing and then replacing. Quite a tedious job. The fruits look so beautiful. I photographed them yesterday. Today's rain revealed various weaknesses. A gutter downpipe goes bang through the centre of the apricot, but is evidently blocked, as the gutter was chucking it over the top, straight on to the apricot itself.

After a rain like that is the ideal moment for pulling weeds out of paving cracks, so I had a spell for 1½ hours, up to 7.30pm, on the terrace, working until my bushel-capacity trug was full to overflowing. Having expatiated in my last letter on the beauties of the wand flower, *Dierama pulcherrimum*, this was my principal target, as it seeds itself so freely and you can have too much of it. The corm is very quickly drawn to a depth of 10cm (4in) or so. All I can do is grasp a fan of leaves and tug. They break off just above

the corm. I hope that will be enough to do the trick. The myrtle
has started blooming. How I love it and its scent. There's probably
a few thousand buds to come. I have been very stern with the
architect in respect of not damaging it when the house repairs on
that wall start, this autumn. They'll be cursing it (and me). But it is
veteran, older than I am and either a cutting struck from a wedding
bouquet, as was customary, or the cutting of a cutting . . .

The chief scent, floating all over the garden, this past week, has
been from the weeping silver lime, down by the lower moat. It is
smothered in blossom this year – just about the last lime to flower.

Tony Schilling, telephoning the other day (he and Vicky are
coming over to lunch with his daughter, Tara, whom I've not yet
met), said he'd heard it reported that I was seen planting. What
could I be planting at this time of the year, he wondered? Well,
Fergus and I like to keep the garden looking good right into
October, so there is plenty of replanting to do as, for instance, in
front of the house, where we have now thrown out the Florestan
carnations, which we treated as biennials. They're never much
good a second time, not having retained any non-flowering
shoots with which to make a subsequent display. On Friday, I was
replanting with marigolds (I know you wouldn't plant marigolds,
but I don't think you would disapprove of this one, which makes
a sensibly large plant, so that its large blooms are in proportion),
interplanted with nasturtiums – a new variegated-leaved seed
strain. It isn't bushy, but runs or climbs, and it doesn't have such a
tendency to hide its flowers beneath the foliage as 'Alaska' – so I'm
told. We shall see.

In the Exotic Garden, we have planted some begonias that we
admired on David Rhodes' and John Rockcliffe's stand at Chelsea.
Ordered then, they have just arrived and although I'm sure they
are intended entirely for cultivation under heated glass, I find that
such plants love the conditions outside at this time of the year.
Streptocarpus are another example and a number of tender ferns.
Of course, we shall lift, pot and house them in October.

The Exotic Garden goes from strength to strength, I have to say. You hazard that it may be more restrained this year, but that must simply be because it hadn't yet reached its peak (or trough) when you were here. Not only have we far more dahlias in bloom, now, but the large-flowered cannas are just opening. Any restraint I may appear to be exercising is on account of the heavy emphasis we lay on foliage. Bold foliage, but still foliage.

Returning to your telephone call. You feel sorrow and dismay at Geoff Hamilton's death. I agree with all the praise you lavish on him but must say that he meant nothing to me. In all his years with the BBC, he never once suggested that I should take part in a programme. That happened only last autumn, when he was ill and off work and Stephen Lacey was his stand-in. I think Geoff was egocentric and nervous of competition. And, although he had a sense of humour he didn't show a shred of it on any programme I saw of his. There is a difference between being serious and solemn or earnest. Undoubtedly he succeeded, but at a mundane level. *Joie de vivre* was not for him.

You say your second sowing of peas went down to mildew. That always happens, in my experience. This year we put on a protective spray and we got an excellent crop without that trouble. We also sprayed our sweet peas, for the same reason and certain mildew-prone clematis – 'Jackmanii' and 'Sir Trevor Lawrence', for instance.

And the limoniums. There are some mildew-prone plants I can no longer be bothered with. Such are the monardas, which never used to be afflicted – and roses, of course.

The prolific moth you write of, that flies and feeds by day, is the silver Y. Unfortunately Janet is right. Its caterpillars do eat our plants – their foliage, not their roots, like vine weevils. I also notice that large white butterflies are laying their clusters of pale yellow eggs on my seakale. Also, no doubt, on the brassicas. But the butterflies are a delight this year, aren't they? There's just been a hatch of common blues in our meadow areas, and we've only just started cutting the grass. Fergus and Jon Arnold, whom we call asparagus legs (he was a student at Wisley, last year, in his year out from college and very hard working) were cutting the grass by the front path, today, in the rain. Their legs and feet got soaking. Fergus said the rain did hamper them, somewhat, but it didn't stop them. As it is Monday and we weren't open to the public, it was easier for them to get on with the job and not to be worried about making a mess on the front path.

Goodnight, Beth. It's now 11.30pm and I've not felt a bit sleepy, but shan't need rocking.

With love, Christo

Tuesday 13 August
Yesterday's rain came to 40.5mm – that's more than 1½in. I hope you got it. Oxford remained dry all day.

Steve Brooke is back from a week's holiday, during which he visited your garden, and talked to you, which pleased him.

—⚜—

Wednesday 28 August
Dear Christo,

Your letter lies beside me on my table waiting my reply. Thankfully I have at last a free morning after days filled with events and visitors. We are only four days from 1 September. Autumn has already sneaked in. This morning heavy white mist hid the garden from view until past 10.00am. I am glad for it, for any drop of moisture which falls. Yesterday, thunderstorms rolled all around us, the skies were black with cloud and any minute we thought we would have to run for shelter. Not far away the heavens opened, but nothing here. Since the beginning of March – six months – we have had 127mm (5in) of rain. But here, at least, the effect has not been as bad as last July and August because we have not had such high temperatures.

If only there were two of me to get round to writing to you more often. I find it both fun and stimulating to write about life beyond gardening. There are millions of words poured out every week in new garden books, magazines, TV and radio programmes. (Who can take it all in?) Personally I think we may have a wider approach to garden design if we have been helped to appreciate other forms of art; to be aware of basic principles – balance, repetition, harmony and simplicity – which apply to all forms of creativity. To look for these ideas in painting and architecture, or hear them in music, has certainly influenced me as much as knowing whether to put a plant in the shade, or in full sun.

Going to Glyndebourne with you has been part of this education, watching and listening to the very differing productions on stage as much, if not more, than seeing how the garden has developed and improved over the past few years. As for being elitist, I agree with you, we all are, who aim for a high level of attainment, whatever we try to do. Unfortunately, the word is generally accepted to apply to events reserved for those who are sufficiently wealthy, or move in the right social circles. I am glad to hear that Glyndebourne, like the Proms, makes provision for children and anyone else who cannot afford expensive seats, to be thrilled by its high standards of achievement and feel, as you say, those 'wonderful emotional shivers' brought about by the entire presentation. I am sometimes asked if everyone attending Glyndebourne wears designer clothes (silly question since they know I don't). The answer is decidedly no, but I would not care to comment further, except to say I enjoy watching how other women dress; some I admire, some surprise me, others are nondescript.

But I'm not nearly so interested in fashion as I am in plants. Few outfits attract me as do the exotic colours and shapes of flowers we grow, and owe especially at this season, to South Africa. All this month I have been impressed by the sculptured beauty of agapanthus, crinum, crocosmia, galtonia and kniphofia, all rivalling the glare of the sun. Their strong colours look wonderful in massed groups. Our nursery stock beds are perhaps the most exhilarating place to see them, hot patches of colour, undiluted, possibly as they may appear in the wild. I have seen kniphofias in South Africa, as we might see kingcups massed in a damp meadow. They grow and flower in the wet season, vanishing entirely when the searing drought comes, as do the zantedeschias (arum lilies), which I also saw in roadside ditches.

We have a wide range of pokers, from the 2m (6½ft) tall *Kniphofia* 'Prince Igor', screaming orange-red, to the cool creamy-yellow of *K.* 'Little Maid', less than 61cm (2ft) tall, which appeared among my seedlings here many years ago. The season extends over many weeks. Some varieties are already in seed, others not yet open.

Crocosmia hybrids seem to be running away with themselves. I'm sure we have too many, beautiful sheaves of flaming colour as they are, there must eventually be some selection of the best. New hybrids of agapanthus also creep into my nursery stock. Some are really exciting with good form and vibrant colour; others only slight variation on a known theme.

Among the whites I still think *Agapanthus* Ardernei Hybrid is one of the most elegant, with loosely held heads of flower faintly touched on the tips of the petals with rosy-purple. I believe you have it in the Sunk Garden. Even more spectacular is one given me by the late James Russell when he was at Castle Howard. (What fun we had listening to him and his sister when they were living in the Bothies at Balcarres, tossing the ball of memory back and forth, almost oblivious of us, as if eavesdropping on another time and place.) Jim said his *Agapanthus* 'Albatross' had been growing for years under a warm wall at Castle Howard. It makes huge spheres of white flowers, delicate in effect because the flowers are recessed on stems of varying lengths. We have grown it here, for safety, in tubs, protected in winter, but a clump tried out in the Gravel Garden survived last winter and is carrying one flower stem, so maybe it can be considered hardy in well-drained soil.

Having just popped out to check my tubs I was startled to find them 'missing', but David appeared and put me straight. He divided them this spring, and stood the pots in a different place. They made plenty of foliage, but few flowers only just opening. Normally the tubs are spectacular with well-established clumps and flower stems standing head high. We also looked at our plants potted for sale; good foliage, but few were flowering. These plants, like hostas, and possibly other fleshy-rooted plants, take some time to settle down and produce flowers abundantly. In the Gravel Garden the agapanthus we planted four years ago have been most effective this year, despite two very dry summers – big bold clumps crowded with rich blue flowers, tempting me to say we must plant more, but David remarked, rightly so, they do not last very long (unlike crocosmia and kniphofia, which produce new buds over a long period). However, I find the seed heads decorative, both green and bleached, so I think we can spare space for a few more, and then must wait patiently for the effect we seek.

Much quicker to fill a gap in dusty August will be extra plantings of eryngium and echinops. Good forms of eryngium, including *E. planum*, with wide branching heads of thimble-sized, deep-blue flowers, and *E. variifolium*, whose deeply carved leaves and long, narrow, spiny ruffs are almost totally silvered, will replace some of the anthemis which would respond gratefully if moved to richer living conditions. Galtonias, tall summer 'snowdrops', have fared better than last summer when their wax-like petals were literally 'melted' in bud. I think they need well-drained soil, with plenty of organic matter, in full sun. Once again, they look best here on the nursery where I can walk between blocks of *Galtonia candicans* over 1.25m (4ft) tall, hundreds of stems carrying snow-white bells. *G. viridiflora* and *G. princeps* are shorter, pale delicate jade green.

I cannot leave out the crinums, although they don't suit everyone's taste, being perhaps over-large and untidy, I admit.

But on the south wall of my greenhouse, two huge clumps have been making a spectacular show, possibly at their best now, but will continue for weeks yet. I think they are both forms of C. x *powellii*. The white form has the most beautiful wide open lily-shaped flowers while the pink form has slightly narrower blooms, pale inside, striped with deeper pink down the backs of the petals. On one stem I counted 15 potential flowers, with buds emerging from the sheath holding them to the top of the stout stem. I gave up counting the stems after I reached 50.

The downside to this plant is that it does need grooming; nipping away the spent flowers which dangle like dirty rags spoiling the pristine effect. The masses of long, narrow leaves can also become ratty and tattered at the edges. Tidying up this plant gives me great satisfaction and doesn't take long; thankfully few plants need it. The pot gardens need more; pelargoniums and argyranthemums are a pleasure to grow – the luxury is having the time to deadhead them.

Writing this letter is showing me we are building collections of plants in spite of ourselves. I used to think it mad to boast of having x hundred of this or that. Fine, maybe, if you hold the National Collection, but how can you care for them all and maintain an interesting garden as well? Running both a garden and a nursery, I am pulled both ways, but I do have the advantage of a dedicated nursery staff, with individuals who like to take over certain species.

At this moment our sempervivum collection is drawing attention to itself. Interested and well-informed visitors sometimes return with new variants in exchange for some of ours. Sempervivums need to be well presented. People with rocky hillside gardens have the perfect setting. Flat Essex needs more effort. We have, alongside the greenhouse, a long raised bed (concrete blocks instead of natural stone). Last year Emily planted it with about 49 different kinds from big potfuls. Already they have spread considerably, and will form a kind of mosaic effect before long, each similar in growth yet fascinatingly individual, like the scraps of fabric we use to make a quilt. Running between them are silvery mats and mounds of the New Zealand raoulias, and a couple of golden variegated yuccas, not more than 46cm (18in) tall, make interesting verticals instead of the inevitable dwarf conifer. They are our stock plants and will be prevented from over-running each other by, I hope, Emily, whose task it is to carefully record their names in her stock-book and pot them up for sale. Emily, now 21 and highly motivated, first came to me when she was 14 years old. She was our Saturday girl, running errands for the customers, yet even then she arrived an hour early in order to have time to look round the garden, to see how it changed from week to week. We could do with more Emilys.

Over this Bank Holiday weekend we have had our eldest grandson, Daniel, and his girlfriend, Liz, staying with us. Both are 25 and met at Nottingham University where Daniel is studying electrical engineering, hoping eventually to be involved in finding new sources of power. Liz is studying Russian and Spanish. Both are now well motivated after several years out of formal education, yet both have benefited enormously by meeting, mixing and working with all kinds of people. Daniel does anything to help finance his education, from building work to packing loaves in a bread factory. Having been brought up with home-baked wholemeal bread, he told us with astonishment of the tiny amount of dough in the bottom of the tins emerging out of the ovens as a full-sized loaf. The 'staff of life' consists now, it seems, mostly of air.

Over the weekend we ate my first picked sweetcorn, happily suffering burnt mouths as we bit into crisp, sugar-sweet kernels glazed with slightly salted butter. Nothing tastes like cobs freshly picked and rushed to the boiling saucepan or steamer.

Giant puffballs appeared providentially in the garden so, for a first course at lunchtime, I cubed one and tossed the pieces like croutons into a large heavy frying-pan where olive oil flavoured with garlic was just hot enough to make them sizzle nicely, turning them

over and over to make them shrivel and brown slightly. To follow
we ate a platter of cheeses with fresh-made bread and a vegetable
salad, made of diced courgettes – the little round patty-pan type
(all courgettes are delicious raw, much nicer and easier to digest
than cucumbers), little tomatoes, 'Gardener's Delight' and 'Golden
Sunrise', all held together with a curd sauce instead of mayonnaise.
Any smooth curd cheese, quark, fromage frais or drained yogurt can
be thinned slightly with a little cream, a spoonful of olive oil, or even
water, then flavoured with any herb, but I especially like summer
savory, much like thyme, but fresher and more tender.

Our *pièce de résistance* over the weekend was a dish of quail
cooked with wine, red onions and little tomatoes, served with
knitting needle-thin French beans and purple and white potatoes.
These were 'Bishop's Choir Boys' and 'Pink Fir Apple' potatoes.
Daniel helped me dig them. The 'Choir Boys' (lovely name!) have
black skins but, when boiled and peeled, retain an extraordinary
deep violet colour all the way through. They do not have such a
remarkable flavour as some purple potatoes I was once offered,
but are pleasant with a firm texture – almost like chestnuts – while
the effect on the plate could be called electrical! Left-overs, mixed
with other vegetables dressed with olive oil and herbs, suggest
unexpected colour schemes for a cold buffet.

Is it any use hoping you and Fergus might find a spare day to
come and see the garden and provoke me into making you an
eccentric lunch?

Much love, Beth

- &&& -

Saturday 7 September

Dear Christo,

I've just walked through the potting shed to find your big,
generous parcel of *Paeonia mlokosewitschii* seed on David's bench.
Thank you very much. The seeds will be sown on Monday, do not

fear. The sooner they are sown, when the beautiful pearl-black skins are still soft, the more likely they will germinate this coming spring. When the seed coat becomes hard and stone-like the seeds rarely germinate until the following spring, 18 months after ripening. If you have only a few seeds to bother with, you can file the coats gently to allow moisture to penetrate. Once germinated it then takes four to five years for us to grow saleable plants, which are likely to flower within a year or two of purchase.

Gardeners who rely entirely on buying already made plants may be forgiven for thinking such plants expensively priced (others include trilliums, veratrums and some arisaemas). I sometimes explain, you can have a baby, put up with sleepless nights, two-year-old tantrums and the rest, before you send it to school, aged five. Plants are not so intrusive, but some need the same sort of regular care for several years before they are ready for sale.

On the table beside me is something which will take us a very long time, I suspect, to build up available stock. A single bulb was brought to me by Gordon Collier, the enthusiastic plantsman from Titoki Point who looked after us when we gave some talks together in New Zealand. It is the double form of *Galtonia candicans*, quite extraordinarily beautiful. Do you know it? I don't normally think doubles are an improvement on plants, but in this case I am bewitched. Imagine a tall, strong stem carrying upwards of 20 flowers, each looking like a perfectly formed rose, with layer upon layer of white petals enclosing faint green shadows. This year we have had two flowering stems. I cut one for Andrew to see, putting it in a green glass vinegar jug (it suits the tall bare stem since it resembles a large bulb), and added a few young leaves of *Yucca flaccida* – I could not possibly take away the galtonia leaves, and thus deprive the bulb which we need to increase.

Another simple arrangement I've made with exotic flowers is by using the new Princess hybrids of *Alstroemeria*. Not being familiar with them myself, I am enjoying them placed in a wine decanter where their graceful stems arrange themselves and need nothing else. It seems this strain of alstroemeria, as opposed to the familiar Ligtu hybrids, is good news in the florist trade, with nurserymen putting down acres of them under glass where they flower almost all the year round. Mine are in shades of cream, rose-pink and an unusual tawny-pink, with dark maroon pencilling on the inner petals, each delicate and beautiful as a fine-lined painting.

It would be hard, I think, if familiarity bred boredom with such exotic shapes and colours. But I suppose, like sweetcorn and French beans being offered all the year round in the supermarkets, the same could apply to flowers grown in controlled conditions out of season. This year we planted some of these alstroemerias in the Gravel Garden as an experiment, to see if they will survive both summer drought and winter cold. So far they have surprised us by the amount of growth they have made, and are flowering repeatedly, albeit with shorter stems than the ones we put into pots as an insurance, which are providing me with long stems for the house.

Something else which has been oblivious to another dry summer in the Gravel Garden is *Atriplex halimus*. This week I took a piece up to Andrew in his little hideaway where he is now working on notes he made in Morocco when we had a winter holiday there about 40 years ago. He is also using a book published in 1939, *Marokko und Westalgerien 1936*, Rubel and Ludi, where he is obliged to translate both German and French botanists. There, in a photograph showing desert conditions 'les plus arides', was an area heavily colonized with this shrub. It seemed such a coincidence to find this information with Andrew just now, since this plant has been much admired during the summer for its vigorous and bright appearance, its long shoots covered with heavily silvered, shield-shaped leaves. Its flowers, opening now, are insignificant. Andrew reminded me (and I recall from long winters past), it will not stand severe cold. Because our plants are grown starved and tough in free-draining gravel, they were not harmed by last winter's cold, about −6°C (21°F), but we overwinter young replacements in case they become necessary.

I made a bad decision over our young French artichoke replacements. These were taken off the old plants towards the end of March, and planted into deep trays while they found new roots in a sheltered environment – actually on the floor of the propagating house. After some weeks I noticed how well they had come on, lots of new leaf showing, so I asked Eddie to row them out for me. A day or so later I went to see how they were and was appalled to see them lying flat like dead day-old chicks. A disaster! I should have checked myself to see how well rooted they were, and in any case advised Eddie to cover them with Netlon when planted (something we often do when planting-out conditions are unkind, usually too hot and dry). Poor Eddie was mortified. I am still cross with myself. But we both have learnt a hard lesson. Fortunately, we have not lost our entire stock of two varieties, but we have lost a valuable year's growth. A constant problem in nurseries is lack of sheltering space at vital times. But, next year, I suggest the young offsets are potted on from the deep trays, then sheltered under Netlon for the short while they will take to root securely into the pots before being planted in the open ground.

In the meantime, we have not starved. With a lot of compost, and a little watering, the vegetable garden has cropped much better than last, with similar low rainfall, but lower temperatures, around 20°C (68°F), rather than up around 30°C (86°F). I can hardly keep up with picking raspberries for freezing (and eating). 'Autumn Bliss' and 'Fall Gold' looked dreadful last summer with both mildew and red spider. No sign of either so far. Tomatoes, too, are cropping well; 'Gardener's Delight' and 'Sungold' hang in such heavy trusses it seems a shame to spoil the picture, but pick them I do, some to give away, leaving plenty to skin, liquidize and freeze. The first crop of sweetcorn, the first cobs always the best, are already frozen. My daughter Mary, a very enthusiastic gardener, helped me pick the laundry basketful. Then we stripped off the husks, bagged them, and had them in the freezer, all within a very short time, to keep them sugar-sweet. If you couldn't freeze them you would need a huge family, or party of friends, to eat them at their peak. We put 40 into the freezer. Fortunately the secondary ones don't seem to come all at the same time.

Sunday morning, 8 September
Yesterday afternoon, hidden from visitors to the nursery by a waving mass of stock plants in bloom, I sat on an upturned bucket near the open tractor shed, where my onions and garlic had been spread on wire netting frames, under cover, to dry. It is a form of escapism, I suppose, to feel the September sun hot on my creaking shoulder, as I rustle off the old dry skins and withered leaves, seeing the trays fill up with golden- or purple-skinned onions, checking they are firm and free of mould. This year I have also collected those funny little clusters of tiny onions which appear on the top of tall fat stems, Egyptian onions, also called tree onions. I hadn't thought of a use for them before, but now I value them as a flavouring, chopped raw into salads or dips without needing to waste half a normal onion. It has been useful to find this onion illustrated in that excellent book *Vegetables* by Roger Phillips and Martyn Rix.

From my young fig trees, planted in half wine-butts, Andrew and I have shared all of four small, dark red fruits. You can't imagine how sweet they tasted, every chew savoured! Next year, I will refrain from planting creepy-crawly annuals in the same containers so we can heavily dose them with well-rotted farmyard manure to encourage better growth. We haven't enough sheltered wall space to grow them in the ground.

I wish I could take you on a quick dash round the garden, but actually it would take all day! After 29mm (1in) of rain last weekend, there is suddenly so much to see. (It also produced a huge crop of mushrooms over the mown grass of the overflow car park. Needless to say, some of them ended up in the freezer, cooked in a mixture of oil and butter: black savoury tubs full of flavour, far tenderer than the rubbery things one buys in the supermarket.)

Everywhere looks fresh and wonderful. With colour coming in fast all around, it is such an exciting time of year building up to the great climax when Michaelmas daisies, dahlias and all will stand in defiance against the threat of frost, until the trees and shrubs take over with the final burst of colour – and then the carnival is ended. Winter will bring other stories – many I hope for our letters.

This has turned into a very wordy thank-you note. I shall stop now.

Love to you all at Dixter, Beth

–❧–

Saturday 14 September

Dear Beth,

It is Saturday afternoon and brilliant. I am sitting with the door open into the garden and am hearing the voices of visiting public. I had to go through the Great Hall to fetch this laptop word processor and a party was just about to start a house tour. A man whom I was close to opened a door of the old oak court cupboard, to see what was inside. I spoke sharply to him, reminding him that this is a private house. Sometimes the public make me feel that Dixter is being soiled.

Today is our local horticultural society's autumn flower show in the village hall, and more people have entered with more entries than for quite a while past, which is encouraging. Much depends on the weather in the run-up. This time, for instance, there are roses, whereas last, in July, the weather had ruined them. In all, the display looked really jolly. Long may these occasions last. They are under constant pressure from the urge to be out and about in motor cars, rather than to contribute to village life.

Olivia (my niece), who has been on one of her all-too-rare visits from abroad for the past nine days, helped me down with my bulky exhibits – huge containers of shrubs, perennials and annuals. There was so much to pick. I feel certain that the garden has never been so good at this time of the year – thanks to Fergus. Visitors have been appreciative.

Day before yesterday, Olivia and I, with members of our horticultural society, went, by invitation, to see the latest method of picking hops, at the most progressive farm in the village, belonging to the Cyster family. They have been around in Northiam for longer than the Lloyds, and three of them were at it: two brothers, in their 60s, and the son of one of them, who is, however, more academically orientated, so it is doubtful whether he will make the practice of farming his career.

However, on his parents' farm, they not only grow and dry hops, but make beer also, which is from their own malted barley, their own culture of yeast and their own, deep-bore-pumped water. They have a milking herd and distribute their own milk and cream. I do admire such people.

There used to be seven hop growers in Northiam; now just one, the Cysters, and there are only five left in the whole of Sussex. But there is a rising demand for British hops and British-style beer (rather than lager) from various parts of the world, including America, so by no means is all gloom, on that front. The new machine (rather like that log felling machine we watched together in Canada, some years ago) is fascinating to watch. It bestrides the row and gobbles up the hops and some foliage (later mechanically sorted out by a blowing device), leaving the bine in position, so that the plant does not find itself suddenly cut down, while still in full growth, but is, in part, anyway, able to complete its natural growth cycle with a proportion of undamaged foliage.

Drying is performed by burners, rather like vast blow lamps, and takes between seven and eleven hours, just as it always did. The dried hops are then pressed, not into round pockets, as of old, but square in section, though roughly the same length. The hops are mechanically sown into their canvas jackets. There is a lot of dust around and I found myself in trouble with coughing, even in that short space of time. Of course, the whole harvest is quite quickly over. The acrid smell of hops is tremendously nostalgic, to me, from the time, up to my 18th year, when they were dried in our own oast house, from our own hop garden.

Fergus has been hyperactive since his return from two weeks in Turkey, where he and his brother visited their mother. A week hence, he will be on his first trip to the USA (organized by Tom Cooper, who edits their premier gardening magazine, *Horticulture*), giving two or three lectures. Amanda is going with him, so it will be an exciting experience.

As a consequence, he has been working up to dark and over the weekends, too. He was selling in the nursery, last Sunday, and had a mother and daughter making small purchases. After the mother had bought one plant, the daughter suggested that the old lady might also get a *Cestrum parqui*. No, with her walking stick, she couldn't manage that. The old lady reminded Fergus of his grandmother. He said she could have any plant of her own choosing, as a gift. Beth, she was transformed! The stick was tucked under her arm and she eagerly went from plant to plant till she had made her choice – an osteospermum. Fergus was tickled, you may imagine.

Badgers are being a nuisance, in the garden. A German girl, who is working for us for a few weeks, saw no fewer than four of them, while in the garden soon after dark. They have eaten every one of two rows of carrots that I was depending upon to supply me for the next six months. Small holes indicate where each of them was.

Last time I attempted to grow sweetcorn, they scoffed the lot, just as they were approaching the moment of harvesting the first cobs. So, this year we have grown them in the raspberry cage, turning out the 'Fallgold' raspberries, to make room. Birds are scarcely interested in the autumn crop, so cage space is wasted on them. Next year, we shall have to grow the carrots inside the wire cage, likewise. I hope the badgers won't burrow their way in.

I'm wondering what I shall do with the sweetcorn crop when Olivia has gone. I note that you removed the husks and then froze the cobs, but our freezer is far too full for that and I think I should strip the corn off the cobs and put it into small bags. Actually, as a vegetable, I do find corn excessively sweet. A little goes a long way.

Now to take other points from your last letter. Do you not grow shallots? We have had a wonderful crop and the left-over from last year's is still usable (for the dogs' lunches). You are using your tree onions to include, raw, in salads. I find that I can digest shallots, raw, when finely chopped, and garlic also (when there's no danger of being unsociable), but not onions. Of course I use a lot of onion in cooking, but I see no point in growing them, as they are so readily available. They seem not to keep anything like as well as shallots, so I just buy for my immediate needs when shopping.

You write of skinning the tiny tomatoes, like 'Gardener's Delight' and 'Sungold', before liquidizing and freezing them, but isn't that a tedious bore, or have you some magic method? For culinary purposes, I wish I was more successful with a larger, but still tasty, tomato. With your glasshouses, that would be easy.

We have only just harvested the first three globe artichokes of the year. That is a pretty shameful record. As you know, the old plants suffered last winter. As you suggested, we rooted the offsets under protection, but when it came to planting them out, they hung back for what seemed like months, rather than weeks. They are fine, now, but I rather wonder if our old method of lining the offsets out straightaway, where they are to grow and crop, as we always had, in the past, might not be the better way, after all.

I agree that *Atriplex halimus* can be a beautiful foliage plant, but I found it quite impossible to keep, because house sparrows stripped it of every leaf. I didn't feel like black-cottoning it. I have to do that with *Artemisia arborescens*, early in the season, for the same reason.

They line their nests with these grey-leaved plants. I wonder if their smell has some beneficial effect. Most of them are strong-smelling.

I have never met the double of *Galtonia candicans*, but can imagine it to be a winner, especially as the stems of that species are so sturdy, so there would be no question of the extra weight keeling them over, as sometimes happens with the double white *Camassia leichtlinii*, which I also admire. I want to try the single white form of that species in our meadows, and have saved a lot of seed, for a start. But we shall have to rear the seedlings for a few years before they're large enough to try in turf, which is so competitive. But other camassias, notably *C. quamash*, are a great success under those conditions, increasing both vegetatively, to make clumps, and from their own self-sown seed. Even if only one seed in 500 succeeds in germinating and making a new plant, that is still a success when one is talking in terms of many thousands of their own-set seeds.

It is the same with the snakeshead fritillary, *Fritillaria meleagris*, which my mother used to sow in boxes, then prick out, finally planting them out with a bulb-planter and some old potting soil, to give them a good start. Once they are fully established, nature does the rest. Such a satisfying style of gardening, but one must start with the right turf, bordering on starvation conditions, so that competition from coarse elements like Yorkshire fog, cow parsley, docks and nettles does not swamp the weaker-growing additions.

We have just mown, for only the second time this year (March was the last), the topiary lawn. That has been allowed to revert to a meadow condition for two seasons now, and it has been notably more resistant to drought, as a consequence. Because I never fed it the turf was weak, but that is ideal for a meadow in which a wide range of species is to flourish. Many 'weeds' have moved in and the white clover was amazing, with its honeyed scent. Now, we have raised a batch of hairbells, *Campanula rotundifolia*, from seed and they are already strong, flowering plants, individually potted. We shall plant them into the turf, when rains have made it easy to take plugs out with the bulb-planter.

Helen Dillon was here for a day and a night, recently, and I had such an appreciative letter from her this morning. Really encouraging, when it comes from an excellent gardener, like herself. 'The borders have great presence', she writes, '– I can't define exactly what it is you do to them [neither can I!] – no question of wuffling along in subtle colour schemes – perhaps it's that you are more aware of shape than most gardeners.' Perhaps that's right, and with you also. The placing of plants in relation to their neighbours is so important and so fascinating, colour being only one aspect to consider. Heights, shapes and textures, as well as season of comeliness, are all factors to be considered. Up to a point, it comes instinctively, but thought is more dependable than instinct, while experience (or discovery, when they are new) of your plants' preferences is most important of all.

I love the bumpiness of my plantings and the way it is possible to place a tall, but thin-textured plant quite near to the front, while channels of low-growers may appear as you approach and lead you to the border's back or centre. The difference between spring, when much growth is still low and this can be taken advantage of with bulbs, for instance – between that and the fullness of summer is very marked. Continuity of interest is a subject that I find specially interesting, and the devices for obtaining it, some of them quite labour-intensive, admittedly, but by no means all.

Beth, I wish you would try *Crinum* x *powellii* under water, in one of your ponds. I have had it in the Horse Pond for eight years at least, and it flowers there before those in the borders. However, it is near the bank and gets too much competition. I think one should plant a larger area. I got this idea from the photograph in a book by Martyn Rix, which showed crinums in the wild, flowering in a bog area. It might dry out at other times of the year, but wouldn't need to. I can't help thinking that the very long crinum bulb is so designed to bring the neck out of water while the roots and much of the bulb itself remain in goo.

You write of the sturdy South African flora that are a standby in our late summer and autumn gardens. I shall always remember seeing a large area of wild kniphofias flowering in a boggy place,

when I was travelling from Kenya to Uganda, in 1946. I grow
quite a number of them, but one can have too many of those
producing a huge spate of blossom, which is out and over in a very
few weeks. In contrast are those which carry on with a succession
of flowering spikes. Your *Kniphofia* 'Little Maid' is one such. I
have a tremendous battalion of its creamy, greeny flower spikes
that has been a sight for three or four weeks already, and shows
no signs of tiring. But, to make an impression, I think one needs
a generous planting. We made ours only last spring, I may say, so
they established quickly.

We are nearing the end of our 'Victoria' plum crop, picking
them as required. My great niece, Giny, Andrew and their family
of three, came for a night, last weekend, and I suggested they take
some Vics home with them. The orchard has now been shorn; the
tree is quite young and I told them that the easiest way to collect
the out-of-reach fruit was to shake the tree. Young John, aged
five, thought this a great idea, and shook like billyho, the fruit
raining on to his back. Pip rushed off for his camera. I hope he
captured something.

The dogs are no less fond of fruit than I am (that seems to be
their rule with all food) and station themselves under the tree for
quite long periods, waiting for the wind to blow them a feast.

Much love, from Christo

--❀--

The Sunk Garden in spring. The pond is home to great crested newts and as the season progresses its edges become covered with yellow bird's-foot trefoil.

Riotous purple and gold *Crocus vernus* with native Lent lilies, *Narcissus pseudonarcissus*, in the front entrance Meadow Garden.

Lily-flowered *Tulipa* 'Ballerina' combine spectacularly with lime-green *Euphorbia* x *martini*.

Striking plant combinations at Great Dixter. Above: *Helleborus orientalis* Early Purple Group and white snowdrops, *Galanthus* 'Atkinsii'.
Below: Frothy *Ammi majus* with blue larkspur.

Above: Self-sown *Eryngium giganteum* in front of *Melianthus major*. Below: Pushiest of the pokers, *Kniphofia uvaria* 'Nobilis'.

The flowering *Aster lateriflorus* var. *horizontalis* reaches its peak in October in front of Great Dixter's signature Peacock Topiary.

Above: Winter–berrying *Cotoneaster horizontalis* with a female *Skimmia japonica*. Below: Ghostly grasses rimed with frost in late winter.

Thursday 19 September

Dear Christo,

I can imagine how you felt finding someone peering into a cupboard in the house which also happens to be your home. It is a penalty we sometimes pay for opening ourselves to visitors. Mercifully, most of them would not dream of doing such a thing.

I feel my garden is still very much mine which I love to share with sympathetic gardeners. Often when I am a bit tired or depressed, a chance meeting with kindred spirits will revitalize me completely, but when I come across someone walking across a flower bed 'looking for a label', I can feel a sudden surge of rage and despair, as if they were trampling over me. The garden may be open, but it is not a public park, nor should public parks be treated with disrespect – please keep to the paths! Fortunately most people give us a lot of encouragement by their interest and appreciation of what we do.

I was fascinated to read about the Cyster family still carrying on hop growing and making beer as well. Long may someone continue the business. Andrew and I were talking recently of the old family firms we knew 50 years ago in Colchester, many gone now, with names like Forsdyke and Bonner, Oliver Parker, Sparling Benham & Brough. Somehow, Tesco and Sainsbury don't have the same ring, even though they do provide good service, but the personal friendly element when life seemed less frantic has gone.

There certainly is a growing interest (not to say concern, after all the scandal of BSE) in how food is produced. Hardly anything which is expected to have a 'reasonable shelf-life' can be free of preservatives, quite apart from whatever has been done to keep it free of pests and diseases. I often wonder what really goes into the mountains of beer cans (and wine bottles) in the supermarkets. As with so much else offered in gaudy packages, all is consumed apparently without ill-effect, but next time I am in Dixter I would love to visit the Cyster's farm, and taste some of their wares. Every day I pick fresh salads and vegetables I feel privileged to be able to feed the family and friends from the garden. I love the growing and then the walk back to the house with a trugful of wonderful colours and flavours.

The maincrop carrots have just been harvested and safely stowed away in our little 'cellar'. (I think I wrote to you about it earlier in the year, a small square pit, lined with concrete slabs, the vegetables layered between dry sand.) This year I chose from Thompson & Morgan's catalogue a variety called 'Bertan', F1 hybrid. I often wonder how to choose from so many new introductions, but these I can really recommend. Large can mean inferior, but these are large, for my soil anyway. One is almost enough for Andrew and me, yet they are very sweet and flavoursome, and have escaped attention from the carrot fly, thanks to being covered with fleece throughout the growing period.

I do grow shallots, but have never had enough to last through to the next crop. Do they not sprout green leaves, as do home-grown onions, and potatoes in early spring? Is it true commercially grown onions and potatoes are sprayed to prevent this happening? It may not be harmful but I prefer growing different types of onion (an old habit dies hard!), the dark red Dutch ones, in particular. They look so attractive, especially round a pheasant cooked in red wine.

Skinning tomatoes is no problem. Just pour a kettle of boiling water over them until the skins split, refresh them under the cold tap, and the skins then slide off easily. Some people bake the tomatoes to concentrate flavour and reduce the liquid. Sounds a good idea, but I like to cook mine as little as possible.

Friday 20 September

Bah! I am perished with cold, my spine chilled to the marrow, after standing out in the equinoctial gale which has been raging through the garden now for more than two days. Out of the East of course. Yet two days ago Andrew and I sat having tea on the lower steps by the house, facing the ponds, basking in low, mellow sunshine, purring at the peaceful scene, backed with tall feathery swamp cypresses, arching bamboos and huge scallop-leaves of gunnera. Around the water's edge, these three are dominant among a hundred other shades and textures of green, so vivid now in the autumn light, with waterlily pads pretending to be cake doilies, laid out on a dark polished table.

Today the scene is wild, so much tossed and tumbled, the lawns littered with oak twigs and leaves, even small branches, while the leaves of *Betula jacquemontii* speckle the grass with green confetti. Yet, tomorrow may well break calm and innocent as it did in our fruit-farming days, when we woke to find the ground beneath the trees carpeted with apples we had planned all year to harvest. But Andrew taught me to look up and see the major part was still left on the tree. Usually, the smaller apples were whipped off the ends of the branches. Like blood, comparatively few apples spilt look like a lot.

Until the frosts come, whatever the weather, the pot gardens continue to brim over with colour and shapes, probably because they are in sheltered situations, and cosseted almost daily. How can I share them with you without boring you with a long list of names? Perhaps try to give an overall impression?

Looking from the house, or sitting on the south-facing paved area, the view makes me think of a stage set, furnished all the year round, but changing with each season. The lower garden, sloping away, provides a backdrop at this time of year of dark oak and silvery willow. Close to, shrub planting creates a Mediterranean scene, with dry, drought-tolerant plants, many grey-leaved and aromatic. By now, any star performers in this part of the garden have vanished into the wings, but the stage is still beautiful to watch each day as warm autumn sun spotlights the huge tree heather, *Erica arborea*, crowded now with acid-green, flame-shaped young shoots. A strategically placed pot of the grey-leaved *Agave americana* strengthens the planting and repeats in a lighter shade of grey the structure of a large *Yucca gloriosa* planted at the top of a shallow flight of steps. Strong shapes such as these, sometimes a tree or splendid grass, often take the place of sculpture or architecture in my garden.

Feeling enclosed and protected we sit at the table under the magnolia tree and enjoy, to our right, a colourful crowd scene of brimming pots, bowing and smiling cheerfully at us in the sunshine.

Pelargoniums in coral-red and salmon shades jostle with the lemon-yellow daisy, *Argyranthemum* 'Jamaica Primrose', all woven through with *Helichrysum petiolare*, both the grey- and yellow-leaved forms. To prevent too many flowering plants looking like an ice-cream soda, I use bold foliage plants set among them, to make strong accents. A large cordyline crowns the group while a phormium with green-and-white striped leaves echoes a particularly handsome pelargonium whose green leaves have broad cream edges. Dark accents are introduced through the chocolate-coloured rosettes of the tree-like *Aeonium* 'Zwartkop', while low bowls of grey succulents, looking like cool marble, spill on to the paving.

To the left of this large group is another smaller group of pots whose occupants merge into *Romneya coulteri*, still producing huge white poppies, repeating potsful of white-flowered pelargoniums and the white daisy flower, *Argyranthemum frutescens*. Here, the upright branches of the tree poppy are linked to the pots by trailing stems of grey-leaved *Helichrysum petiolare*. Behind them the claret-leaved vine, *Vitis vinifera* 'Purpurea', tumbles from the end of the bedroom wall, repeating the purple-leaved aeonium opposite.

You asked me about the pot gardens outside the little yard overlooked by the utility room window. Several years ago you astonished me by rushing for your camera to take a picture from inside the house of the red cannas and the variegated form of *Arundo donax* soaring up above the window. This year we've done something different. We have made two large groups in the angle formed by the office wall and window, facing south, and the utility room facing east. By this time of the year, it forms such a jungle there is only a tiny path for me to reach the back door. The main eye-catchers are velvety, beetroot-red petunias, rose-pink pelargoniums, an enchanting little lilac-pink nemesia, which never stops growing and flowering, and the pink *Argyranthemum* 'Petite Pink'. Again, the froth of colour is relieved by the dark rosettes of aeonium, while jumping out at you are the bold and beautiful leaves of *Plectranthus argentatus*, heavily felted with fine silky hairs. Each morning, I open the door to count the deep blue convolvulus flowers trained round the windows. We've given up trying to grow the super one with the light sky-blue flowers, *Ipomoea tricolor* 'Heavenly Blue' – it sulks too long in early summer if it's the least bit cold.

It's a great relief after the drought to walk now in the Gravel Garden. During August we had, in little offerings, not much more than 15mm (½in) of rain at a time, a total of almost 80mm (3in), very surprising and most welcome. All the plants responded like mad. It is wonderful to see it so colourful, a haze of pink, blue and mauve flowers, interwoven with new foliage which will clothe the area all winter. Ballota and santolina look really handsome now, after being well trimmed in July. *Caryopteris* 'Heavenly Blue' forms large bushes crowded with spires of intense blue flowers, while the second crop of catmint, *Nepeta* 'Six Hills Giant' and the paler *Calamintha nepetoides* (still crowded with bees) make softer washes of colour. An amazing little linaria called 'Antique Silver' has spread several yards along the gravel edge into the hoggin base, looking as if it had the best of conditions. It makes frothy trails of greyish-blue flowers, set off by late blooms of a creamy-yellow poppy, *Eschscholzia californica*, seeded among it. Another invader here is *Clematis orientalis* (*C. tibetana vernayi*), blown in from elsewhere, its sharp, lemon-peel-thick petals and silky seedheads tangling over bergenias and other off-season plants which don't seem to mind the intrusion.

Introducing warm tones among these cool colours are many sedums – wonderful plants, I am so obliged to them, for they are among my most successful tolerators of drought. The well-known *S.* 'Herbstfreude' ('Autumn Joy') is making bold impact, but so too is a newcomer originating from Ewald Hugin, of Freiburg in Germany, called *S.* 'Matrona'. Equally robust, its large heads of rose-pink flowers are intensified by dark green leaves with leaf edges and stems stained purple. Altogether an exciting new plant. Poor soil might be an advantage. If too well fed the large sedums can grow leggy and then fall apart with the weight of their flower-heads.

Edging the curve of one of the island beds is a planting which looks like a patterned shawl dropped on to the pale gravel. *Sedum* 'Bertram Anderson' has clusters of wine-red flowers set against blackish-purple leaves, all weaving through little *Gypsophila repens* 'Rosa Schönheit', still producing sequin-like dots of tiny pink flowers, while the snake-like trails of *Euphorbia myrsinites* form a tassel-like corner.

Euphorbia seguieriana subsp. *niciciana* provides that much-needed touch of acid green – what a long-lasting plant it makes. Throughout the whole length of my dry river-bed garden, *Verbena bonariensis*, seeded in groups here and there, sometimes by the path edge, sometimes in the background, makes graceful screens of purple, both softening and structural, with its bare green strut-like stems carrying clusters of tiny purple flowers for weeks on end. Particularly attractive is where it tangles with the white moth-like flowers of *Gaura lindheimeri* emerging from a patch of the white-flowered *Sedum spectabile* 'Iceberg'.

While writing this I've just realized that almost everything flowering now at the end of September in the Gravel Garden, creating such a welcome summery effect, consists of tiny flowers, held together in dense jewel-like clusters. Grasses wave for attention, but must wait for another letter. I can't bear to rush them.

Before I leave you, let me say how thrilled I am Fergus and Amanda are going to Boston. They both deserve to have a wonderful time, and will, I have no doubt. I shall never forget my visits there, the excitement, especially in the fall, of seeing the unbelievable red and yellow of the maple leaves, and meeting new people who quickly become friends, through the love of plants. I would love to hear Fergus giving his talk. He has such a passion now for plants and placing them. With his warm and outgoing personality the Americans will love him.

Much later . . . Walking out to inspect the damage from the gales (not so bad as it might have been). I've just found nine seed heads of *Paeonia obovata* var. *alba*, each opened wide like a big, three-petalled flower, holding a sticky mixture of fertile blue-black seeds set among the bright scarlet unfertilized seed cases which are empty. The hard seed receptacle has a rumpled purple lining where the seeds have nestled. Emily thought they would look nice on top of our bowls of potpourri. She helped me pick out the seeds and count them. 157! We have never had so many, all from one plant. It is perhaps the most beautiful of all single peonies, white and globular in shape, like a blown glass bubble. It looks exquisite in half shade, among ferns, with the sweet-scented, cream-flowered *Smilacina racemosa* near by. Do you have it? I will spend the next five years growing some on for you.

Hoping the dogs are behaving themselves – you too!

Much love, Beth

– ❦ –

Friday 18 October

Dear Christo,

You can be sure I did not miss seeing you and Rosemary Verey on the box exploring the familiar paths of Dixter.

Television produces a strange sensation as we sit almost on pins, eavesdropping on people we know well, especially knowing a little how these programmes are filmed, in little bites, with endless stoppings and startings, because an aeroplane has gone over when you thought you had made a really inspired spontaneous observation, or a motorbike revs up half a mile away, or even the wind has upset the sound man. Or maybe (usually in my case) one has had too much to say in the prescribed two and a half minutes for the shot, and needs to be more concise. I could not fault you or Rosemary on that score, but I must confess I did not think the photography did justice to the garden. Neither the camera angles chosen nor the colour effect came up to the programme produced for *Gardeners' World* where you were talking to Stephen Lacey – which just goes to prove that photography is just as unpredictable as gardening. Nothing can be on form all of the time.

There are times here when I am depressed about the garden, possibly because I become satiated with impressions I have every day. Sometimes the responsibility of maintaining it all weighs heavily on me, knowing it is in the nature of things that change must come.

Too often one's mind is cluttered with problems, eyes on the ground, fussing about a few gaps, or messy bits of planting. But recently I have spent time in the garden with Gerard discussing tree pruning and maintenance. Because we went round with our heads tilted backwards most of the time I came to realize how seldom I take in the enveloping framework of the garden, partly because there is quite a lot to see, partly because I may look but do not give myself time to absorb what is happening. Concentrating with Gerard, it was both a pleasure and shock to become aware how spaces have been filled, how large everything has become. Despite dry conditions, many trees and shrubs have grown almost without our being conscious of their progress until now. After half a lifetime of planting in this garden, I stand and marvel at the sheer size, height and spread of some specimens. This is not without its problems, since space is not limitless, as Gerard points out. He has been with me since his schooldays and takes a very personal view of the trees and shrubs he has grown up with. Over the years he has attended day courses on pruning and tree management. From a safety point of view this is essential. It is too easy to buy and use lethal machinery with no knowledge of the correct safety gear to wear, let alone how to handle ladders and ropes. To deal with the tallest trees, including the ancient oaks, we hire a hoist, a bucket seat attached to a Meccano-like arm which lifts Gerard up to about 12m (40ft) off the ground, enabling him to thin a tree or reach dead branches spotted dangling precariously. We do not think the cost of hiring is an extravagance and plan well in advance.

Some decisions are hard. *Cornus controversa* 'Variegata' has slowly made a most beautiful small tree, pagoda-like in shape, its horizontal tiers of widely-spaced branches carrying pale green and cream leaves throughout summer. Planted too close is *Cornus kousa* var. *chinensis*. If left together, the variegated tree will lose its beautiful symmetry, a feature in winter as well as in summer. Yet it was such a painful choice, since the Chinese dogwood is beautiful in flower and has taken so long to establish. But decide we did, to prune and move it in winter when we have chosen and thoroughly prepared a suitable site. We must take the risk of losing it.

A few years ago we were obliged to cut down a handsome green-and-white variegated holly; it was altogether too unwieldy and awkward, smothering its neighbours. It sprouted vigorously from the base and now forms a neat columnar shape which we maintain with careful pruning. Every cut produces a dense effect, new shoots, more leaves – altogether an improvement, especially where space is limited.

The colchicums have been late this year – a good thing, perhaps, extending the season for many weeks. We have quite a wide range, some finished long ago, others are now at their best. They are specially welcome in the Wood Garden where few things flower at the end of the season. Colchicums are really mountain meadow plants, appearing in the short turf of the high meadows scythed for hay, but I have planted them in sunlit openings, in big bold drifts, outlining the pathways. The impact of so much luminous purple and white is exciting in what could now be a rather sombre scene. They are supported by carpets of vincas, ajugas, *Tiarella cordifolia* and, less well known, an evergreen strawberry, *Fragaria chiloensis* 'Chaval'. This makes perfect ground cover in a woodland setting where there is room for it to spread dense carpets of small shining green leaves. A good setting too for the scarlet, juicy berries of *Arum italicum marmoratum* and pale green leaves still looking good on Mr Bowles' golden grass, *Milium effusum* 'Aureum'.

I love the true autumn crocuses. Since so much of the garden is sandy or gravelly soil, I think we lose many crocuses to mice. In our first garden, on heavy, chalky boulder clay they increased, making wonderfully colourful patches in both spring and autumn, but here I look for their return with apprehension. *Crocus speciosus* opens wide to the sun, showing off its beautiful bold veining – dark pencilling on lighter blue cupped petals filled with orange feathered stigmas and stamens. I am relieved to see *C. s.* 'Albus', one of my favourites, slowly increasing in the Gravel Garden. It is thrilling to see these pure white pointed petals mingling among the low mat plants, or just trooping through the bare gravel stones. *C. medius* is another smallish, dark purple flower, good for contrast with *C. kotschyanus* var. *leucopharynx*. What impossible names both to spell and pronounce! But it is a gem, pale lilac blue, faintly pencilled with dark veins. Look inside and you might be surprised to find a white throat filled with white stamens and anthers. It is similar to *C. zonatus*, but this has a yellow throat.

Having enjoyed another good summer's baking in the Gravel Garden the sternbergias are flowering well. Their yellow crocus-like blooms emerge from low clusters of shining strap-shaped leaves, sometimes out of bare gravel, elsewhere from a carpet of *Phyla nodiflora*, which rivals thyme mats in its ability to defy the drought, covered with small clusters of tiny pink flowers all late summer and autumn. Here among the sternbergias, the first snowdrops are in flower, *Galanthus reginae-olgae* Winter-flowering Group. Some people are taken aback by seeing both crocuses and snowdrops flowering now, 'at the wrong time of year'. I know how they feel, but knowing where these bulbs come from, usually the Mediterranean, and even perhaps seeing them in their native surroundings, helps one to understand that it is all right, nature knows what she is about.

Yesterday, we had one of those magical still days, not a breath of wind, the low autumn sun warm on my back, illuminating odd jewels of colour set against a general background of green tones. A cold night had left silvery patterns of dew, like silk scarves, spread across the mown grass. Now the holidays are over, the children back at school, the numbers of visitors drops obviously, but the season goes on, the garden still has surprises while the glory of autumn colour has scarcely begun.

As well as opening the crocuses, a lovely morning brings old friends, visitors who have been coming and watching the garden's progress for many years. Beside the ponds I found Mrs Peter Healing and her daughter. The late Peter Healing often came here in my pioneering days. I have warm memories of his kindness and encouragement and, once, I visited his garden where I was impressed not only by his colour combinations but also by a small greenhouse dripping with clusters of the tomato 'Gardeners' Delight'. Occasionally, I am able to point to a truss on my own plants and say it is almost as good as those I first met in Peter's garden. His daughter rather took my breath away by greeting me with, 'Don't ever die Mrs Chatto' – a trenchant remark since I do find myself worrying perhaps more than I need about the future of the garden.

Then I met friends who used to bring a very old gardener to see me, a man in his 90s, who would walk all round the garden delighted to find plants he knew from long ago. His name was James Christmas. For years he wrote me letters in spidery writing which gradually became illegible. It tells something of his character when I tell you his doctor mowed his grass for him until eventually he was obliged to leave his beloved plants and be cared for himself in a home.

These people, together with the beauty of the day, warmed my heart and raised my spirits. I hope the garden did as much for them.

Do you know *Persicaria polystachya*? If you don't have it I think you would love it by the Horse Pond. It needs space. Just now, beside one of my ponds, framed with swamp cypresses just beginning to turn russet brown, it forms a huge mass of tiny white flowers held in airy clusters, filling the air with a sweet, strange scent. It could be mistaken for a very large shrub. But it starts each year from ground level, producing many stout jointed stems handsomely clothed in large pointed leaves accented with red leaf stalks.

Before I stop for lunch I must tell you about our queen hornet. A few nights ago, Andrew and I had just sat down to supper when she suddenly appeared crashing against the high window at the end of our table. Not relishing the idea of finding her later in our bedrooms, we flapped about, dreading to kill her, yet in no way able to settle down to our meal. Eventually, armed with a long-handled broom I managed to steer her, buzzing like a helicopter, into the kitchen, and between us we gently guided her out of the window. Swing windows don't make such rescue efforts any easier.

Now I will stop. I have to do the weekend shopping. And I'm much looking forward to having you and Fergus to lunch next week. It bucked me up a lot to have phone calls from you both.

Always love to you both, from Beth

— ❧ —

Sunday 27 October

Dear Beth,

What an excellent day that was that Fergus and I spent with you last Tuesday, the weather conspiring to make it ideal. We were both full of your achievements, afterwards. Such a delicious lunch, too, and you present food with such originality – entirely different from those garishly illustrated cookbooks that I find so off-putting.

You told us that we had spent two hours going through the Gravel Garden. Well, it didn't seem like that at all but I can believe you because there was so much to see and to take in. To photograph and to note down. After I'd remarked that *Crocus speciosus* 'Albus' didn't look its best against a background of pale gravel and Fergus had suggested a purple-leaved acaena for it to grow through, I loved your remark, made to me, while taking Fergus by the arm, 'Look what tutors you've got. The pair of us.'

It was certainly the day of the crocus, with clusters of them expanded to the sun. Well, your last letter dilated on them, as well it might, but actually to see and enjoy them first-hand is unbeatable. I am so glad to have *C. medius*, again, which I previously lost through inattention. (It was naughty of you not to allow us to pay for any of the plants we took away – all ones with a special meaning for us – but it was dear, too. Thank you, Beth.) The colour is quite intense, purple rather than mauve and the red stigmata in exciting contrast.

I like *C. kotschyanus* var. *leucopharynx* a lot, with its white centre and 'stalk'. And it seemed to be a free flowerer, which the strain of ordinary *C. kotschyanus* (*C. zonatus*) that I got through commercial sources is certainly not. *Galanthus corcyrensis* is a beauty, its whiteness so solid on an elegant bloom, and I could see (as you related in your letter) that the tiny, mat-forming 'verbena' *Phyla nodiflora* makes an ideal background. Indeed, it was quite a day of backgrounds, with so many good ones for your colchicums. I shall plant some around my tricyrtis, which looks much like your 'Bridgemere' – a 90cm- (3ft-) tall candelabrum of chalices made of six, spreading and upright-facing 'petals', white with purple spots.

Persicaria polystachya is a great plant. I think that is the one that grows by the roadside between Braemore Junction and Ullapool, in Wester Ross. You are the only nursery listing it and I think the expert who named it for you has taken a synonym for one that is better known as another species. Its scent was surprising – I thought of honey.

It is good to see the new plantings on your boundary at the garden's lowest level, but surely, in such a position, which is seen across the garden, the groupings could have been fewer and larger – so many were in threes, fives and sevens.

Returning to the Gravel Garden, I do so like the way you have worked shrubs into your design. 'It will be like this all winter,' you remarked where *Cistus ladanifer* and bushes of phlomis were predominant. It seems foolish, in our climate, for the 'new' perennial garden (whatever that may be) to plug perennials at the expense of shrubs.

Another thing struck me: your Gravel Garden is held up as an example of low-maintenance gardening. It isn't, and why should it be? The best gardening never is, in my experience. You took immense pains with your soil preparations before ever the gravel arrived. Fertility wasn't left to chance. You imposed it, which was very necessary seeing that the site had been a compacted car park. And now, as you relate, when you need or wish to replant, you scrape the gravel aside, remove the tired soil beneath it and replace with fresh. Just what Fergus keeps on doing here. Most new plantings reach a peak in their second year, after which there is a long, slow decline. Not in your case, because you are continually re-thinking and acting on your new thoughts, readjusting for balance and replanting where necessary.

It is Sunday evening and I am alone with the dogs once more, after a busy weekend. Fergus organized one of his volunteers' invitations, in this case so that we could do a major piece of

re-organization on a large stock bed, where we want to get rid
of rows and replant our stock more scenically, in groups. Eight
students came over from Wisley – such a good bunch – and there
were several more besides, including a young woman I got talking
to on the train, the week before. She came with a woman friend
and her husband, a young solicitor, joined us yesterday evening.
Frank Ronan was here, too, and a great help, though he had no
idea, until he arrived, what he was in for. He has given me a copy
of his new novel, not officially published, yet.

Well, the weather yesterday was ideal – sunny with large
cumulus clouds and quite a breeze, but not too much. The work
went really well though I was in the kitchen, preparing an evening
meal for 15: pork stew with olives followed by blackberry and
apple pies – two of them. The blackberries have gone on late,
this year, and I was able to pick over a kilo (3lb) of wild ones
on Thursday, a stone's throw from the garden. They do taste so
delicious and I love the scrunch of their pips.

Today, the weather was really nasty – the tail end, we are told,
of American hurricane Lilli (or Lily?). Wet, grey and windy. Not in
the least deterred, Fergus organized a number of under-cover jobs,
including the removal of an accretion of cobwebs in the roof up
here, in the solar. I cooked three chickens with tarragon, followed
by the largest steamed chocolate pudding I have ever made (my
mother's recipe). The consumers were most appreciative and only
left, reluctantly, around 6.00pm – Greenwich Mean Time, alas.
One hates the clocks going back.

After all that effort, Fergus, quite undeterred, drove up to
London to spend the evening and night with Amanda.

We used and lived in the Great Hall, several bodies sleeping
there, in front of the fire, last night. And I made a large 'flower'
arrangement (berries and foliage and coloured stems, also), in
the centre of the hall, making use of some of the lovely spray
chrysanthemums now in bloom. The weather being mild,
a large fire was all that we needed for heating. I suppose the

central heating will have to go on very shortly, but we've not done badly.

Do think about dates for a November visit, dear Beth. I look forward to that.

Monday 28 October

This evening, at Perry's, he having a video player on his TV set, Fergus and I watched the video made by Bill Clark of you in your garden. Fifty minutes of it. It was so good and the fact that you weren't hustled was good, too, as it gave you time, not only to expound on your philosophy, but also to find the exact way that you needed to express it. Sometimes we waited a couple of seconds while you collected your thoughts, and then out it came. Excellent. And you became more relaxed as the programme unfolded. I know you often feel self-conscious in front of a camera, but here you accepted it and became entirely yourself.

The cameraman was obsessed by your ducks, but I particularly enjoyed the shots he got of the wild moorhen and its chick.

Sometimes colour seemed bleached – for instance of the double kingcups. How difficult yellows seem to be to get right. Photographers, with just their camera, more and more insist on low early morning (particularly) or evening light, avoiding midday sun and clear skies. That in itself is rather artificial. But a TV team has to take things as they come and are mostly filming in the middle of the day. Are there union rules that prevent them from starting early?

Today has been even rougher than yesterday, the depressions being in their third phase. So I have avoided the noisy solar this evening and have remained in the parlour, which is protected from prevailing winds. It is the first time since last May that I have had a fire here.

Much love, from Christo

PS Do think about November dates for a visit.

—☙—

Saturday 2 November

Dear Christo,

I much enjoyed having you and Fergus share the garden with me. We were lucky to have such a fine still day. I loved the way you both lingered over almost every plant. I say plant particularly since there were few flowers in the Gravel Garden, just clouds of *Verbena bonariensis* and little drifts of crocus; touches of colour in a landscape of leaves. To have you both so intent at this time of year was a real pleasure, and a compliment.

Since you were both here, I have met a regular visitor to the garden enjoying the same scene, and she remarked what we all know, that many people cannot find interest or pleasure in leaves for their own sake. She said she had sometimes brought visitors who could not see the point of it. This underlines the point: we only take in what interests us, what can be linked to previous experience or knowledge. When offered a plant at the nursery how many people say, 'But what sort of flower does it have?' no matter how beautiful the plant itself may be.

I saw the superb photographs taken by Steve Wooster of the Exotic Garden at Dixter in the October–November issue of *Gardens Illustrated*. They thrilled me, even though I know from experience how mind-stirring it is to stand among this sumptuous collection at its best. Steve is an artist, too. I do think he finds the most advantageous and unexpected angles, showing off in fine detail the clarity and richness of contrasting colours and textures, all softened by autumn mist drifting through the background.

The Gravel Garden could not provide a greater contrast. Both our gardens, I think, shock people. Not all, thank goodness. Yet I'm sure we neither of us began them with shock tactics in mind. (This is a phrase treasured by journalists.) You have always loved dramatic cultivars and half-hardy plants and have developed and extended that theme. I set myself a project to see what could be

129

done in poor gravel soil with low rainfall. We are both stimulated by the differences in our approach to making a garden, as well as remaining good friends, since we both love plants for themselves.

However, I must take you up on insisting the Gravel Garden is not low-maintenance. In comparison with bedding out, as practised in our public parks, I think it most definitely is, and for the first two or three years we kept records of hours worked there. Perhaps I should explain my theory of maintaining the gardens here. As you know we have about 2 hectares (5 acres) of garden (distinct from nursery stock beds), mixed plantings of trees, shrubs and plants with walkways kept to a minimum. Such an intensively planted garden would involve a big staff to keep it clean and tidy if we did not make full use of different kinds of mulch, combined with dense planting where possible and desirable. For over 20 years, two girls, the same two, Lesley and Winnie, have maintained the gardens throughout the growing season. In winter they help with packing orders for post, or weeding pots from the nursery, but do take the odd sunny day to cut down and groom where needed.

Planting here is laboursome, as you rightly observed in the Gravel Garden. Practically everywhere, we have to improve the soil before we can begin. Because so much of my soil is raw gravel and sand, we cannot just take a few plants, dig straight into the border and plant. We must remove the stones and sand and make a hole (or section) large enough to work in plenty of compost, to give the plant some chance, especially with recent years of low rainfall. As you could see, most of the plants become well established, once they get their roots down deep. But last year, with the great heat 25–30°C (77–86°F), I was disturbed to see even the cistus dropping their leaves, looking tired and bare-legged. This year, with even less water, but lower temperatures, they flourished.

Elsewhere this week David and Doug have been coping with opposite conditions. In the Reservoir Garden, where you said you liked the mixed planting of the large island beds, I originally had dry powdered clay (left over in great heaps from making the reservoir) spread over the existing gravel, hoping it would help make a retentive soil. Well, it didn't, not by itself anyway. Over the years, we have been obliged to remove some of this solid yellow stuff, especially round the border edges where herbaceous plants make a foreground to shrubs and trees. Then we have added compost, old well-rotted manure and sometimes gravel and sand from elsewhere to make a more open mixture for plants to penetrate. At the same time, we are glad of the clay content which increases water retention. One patch we treated like this two years ago was horrendously sticky, so we left it fallow for two years, letting weeds flourish to promote root action. Now, this week, digging it over ready for replanting, we are surprised and pleased at the good, dark colour and crumbly texture of our improved soil more than a spit deep.

Sunday 3 November

Last Sunday was wild and windy. It seemed a good opportunity to deal with the quinces you brought me, comforting to squirrel away a special treat; their scent had met me every time I had entered the kitchen. I decided against making jam or jelly, much as I like them both, but we eat very little jam nowadays, feeling better with less sugar. I peeled and sliced the quinces thinly and put them into half water, half apricot juice with enough pale brown sugar to make a syrup and simmered them gently. When soft I let them soak overnight for the flesh to absorb the sweetness. Next day I put them into containers for the deep freeze. They are good with muesli for breakfast, or make a base for winter fruit salads.

Someone who has never tasted a quince could well be shocked both by its extreme tartness, and its rather woody, grainy texture, especially near the core. Wild pears I believe are also gritty. Horticulturists have worked wonders to evolve such melting texture as the pear 'Doyenné du Comice', but, as I was brought up as a child to stir the jam kettle, both the heavenly scent and rough texture of cooked quince brought back happy memories.

Talking of texture reminds me of our mushrooms. For weeks now, after a few showers and very mild temperatures we have been delighted to find them appearing all over our short-mown grass car park, and better still, the overspill area where they are not affected by car fumes. My friend Janet, the potter, stayed with us last week, on the one really wet day we had, but that did not deter us from going out and filling a basket, enough for supper and for her to take home. After wiping them clean, we cooked them simply, just a little oil and butter mixed, cutting them into pieces so they practically melted into their own shining black sauce. The rich flavour and soft texture made them a dish on their own. They needed neither onion, garlic, a dash of sherry – or anything else I have resorted to – to try to put some flavour into the rubbery white buttons offered in supermarkets.

I'm not going to be put off by your teasing me about making herb teas instead of coffee! I love coffee, especially the smell when it is freshly made at Dixter, tempting me to drink a cup after lunch by the Horse Pond on warm summer days, with Dahlia waiting hopefully to be allowed to lick out the grounds. But sleeping can be a problem for me, with or without coffee. Over the years I have experimented, collecting various herbs, leaves, fruits and flowers from the garden, using many of them fresh as they appear in season. Some, like lemon balm or mint, I hang up in bunches to dry. But this autumn, I have discovered how easily and quickly things dry in the airing cupboard. Even rose hips, the big fat juicy ones, like small tomatoes, from *Rosa rugosa* have dried well. It's a sticky job opening them, removing the calyx (and the odd earwig), and spreading them over baking trays. Each day I stirred them about. By the end of a week they were completely dry: skin, flesh and seeds, looking a bit like dried chillies.

I also preserve the thinly peeled skin from unwaxed lemons, and lots of marigold petals. All these I keep in screw-top glass jars, to add to my teapot, perhaps with a few curled leaves of lemon verbena and a teaspoonful of honey, not to sweeten noticeably, but like salt in a savoury dish, to bring out the flavours. Rosemary and marjoram make comforting teas, too, and of course peppermint. For years I bought tea bags until I found a bag of my own dried peppermint at the tail end of winter. It was so different from the bought dusty bags, so bright and strongly perfumed. I thought how mad to be able to grow all these good things and not make use of them.

If I don't stop now there won't be time to cook two little pigeons for lunch . . .

While the house was filled with a rich gamey smell from the pigeons simmering in a sauce of tomato, red onions and rosemary, I went to the vegetable garden to dig celeriac, to make a purée with just one potato added. Peering round the leylandii hedge running alongside the grass car park, I could see fresh mushrooms had popped up overnight. I picked a dozen, freshly pink and white against the weatherworn shallow-tray basket. What a picture they will make, black and succulent against the creamy purée sprinkled with fresh chervil.

I do enjoy all the stages before vegetables appear on the table – the planning, growing, caring, picking, cooking and eating a wide range of food fresh from the garden. We are fortunate to be able to live this way.

Later still . . . I am concerned about leaving Andrew at weekends now we have the long dark evenings. During the week there are people around to make sure all is well, the fire lit, the log baskets filled. Looking at my calendar I am shocked to find my mid-weeks for November are not free, except for this coming week. Such short notice!

After a quick phone call, I am greatly relieved to find you can have me. Thank you so much. See you and Fergus very soon. I will bring you a piece of *Persicaria polystachya*.

With love, Beth

– ❦ –

Monday 11 November

Dear Christo,

Those were three lovely days for me, with you and Fergus
at Dixter. I wasn't sorry to have left behind a packet of letters
awaiting reply, on my hall box, having left the house by the wrong
door. Now they must wait a bit longer while I say thank you for
the best place to come and relax.

I always enjoy breakfast at Dixter, knowing no one will be
looking for me. Shall I change my mind about jam-making?
Two splendid fresh-made jams on the table almost tempted me
to consider it, but I don't think so. I used to love harvesting the
different fruits of summer and autumn, filling the house with steam
from the jam kettle, but it needs a young family (or visitors such
as your open house), to eat them up. I was very impressed by your
quince jam, leaving big chunky pieces of fruit set in deep coral-red
jelly. I used to cut smaller pieces, resulting in a more porridge-like
consistency! But I imagine, as with marmalade-making, you
have to be sure the fruit is tender right through before adding the
sugar. The bramble jelly which you pushed purposefully towards
me is another Lloyd special, unadulterated by apple. In times past,
I have seen you suspending the jelly bag over the long kitchen table
from a Heath Robinson-like contraption of crossed lathes and
home-made hooks for the four corners, which I suspect has hung
there, from the beam above, since your mother's young days.
That kind of thing, the many old kitchen implements you
still use, little habits and disciplines (taught me also by my
mother), add considerably to the pleasure of staying at Dixter.
It has happened before now that I have transgressed in your
kitchen, throwing away perfectly good greaseproof paper, used
to cover the scales before weighing dry ingredients, instead of
dusting it off and returning it to its proper place. That kind of
discipline I can take. Weren't we both brought up in wartime
never to waste? Sometimes, today, it is all too easy to be careless
of such small matters.

It is a pity, I think, that many garden visitors give up the habit· of visiting by the end of September. Many do so sooner, as holidays are over and children back at school. But gardens can give pleasure (and ideas) right into winter. Of course it takes time, years, to create the bones of a garden which will look good when the flowers have gone. Dixter is exceptional in having the warm russet-red roofs of house and outbuildings, but your father planned and planted great yew hedges and archways, cosy enclosures which you and Fergus are filling now with bold groups of stock plants, showing off contrasting shapes and textures. Again I ask myself, should we do something like that? But no, I think not. We have about 1 hectare (3 acres) of mother plants, as well as the garden, to be tended. I think David, my propagating manager, would not take kindly to having his stock beds dismantled. As they are, the beds can be labelled as well as the plants, so he can send helpers to Bed C14, for example, where he knows they will find what he needs to be dug for splitting and re-potting. When I visit nurseries abroad, I tend to gulp down new ideas with great relish, but I often have to spit them out, or modify them to fit in with our differing conditions, often climatic, but sometimes different systems of management.

I hate strong winds in the garden, so noisy and threatening, especially at night when I lie wondering what will be left of the brittle-branched *Paulownia tomentosa*, or my lovely symmetrical swamp cypresses, which have taken a beating this autumn with Atlantic gales tearing uninterrupted across the neighbouring farm. Gerard comes to me with a sad face to say more tree surgery will be needed. I try to console him, and myself, by pointing out that like yew, taxodiums do sprout again from bare wood, unlike most conifers. Yet we both know it will take years, perhaps as long as it takes for him to see his baby son start school, to grow back what has been lost.

But at Dixter these past few days, protected by fine buildings and hedges, unfettered by responsibility, I could just stand and stare, not only at the planting, still rich and full, albeit with few flowers now, but at the bowl of blue sky, filled with feathery white clouds twisting and dissolving into nothingness, high, high above. Below, slow-moving indigo 'mountains' closed in behind the oast houses, their white caps highlighted against the dark sky, while all the autumn colours of the garden were gilded by the dying of the sun as it sank into a sea of gold.

More and more, as I visit Dixter, I come to realize how wise Lutyens was in planning paved paths everywhere you could wish to walk round the gardens. Whether broad or narrow, they fit the scheme of things perfectly, but best of all they allow thousands of feet to walk round a genuinely private garden without doing a bit of damage. Could he have possibly guessed that, I wonder? Never imagining I would share my garden with other gardeners, and with no formal training in design, I have not made such wise provision. So I must continue to be concerned with on-going repair of grass walks.

Sunday 17 November
This letter lay on my table for the rest of the week, as the same evening I had written it I was to spend the night tormented by a storm which rattled my insides, leaving me drained and empty, fit for nothing for several days. Emily went down with the same bug; it comforted me a bit to find how much it had shaken her. But by the end of the week we were almost back to normal.

We have been collecting up all the half-hardy plants, trying to find shelter for them for the winter. There is never enough room, especially as some, like agaves, grow ever larger. Some are so big now it takes both David and Gerard with sack barrows to lift and wheel them into place. David takes the opportunity to tip them out on to a trolley, take off the new shoots which have been growing round the inside of the pots, and remove lower leaves so they take up less room. Then he re-pots them in fresh compost, so they are ready for next season.

While this was going on, Moira and Emily asked if I had decided what to do with the grapes which hung like a frieze over the potting-shed doors. I had looked at them earlier, their pink-stained, pale green skins almost transparent with ripeness, such a bumper crop this year, yet was feeling too tired to bother. In spite of myself, the decision was made. In no time, two large buckets and two big bowls were filled to overflowing. Rosie joined me in the utility room and when she left for home, Emily took her place. Washing the bunches first in the big sink we stripped off the good grapes, discarding surprisingly few affected by mould, or too small and sour, despite the dry summer. I think the roots of this vine, *Vitis vinifera* 'Fragola', brought to me as a cutting many years ago, must have received some of the run-off as the girls watered their trolleys full of newly planted pots where it was growing against the south wall.

I pressed the grapes through my large mouli sieve, and then poured the juice into squares of muslin tied over two buckets. It took all night to drip through as the pulp was rather thick. Next morning I filled 30 containers with fresh juice and put them in the freezer. The musky flavour, reminiscent of strawberry, is not really retained in the juice, but we all had a tasting and the general verdict was, well worth doing. It was more enjoyable than the oversweet grape juice obtainable in cartons which I had kept by me to compare.

Now I shall call Andrew from his little room in the roof to come and share the fire with me, shut out the November gloom (it has drizzled all day, the terrace is littered with magnolia leaves over a rusty carpet of golden larch needles), make some tea and listen to a recording of Alfred Brendel playing the fourth in a series of concerts in which he played the complete cycle of Beethoven's piano concertos. We have enjoyed all these, absorbed by the genius of both men, Beethoven and Brendel. I like to imagine Beethoven might have been writing these endlessly fascinating pieces when our big oak was a stripling left by a farm labourer trimming the boundary hedge, more than 200 years ago.

Goodnight Christo. Love to everyone, Beth

- ❦ -

Thursday 21 November

Dear Beth,

I was just getting steamed up to write, so am glad that your latest letter arrived, this morning, before I opened the valve. I am so sorry about your tummy bug. It takes the stuffing out of you, as my mother used to say. Do hope it has quite cleared up by now. I was glad to have you here (though not for your sake!) the day I was sick (rare for me), and you were able to be nice to Ian Hodgson while I was still feeling dopey. In fact, I enjoyed your whole visit a lot. You always enter into things going on here, so wholeheartedly. And Fergus is very fond of you, as he should be.

So it is only a month to the shortest day. The darker mornings mean that when I call the dogs and let them out (5.00am, today) I can see the night sky as it will be (planets apart) in the evenings next March, and still totally dark. Venus is drawing to the end of the splendid visibility it has had all this year (apart from August, when it was dodging in front of the sun), but still sparkles low down in the early morning sky. Mars is drawing nearer and getting brighter, at last, in Leo, and will be at its brightest next February.

So, it was a hoar-frosty night and even now, at midday, there is still frost on the north side of the house roof, though other roofs look warm in the unalloyed sunshine – not a cloud in sight. What a storm that was, on Wednesday. I was glad the leaves were off all but the oaks. Autumn colour has been poor, this year, thanks to high winds, but last week we had three perfect days in succession, and on two of them I joined Fergus in Long Border work, for a number of hours. Even Dahlia didn't beg to be let in, but lay with Canna at the foot of the bamboo, *Phyllostachys bambusoides* 'Castillonii' (the one with slivers of green on the flat surface of its otherwise pale beige canes), on the orchard side of the path, sunning herself. I feel so much better when I have gardened, though there is plenty of writing to keep me inside.

When I've managed to 'do' a couple of thousand words in a day, it gives me a sense of achievement. Fergus feels just the same if he has got through a good wodge of garden work, as planned, but too often he is frustrated by unexpected calls on his time (sometimes by me), which makes him irritable. After October's beautiful weather, when we didn't want to tear the garden to pieces, we are faced with extra pressures, now. Like you, we have lifted all the tender things that need to be housed, but there is (unlike you) still a lot of bedding to go out – he's moving foxgloves, just now. And bulbs. Always a bit of a race against boggy conditions (though he works from boards), frost remaining in the ground and ever-shortening days.

I gave a dinner, for the third year running, for staff and spouses, last week, which made us ten – just right for the number of chairs at Rupert Williamson's table. It was a lively evening, though I have to admit to dropping off, towards the end. Everyone expects that! I did a mammoth fish pie, which was excellent, followed by a quince tart, which was not. Pip had done one most successfully, when here last month. It was likewise my first attempt. No trouble with the pastry, but the contents (mainly quince purée) overflowed while cooking, and were a little too dark on top. I mustn't be beaten by that. Pip, although only 20, has a great facility for taking on new recipes successfully. It was the first time he had made pastry. Perhaps if I didn't admit to failures, they'd go away? We had a family friend – she was matron at the London Hospital – who always declared that if you never admitted to having a cold, when external evidence made people ask you if you had, it would never develop into one. Hm.

Fergus drove me to Wisley, day before yesterday, for one of their trial inspections. I was glad to have him, as there was driving sleet and it settled as snow, in the last part of our journey. We were inspecting a trial of intermediate and miniature cyclamen (*C. persicum*) – a very large batch, beautifully raised by Ray Waite. They are such an improvement on the cyclamen we used to know. For one thing, most of them make a feature of their patterned foliage. Then the flowers, especially in the miniatures, are elegant, not clumsy and, in many cases, the original scent has been retained.

Ray is retiring this month, after 15 years at Wisley which, he says, he thoroughly enjoyed. When someone is patently doing a job successfully, he or she tends to be left to get on with it. I knew him ages before that, first taking notice of an exhibit of column stocks at the Chelsea Flower Show, when he worked for Slough Corporation. We got talking and, with Margaret, who also works at Wisley, became close friends. They were guests of honour at the RHS Council's lunch, during the last show at Westminster.

Ray has always been creatively experimental, though many of his practices he picked up from reading old 19th-century literature. For instance: layering a rod from a hothouse vine, into a pot (or several layers from the same rod into several pots). When fully established, the now pot-grown plants can be severed from the parent and will carry a beautiful bunch of grapes, which can be set, as a fruiting pot plant, on a dining table for dessert.

He has also experimented widely in growing plants, mainly annuals, from seed for conservatory display. Things like love-in-a-mist (*Nigella*) which, if treated individually and given their head, will make beautiful flowering pot plants. I only wish he would set all such experiences down in a book, called 'Greenhouse Flowers from Seed', perhaps, so that they are not lost. He would like to do this but has been unable to find a publisher.

Publishers don't like the risk of a new author writing on a new theme. Beyond the well-established authors whom they know will sell, they show minimal enterprise, except, maybe, on a fashionable and politically correct subject like 'Organic Gardening' or 'Gardening with Nature', or 'Women Gardeners Through the Ages', or 'The English Garden', or the 'Englishwoman's Garden', or, maybe, 'The Englishwoman's Ecologically Friendly Garden' (for you, Beth?). An ever-increasing proportion of garden writers today have very little personal experience of the practice of gardening.

Later. Fergus was just about to start replacing asters, on the Long Border, with seed-raised doronicums, interplanted with 'White Triumphator' lily-flowered tulips, when I visited him after lunch with, I have to confess, the intention of interrupting him – just what he least wanted. But, it occurred to me, the weather was so still and dry, ideal for spraying the wall peaches with protective fungicide against leaf curl, next spring. We repeat the spray once or even twice, before flowering starts. (Actually, we should do better, as at Wisley, to erect a shelter above and in front of the peaches to keep them from getting wet, but we're not yet organized for that refinement.) 'Perry will have to do it', said Fergus, reluctantly; 'He's carting logs.' By that he meant that, while it was dry, Perry was moving logs for my fire from where they had been sawn, yesterday, to be stacked in the dry, under cover. Making it much nicer for my fire. I said he could do that tomorrow, even if it was windy and unsuitable for spraying. 'Tomorrow', said Fergus, 'he is . . .', and there followed another important task, scheduled to be done. 'Well,' said I, 'all I know is that the peaches need spraying [I had mentioned this, a few days earlier] and that conditions are right NOW.'

He laughed and interrupted his work to tell Perry to switch jobs. A result of the cool summer, this year, was that the peaches didn't have nearly as much sweetness and flavour as last year, but there were more of them. Hard to get it right. In a really hot dry summer (e.g. 1995) honey bees attacked our peaches and autumn raspberries in quantity, for sweetness and moisture. That didn't happen in 1996.

I have been sent a copy of the 'new edition' of David Austin's *English Roses*. It is lavishly and lusciously illustrated and must, I feel sure, sell extremely well. His style of rose bloom is just such as appeals to me most: flat, full of petals, often quartered, the colours not too hot (though I loved the blooms of a flat-faced, rich hot red variety called 'Geranium Red', now out of the running). Most of the illustrations are in close-up. Those that are growing and have a setting often show up the defects of the straggling rose bush, even though no dead blooms are showing (of course).

Where the roses are being grown in beds on their own, their defects shout loudest. But where combined with plants, especially spire-forming plants like salvias, sidalceas, veronicas and foxgloves, the contrast heightens their impact amazingly. Even so, like the majority of double roses, they hold on to their petals, when faded, and a flower truss looks horribly bedraggled after rain, with each bloom hanging its neck.

They all look as though they must have a wonderful fragrance, exactly suited to their generous inclusion in potpourri. You make potpourri, Beth. Shouldn't it be possible to get sufficient fragrance into the mix without additives, as is the normal practice? They may be natural and 'essential' oils and concentrates but somehow seem a cheat, to me. I remember my mother once buying some orris root, which was a great excitement, but when added to our home-made potpourri, I thought the result rather disappointing. I used to break open the live rhizomes of bearded irises and try to imagine some scent, there, but without success. I don't think we grew the right iris.

Keep well, dear Beth. Winter is never as long as it seems!

With love, from Christo

—❧—

Wednesday 4 December

Dear Beth,

It is already 10.00pm, so I don't know how far I shall get with this letter. I have been in part composing it in my mind, otherwise I should be writing to Roger Highfield (my friend since 1942) in Oxford, he having sent me another book on Gertrude Jekyll. She is inexhaustible.

He has also sent me a publication called *Japan*. Roger was the Crown Prince's tutor at Merton. Her Imperial Highness, wife of the Crown Prince, came over to open the restored Japanese gateway and landscape, at Kew. There are pictures of celebrities standing with hands crossed in front of them. 'Originally made for the Japan-British Exhibition held in London in 1910,' I read, 'it was later presented to the Royal Botanic Gardens at Kew, and is one of the very few genuinely authentic Japanese structures in Europe.' I fail to see how any structure that is a copy and out of its homeland can be authentic, let alone genuine.

I just wish we would stop copying one another. Japan has its marvellous culture; we have ours. I agree that there is much we can learn from them – their meticulous training and care of plants, for instance, born of their shortage of space. That is greatly in contrast to our slapdash ways. Doubtless there are devices that they can learn from us. But this slavish copying, without original inspiration, is a disaster. Imagine if I should meet my Long Border in Kyoto. Home from home? I think not. And Japanese gardens in the West are a disaster.

Romke (van de Kaa, my head gardener 20 years ago) came over from Holland for four nights, leaving yesterday. He loves Dixter and renews his acquaintance every time he comes. He must have taken upwards of 40 photographs – I hardly know what of. But he sees the scene with fresh eyes, and I must say that, in between depressions, the light has been marvellous. He points things out to me that I rather took for granted, though I know I shouldn't and usually don't. The *Cotoneaster horizontalis* are luminous, just now, not just with their berries, which the birds have ignored for the second year running, but, for their foliage, which has also coloured to tones of red, rather different from the berries. The whole garden is glowing with these, all, or nearly all, self-sown. There is one self-appointed spot, against the brick wall of the old pig sty, where a cotoneaster has dark rosettes of *Helleborus foetidus* at its feet. When the sun shines, that looks incandescent, the hellebores highlighting the cotoneaster.

The sky was big today, with white, fleecy clouds in just the right proportion. Like waterlilies in a pond, they shouldn't cover more than a quarter of the sky. Now that the waterlily pads have all but disappeared, the Horse Pond looks twice its normal size, so free and untrammelled.

Fergus is so aware of much work to get through in the garden that he sometimes feels I am in the way. He is right, because I sometimes feel the need to put in my oar (interfere, i.e.). I am finding that when I have a message to put across, I need to put it twice. This, at my age, is tiresome, because remembering (a) what the message is and (b) to communicate it at the right moment is quite an effort. Thus, to Fergus, when giving the meadow areas either side of the front path their final cut, to remember to include the half-moon outside the gate (where the Mount Etna broom and medlar are), in this exercise. Days later, I see that the half-moon is still uncut. I need to remember, at the right moment, to point this out. But Perry is engaged in giving the orchard its last cut. 'If that is interrupted, the piles of grass he has left for collection will make the turf beneath them pale for lack of light,' Fergus points out. 'How long will the half-moon take to do?' I enquire. 'Half a day,' says Fergus, not wishing to underestimate!

But there is another area that is shaggy, an awkward, up-and-down piece among lilacs outside the heating chamber, as I have always called it. (Perry invariably corrects this to boiler room, but I can't be bothered to change that sort of unimportance.) In the end, a compromise: since scaffolding may have to go up at any moment outside the boiler room, so that the timbers of the house from Benenden (brought to Dixter 1910, but built 1500) can be replaced, it is agreed that Perry can break off from the orchard to do this, but the half-moon – not till later. Bulbs are already showing through, in the meadow areas, I may say, so there is an element of urgency. Fergus hates to have his plans interrupted. Why can't I disappear for a day or two and let him get on with things? But that is momentary. His moods change like the sun's with the clouds. Soon, he'll be wanting me to discuss the next plans for planting and interplanting in the Long Border. I want to be in on that, too.

Another example: I told Perry a faulty washer needed replacing on the kitchen hot tap. I'm always being told that if this is left too long and you simply try to tighten the tap, while turning it off, harder and harder, the bearings wear out and the whole tap has to be replaced. Perry heard, said yes and did nothing. It was only the first time of my saying it. There were other things to do. So, after a few days and with the tap still dripping, I have to crank up my memory into saying the same thing at the right moment, a second time. Perry, having brought in the fire logs, does it immediately. I bet you don't go through these situations, Beth. The moment you speak, action is taken.

How's your rainfall? We had 125mm (5in) in November, by far our wettest month this year. August was second wettest. December yet to come, of course. Areas that show they need draining, notably alongside the front path, are flooding again. We delayed doing anything about this last winter, because of other claims on our time. This winter, I think Fergus has resigned himself. Action will have to be taken. Poor fellow, torn this way and that. Lucky me having someone with such a conscience by my side.

Relationships between people who see each other all the time are not simple – and never static. I love Fergus dearly and he does me, but the exigencies of existence and proximity are constantly throwing up new situations that cannot be ignored. Far better that way than just jogging along.

I have written some 2,400 words, today, for my *magnum opus* (can't discuss what that is, until it has got further), so that gives me a certain sense of achievement. Roger once told me that in Oxford, if you find yourself talking to a stranger at a party, you only have to ask 'And how is the *magnum opus*?' for the floodgates of conversation (or monologue) to be opened. A couple of years later, when Roger had come on a visit. 'How is the *magnum opus*?', I enquired. All unsuspecting, he immediately entered into details of what he was working on. I enjoyed that.

With love, from Christo

—✿—

Thursday 12 December

Dear Christo,

Two letters from you, fun to read, but now with my head full of things to tell you, as well as points to raise on your letters, I am in a whirl, unlike you who I've seen sit down at your laptop, your fingers obediently following your well-ordered thoughts, and an article ready for the day's post well before the pre-lunch drink tray appears.

Perhaps I'll begin at the deep end and plunge into your pool of despair (well, a puddle really), concerning staff not always able to do things right away, or more justifiably irritating, forgetting to do them at all! Getting grass cut in good time before bulbs appear is important, but it depends partly on the kind of bulbs. Daffodils don't have to stand above manicured grass; a bit of companionable weed, especially if it's Queen Anne's lace, can enhance them (crocuses might be different), but we fell behind this year in strimming the grass where cyclamens are thriving. Gerard had to strim round them so the effect of little posies embroidered over green canvas was marred by whiskery pieces. But I know next year he will not let that happen.

I feel, just as you do sometimes, a sense of anxiety (have I arranged for this or that to be done?) when I'm bogged down with work indoors, the weather too maybe pinning me down. To help myself, because otherwise I know I'll forget, I write little notes on scraps of paper to hand around, reminders of this or that I would like to have done, reminders of things I should be doing myself. More detailed notes go on to sheets of cardboard. They last longer, can be referred to. We both are blessed with good people in our teams who are not only enthusiastic and hard-working, but who take their responsibilities seriously. We need that. And it takes time, years of devotion, to achieve. Running a garden and nursery is a highly complex business requiring intelligence and initiative.

You know all of this, of course, and you do give your staff the opportunity to grow, to develop their potential.

I do sometimes wonder whether large and complicated gardens such as ours will be a feature in the 21st century. They cannot, I think, be run by committees, or the work put out to tender for the cheapest rate. Large, good gardens need inspired leadership, with concern for everything involved, both the plants and the people who care for them. I am thinking of gardens you and I have visited in Scotland; one in particular, where the owner, now paralysed after a stroke, had planted magnificent trees and shrubs, 50 or more years ago. It was September and I remember golden light falling through a huge cercidiphyllum, with leaves about to fall, translucent in tones of cream, pink and copper, smelling faintly of strawberries (mine never colours like that down here in Essex). But the garden had a sad feel; one lonely young gardener without a leader, fumbling his way round, proudly showing us sun-loving plants he had chosen to put against a tall, shady wall. Woodland plants, with the Scottish climate, would have been much easier to manage and would have looked spectacular.

Of course, we know another Scottish garden, Balcarres, where Lady Crawford's enthusiasm and drive makes up for a whole team of gardeners, as she sweeps Donald, her gardener, before her, cutting great swathes into virgin land, filling it in no time with massive and beautiful groupings of herbaceous plants and ground cover.

Professional gardeners (other than dedicated loners) like company, they like to be part of a team, ideally with an enthusiastic boss or head gardener to lead them. My mind goes back to Fergus, some years ago now, studying cattle at Wye College, if my memory serves me well. He had the luck to stumble into Dixter and be mesmerized by plants . . . and you! And so make a complete turn-around. To create a large and interesting garden is costly, as we know, who have to pay our way by individual effort. Who can tell whether such gardens will be part of the 21st century? But there are, and will be, many smaller gardens, of both artistic and botanical merit, made and maintained by knowledgeable enthusiasts, particularly as people are retiring or are made redundant early in their lives.

Now I'll climb down off my pulpit and tell you about my potpourri. Potpourri has become ubiquitous. At worst you might find, in some hotel bathroom, a bowl of dyed woodshavings smelling horribly of cheap perfume. The real thing is much harder to come by. There are no doubt secret recipes as there are of fine liqueurs.

Several years ago I was sent a small packet from a shop in Florence. I still have its contents preserved in a lidded jar, together with the little note from my friend and the sheet of delicate tissue paper printed with the name of the supplier, Officina Profumo-Farmaceutica di S. Maria Novella, and a coat of arms inscribed 'Casa Fondata, Nell Anno 1612', all impregnated to this day with a sweet, spicy, heady perfume. I have it beside me now, perhaps two handfuls of brown petals, leaves, seeds and tiny rosebuds, and I marvel, every time I take a deep breath, how fresh and intense the scent remains, completely unable myself to capture anything so fine and lasting.

I suspect it was made by the Moist method. Basically the petals of scented flowers, such as roses, are packed into a jar between layers of sea salt, and tightly sealed for some weeks before other ingredients are added. Although this is the best way, I understand, to preserve delicate perfumes, the disadvantage is the loss of colour, the whole mass becoming brown, like compost – and smelling no different, if you get it wrong, as I did on my one and only attempt.

The Dry method can keep both the colour and scent of many flowers and leaves. A few weeks ago I assembled all the bags of scented leaves and flowers Emily had collected and dried for me over the summer months. Among the ingredients I most value are rose petals, lavender and monarda, together with scented leaves like *Calamintha nepetoides*, *Aloysia triphylla*, rosemary, lemon balm, and rose-scented geranium. For colour and fun, I add dried rosebuds, nigella seed-heads, brilliant blue delphinium petals, scarlet pelargoniums – collected when deadheading – rosettes of the double blue and purple cranesbills, and the exquisite hop-like flowers of *Origanum rotundifolium*. To all of these, I add crushed spices: cardamom, cinnamon, allspice and nutmeg. You need enough spice, but not too much or it could smell like mincemeat.

Next you need a fixative, to help retain the volatile oils. I slice rhizomes of *Iris* 'Florentina', dry them in the airing cupboard (it takes about a week), then smash them into powder in the liquidizer. My nose, I have to admit, does not recognize the strong smell of violet that this root is reputed to have, but it goes into my mixture, hopefully, as a fixative, together with some powdered lemon and orange peel.

This year I discovered gum benzoin, a sticky perfume from a tree native to the Far East, and have used some of that. Without any additional perfume, I put several plastic bags filled with this mixture, tied at the neck, into a small spare room and closed the door. A few days later, opening the door, I was surprised by the fresh aromatic scent filling the room.

To the remainder of my mixture, I added (in spite of you shaking your head) some essential oils obtained from a reputable source. They were all oils of the plants I had included: bergamot, lavender and rose geranium. Together with little muslin bags I'd filled with silica gel to absorb any hint of moisture, I packed this colourful scented mixture into large glass jars, to mature. Now and then I open one and take a big sniff. It is delicious and very pretty. But not from Florence.

Outside is different (too cold and dank for any scent, not even of fallen leaves). This morning I met Winnie and Lesley tidying up in the Wood Garden in a slight drizzle, everywhere silent and still, the sky leaden. Yet the scene was beautiful, an astonishing amount of colour; everywhere shades of copper against the vibrance of evergreens. I can't remember the oaks hanging on to their leaves for so long, together with quince-yellow leaves of flowering currant,

yellow-ochre of *Lunaria rediviva* and *Physocarpus opulifolius*
'Luteus'. The birds haven't yet touched the pink-flushed bundles
of white berries strung on crimson threads, which weigh down
the branches of the Chinese mountain ash, *Sorbus hupehensis*. By
the reservoir, tall swamp cypresses pierce the sky, their steeples
rusty with leaves not yet fallen; liquidambar still wrapped in
crimson maple-shaped leaves, lovely beside great ivory plumes of
Cortaderia 'Sunningdale Silver'. All these scenes lifted my spirits,
and Winnie too, busy with her tidying said, 'However much we
cut down, there is always so much left to see here in the garden –
nowhere is bare.'

You mentioned rainfall. We have had almost 150mm (6in) since
the beginning of October – nearly as much as we had in the whole
of last winter. We divide our year, for recording rainfall, into winter
and summer. This is how they stand for the past two seasons:

	1994–95	1995–96
Winter (Nov–Apr)	395mm (15.54in)	203mm (7.93in)
Summer (May–0ct)	165mm (6.53in)	163mm (6.42in)
Yearly total	560mm (22.07in)	366mm (14.35in)

Although the rainfall for this past season was one of the lowest
since we have made records here, 40 years now, the garden was not
so badly affected as in the previous summer when the temperatures
were abnormally high, several times reaching 32°C (90°F).

I am enclosing a cutting taken from *The Times* this autumn,
referring to weather conditions on 15 October 1921. The concern
expressed then over 'exceptional dryness, sunshine and warmth',
and variation in rainfall making all the difference between 'famine
and plenty', could have been written anytime during these past
two very dry summers. It is not possible for us to pontificate from
our tiny vantage point on major changes in the weather systems.
We must just do our best to adapt to what happens in our lifetime.
Quite apart from meteorological changes the human race must
also be aware that lack of water will be catastrophic if we do not
change our ways.

In summer I sometimes quail when I hear visitors telling my staff how lucky they are to work in such a lovely place, knowing only too well what they have to put up with in winter: dark mornings, penetrating cold and wet, ice on the puddles. Yet, week by week, the work gets done, a cycle of events rather like the curriculum of the classroom, working together in little teams to prepare for the next season's performance.

To cheer ourselves up and the visitors who come at this time of year, Debbie and Emily collected some of the prunings made by David and his team in the garden, to decorate their workshed as they do with fresh flowers in summer. Outside my front and back doors, I have two large earthenware pots. Inside are plastic buckets filled with loosely crumpled wire netting. In these I make my winter arrangements, not Christmassy arrangements, mark you; they last well into the New Year, to welcome early visitors. I use a mixture of evergreens and deciduous, plain and variegated. There is the blue cypress *Chamaecyparis lawsoniana* 'Triomf van Boskoop', pale ivory variegated privet, the large-leaved ivy, *Hedera colchica* 'Paddy's Pride' (now 'Sulphur Heart'!). Bold, glossy rosettes of *Magnolia grandiflora* relieve the startling yellow variegation of *Aucuba japonica* 'Crotonifolia'. To warm the group, I found the terminal sprays of *Mahonia japonica* turning scarlet, beautiful to look at, but a little sad because it means the bush is dying (probably damaged by drought). Tall crimson-lacquered stems of cornus pick up these red tones, together with some pieces of *Skimmia japonica* 'Rubella' whose deep red buds are attractive now. Several handsome, blue-grey heads of my favourite, *Euphorbia wulfenii*, pull together all these contrasting tones and textures.

Thank you for your Christmas wishes. We shall see our daughters during the break, but be quiet here most of the time. I welcome that for myself, but for Andrew it is a must: he is becoming increasingly frail, but remains clear-headed. That is everything.

I shall think of you and Dixter and imagine the Great Hall full of warmth, good smells and young people sharing with you the traditional spirit of Christmas.

With good wishes, now, and for the coming year, and a hug for everyone, from Beth

– ✿ –

Tuesday 31 December

Dear Christo,

It's the last day of 1996. Outside we have a Christmas card snow scene; inside I sit thinking of you at Dixter, imagining you too will be frost- and snowbound. I have just been out to feed the birds. Keith has made me a bird-table with a roof to keep off the rain and snow. This morning it looks like a little Swiss chalet perched on the topmost pot of my group of large terracotta pots, all emptied now of plants and soil. Blue tits, great tits, coal tits, chaffinches, robins and green finches all take their turn till hustled away by bustling blackbirds. The timid song thrush waits till last, hiding beneath shrubs. Everywhere in the fresh snow there are footprints of birds and animals, some I recognize, others I don't.

From Andrew's study window, up in the roof, I look across the fields and see our neighbouring farmer carting out hay to feed a flock of sheep huddled, mud-coloured, against the glistening snow. He had intended them to survive on turnip-tops (sown after the wheat was harvested), smothered now in drifted snow.

So far we have only had dry snow flurries, blowing like a sandstorm across the nursery. The wind is bitter (straight from Russia, so the papers say), but it is brilliantly sunny, even warm on my face as I sit by the window looking out on to the garden. The bleakness of winter is relieved by patches of green; feathery bamboos, various conifers and evergreens, and the bright green algae growing along the shady side of oak boles and branches all illuminated by the long, slanting rays of sunlight. In contrast, leaf-losing trees and shrubs form delicate traceries of buff, brown and black against the blinding whiteness of the snow.

Tall columns of miscanthus grass, bleached and dried, sway restlessly beside the frigid ponds. The ducks and moorhens have disappeared, probably flown to the open salt water only a few miles from here, since the River Colne is tidal as far as Colchester. Nothing here now for the heron.

All this will be another test for the Gravel Garden. During the first three or four winters, we had very few frosts, certainly not enough ice to bear a duck. Even then, the temperatures, especially the wind chill, could be damaging. (Lowest temperature recorded on the south wall of the potting shed, −11°C/12°F.) With protection in mind, as well as looks, we haven't yet cut down much. The massed heads of *Sedum maximum*, normally contributing the rich, dark colour of coffee grounds, today have little snow hats, reminding me of sugar-dusted mince pies. (David Ward made me a dozen for a Christmas present, as well as producing some home-grown eggs.)

Before Christmas, I was picking twigs of the sweet-scented, cream-flowered shrub, *Lonicera* x *purpusii*, to put with the shining leaves and green flower buds of *Skimmia* x *confusa* 'Kew Green', and the snowdrop we used to call *Galanthus corcyrensis*. (This grows wild in Corfu, Sicily and Greece in thickets on limestone hills, where it flowers naturally in autumn.) We are now obliged to call it *Galanthus reginae-olgae* subsp. *reginae-olgae* Winter Flowering Group. (See *Plant Finder*!) It is far superior, I think, to the snowdrop we have always known as *G. reginae-olgae* which flowered earlier, but grew feebly in my garden and has since passed away, unlamented. Perhaps I did not understand its needs.

The later form grows strongly, with large, well-formed flowers. It has been in flower since October, and still I could find a few late stems for Christmas Day, to put by Andrew's chair. On the hall floor I put a copper pan filled with pots of bronze and speckle-leaf begonias (from our small heated greenhouse), and tucked among them a few stems of the peach and apricot alstroemerias I told you about earlier. They continued to flower in pots in our propagating house all autumn, until we cut them down to rest until spring. Those we planted in the Gravel Garden vanished after the first frosts, but they were well mulched with gravel, so we hope to see them reappear in spring.

Usually I don't bother with fresh flowers at Christmas time. I prefer the evergreens from the garden. One or two bold groups, similar to the pots I make outside, have taken the place of the Christmas tree we had for all the years when there were children and grandchildren to delight. But the holly and ivy remain, twined around the grandfather clock and along the picture frames. The colour and atmosphere of Christmas past and present is for me in the many cards grouped on every surface that can be swept clean to make room for them. Big family parties are too much for Andrew now (and for me too, if I am honest), so the family visit us in small groups, while we enjoy the company of an extended family through the beautiful cards and their messages.

The vegetable garden looks forlorn, brassicas drooping, leeks collapsed. Thank goodness we dug artichokes and leeks before the ground became rock hard. Carrots and beetroot are safe and available from the little 'cellar'. So too is horseradish which I grate into sour cream or strained yogurt, together with chopped chervil, parsley or dried summer savory. Sometimes I add a little onion, or finely chopped red pepper – but I remember, you cannot eat peppers. This tasty mixture I drop into bowls of bland vegetable soup, use as a spread on bread, or mix into grated carrot for a salad. Provided you do not use too much horseradish it does not cause that excruciating pain in the nose as did the horseradish sauce (Mrs Beeton's version) which it was my task to make, as a child, to go with roast beef. This way of using it, less hot and bringing out the aromatic flavour of the root, is a new discovery for me.

Lettuces in my tunnel, I have to confess, are slowly going down with botrytis, because I don't spray them, of course. I watch them carefully, whipping out anything which looks as if it might keel over while it still is good to eat. But two chicories, the narrow red-leaved 'Treviso' and the big creamy-green 'Sugar Loaf', are my standbys, together with rocket and landcress. Up till Christmas I was cropping the young tips from especially lush carpets of chickweed, using them chopped like parsley. But they will be gone now.

All this domesticity over the holiday helps take my mind off decisions I should be making. The catalogue must be revised, descriptions written for new introductions, all to be ready for printing in February. Rosie has already spent dark afternoons trawling through it with the *Plant Finder* beside her to discover yet more outlandish names for well-established favourites. It wouldn't be so bad if the new ones were pronounceable, or even spellable. But I expect that is what most people think when they first come across Latin names. We forget that feeling of helplessness we used to have at the prospect of ever learning the language of plants, until we meet something totally unfamiliar. Remembering it depends on whether you can fit the new word into a recognizable pattern.

Most worrying this minute is the thought of finding work for six men and six women, returning in two days' time, all engaged outside in propagation or maintenance. Already David has filled the propagating house with trolley-loads of pots to be weeded. Left overnight to thaw, they can be dealt with next day.

Normally finding work is not a problem. But everything frost-bound and snow-covered is different. Debbie and Emily can make root cuttings, provided roots can be dug. We may have to work half-days; getting home before the roads have become sheets of glass is no bad thing. But I am concerned for those whose wage packets are the main support of the family. Somehow the problems will be overcome. My acute anxieties usually turn out to be unjustified.

I often think of you when I am feeling apprehensive of the future; your determination to keep going at all costs encourages me. But a winter visit to Dixter is very different from summer. I know you have your oases of warmth – the big open fireplaces in the solar and in your writing parlour, encircled by your own handstitched, tapestry chairs – but to reach these oases of comfort one must walk the length of the Great Hall, when I am glad of every extra layer of garments I have brought. I have also enjoyed the comfort and delight of a fire in my bedroom, maintained from a store cupboard just outside the door. Such peace it was, to sit there for a while, watching the flames light up the dark recesses of the room, the logs crackling, the soft wood ash collapsing as the room darkened, when I climbed into the four-poster bed and went straight to sleep.

For you, maintaining the fabric of Dixter is an on-going responsibility. Again, I have observed your stoicism in the face of inevitable expense. Have the repairs to the foundations already begun? I hope it is a good feeling, of relief, to have decisions made and plans laid, as we go into 1997.

My warmest wish for you, for the coming year, dear Christo, is continued good health, allowing enough time for yourself, as well as the happiness you give to others.

Much love, Beth

—❦—

Part Two

Wednesday 8 January

Dear Beth,

Evening, and I am in the solar with the girls, under a rug, all keeping each other warm. I have just been listening to Shostakovich's 4th Symphony – the last 40 minutes of it, that is. I know nothing about it and have never heard it before, but it is invigorating stuff. Full of threat, but energy too, a little tenderness, and even some Viennese waltz music, now and again. I have to send my application for tickets to Glyndebourne, and have left it late to ask you about dates, but shall keep a space for you anyway, which someone else can fill if no good to you, for *The Makropulos Case* (Janáček), which you were unable to come to when this production was new, two years ago. You know the Janáček idiom and I think you'll find it as moving in its way as *Karya* and *Jenufa*. Anja Silja, the sexton in *Jenufa* who murdered J's infant for the sake of family honour and was haunted by her crime thereafter, is the star in this opera. Imagine being condemned to live indefinitely, being reborn every generation as a beautiful opera diva, attractive to many men. She has become utterly cynical and longs only for an end to it all. It is a wonderful production and a shatteringly moving opera, though it opens dryly enough. I do hope you can come. Fergus and Amanda, and Stephen and Judy Anderton will be there. Stephen is very glad to be shot of English Heritage (so much work and travel that he scarcely saw his family and the pay was poor) and to be his own master, though the hazards of that situation are always daunting. But he has regular slots in the press (writing on gardening every Saturday for *The Times*) and I expect other media outlets will be forthcoming, as he has an attractive personality and is not afraid of publicity.

Two letters from you since I last wrote, more than a month ago, so lots to catch up on. First, thank you so much for the bag of potpourri. Whatever I might disapprove of in its contents, it smells delicious and looks delightful. I somehow hadn't thought of adding ingredients purely for their shapes and colours, but it's obvious once pointed out. It looks so pretty. Amazing how the smell of lavender persists. My mother made lavender bags to put in clothes drawers, when I was very young, and they still smell nice after all those years.

You write about gardens in the future and whether large ones like ours will be able to exist. Will there be the people to afford to own and keep them up to scratch? It is in the private sector that most inspiration is to be expected, because there are not the shackles of rule by committee. Two people, bouncing ideas off one another, is ideal for a gardening enterprise, but with help from auxiliaries, likewise inspired in their way. It will become more difficult, but creativity will out, one way or another. Even in the public sector. Look what Stephen Anderton, himself, achieved at English Heritage's Belsay Hall, Northumberland. There were the old bones of a wonderful garden, but he injected new blood in its veins. He instigated the new local croquet club to take possession of the old tennis court areas. He organized plant sales, he opened up the overgrown west quarry and did an immense amount of new planting. There will always be outlets for persistent individuals like him, though they also need a bit of luck. Largely, however, we create our own luck.

The scene in public gardening is very dismal, with so much funding withdrawn and the system of tendering, which rules out the sense of community and pride engendered by a resident team. There was a good deal of protected dead wood in those teams, but by and large, many of them did a splendid job. Brighton Parks Department was justly famed, when Raymond Evison (not the clematis specialist) and his team were at its head. Stanmer Park, where they had their production area, seemed a model of its kind. That has gone and the scene is pathetic: many areas of activity have been and are still being closed. Is it, perhaps, because Brighton itself is less important as a resort, now that so many people travel abroad for their holidays?

Still, even with shortage of means, the spirit of adventure will never be quenched. There will always be plant enthusiasts, finding some sort of outlet, and others who want to create a beautiful scene with plants. And enthusiasm is infectious. Such as you and I can engender it in others, sometimes more gifted than ourselves. Fergus, incidentally, had moved out of agriculture, in his studies at Wye College, and into the horticultural field, before ever I met him. His first visit here was with an organized party of horticultural students. He, with his henna-dyed hair, and Neil Ross, who has since emigrated to New Zealand and is with our inspired mutual gardening friend, Beverley McConnell, stood out from the rest. You know how attracted I am by young talent and so are you.

For parts of the past three days we have been working on this year's new plant catalogue. Of course, it is trivial compared to yours, but it still causes us a great deal of discussion, not to say worry. We go through it plant by plant and often discussion can last for five minutes on one item. About supplies, about where to grow stock and how much and whether we need to buy in. We don't like buying in, any more than you do. It creates one more imponderable between the making of the plant and its final outlet. The more cogs in the wheel, the greater the chances of something going wrong. But we do buy in, just the same. Sometimes to tide us over till our own production has got its act together. There may be a greater demand than we had anticipated. Or we may have a fatally attractive plant in the garden, like *Ceanothus* 'Puget Blue', which we are bad at propagating ourselves, but for which the demand is huge. *Osmanthus delavayi* is another and *Cornus alternifolia* 'Argentea', to whose propagation by grafting we are not geared.

All through this, Fergus is taking notes and looking anxious. He takes the burdens of responsibility very seriously, which enables me to take them more lightly, thank goodness. But I am still very much involved. I don't want to become a cipher any sooner than my decline in energy and intellect make necessary. When Fergus has got away for a few days, he returns a different person. He went with Amanda to her parents in Cheshire, for the weekend after Christmas, and was drawn into a funeral, in Wales, for an old lady of 105. While they were waiting for events to get moving in the church, he turned to his neighbour and asked him if he would like to hear a dirty story. The man cast his eyes heavenwards and said he thought they'd better wait till they were outside. Fergus loved the gesture.

Olivia and her German husband, Peter (he's good news), were here for Christmas. Fergus was too, bless him, looking after wood for the fires, vegetables for meals and all that, and his brother, Edgar, and his brother's partner, Victoria. Such a nice gathering, large enough to be fun but small enough to be able to talk and think. We had a small Christmas tree here, in the solar, and Olivia decorated it with our old collection of ornaments, so much more attractive than what are on offer today. One box of glass birds with fine-spun glass tails is marked in my mother's hand 'Glass Birds bought at Harrods with Xr. [my family abbreviation] 1936'. I was 15.

On New Year's Day, another section of the family came to lunch: my great niece, Giny Best, with Andrew and their three children; and Chris Lloyd, my great nephew, with Gins (both girls are Virginia) and their infant daughter. There were two infants, in fact, one born July 1995, the other October. The October girl usually frets for most of the visit, but since her cousin, Angus, was fretful himself, she looked calmly on, as much as to say, what's he making a fuss for? I gave her a musical box, which plays 'Ba Ba Black Sheep' till you go round the bend, and him a train of the kind you drag. Both were made of wood, not plastic, which makes a refreshing change, nowadays.

Like you, we are truly into winter; about 7.5cm (3in) of snow has been lying around for the past 10 days. It has been worse, further east, in Kent, where Jack Elliott told me on the phone that they had 20cm (8in) and snow ploughs were busy. The cold enables me to freeze my ice trays in the larder, instead of the fridge, and the cubes so made are beautifully clear, not cloudy, as normal.

The house certainly is cold, with mere islands of warmth. I had a roaring fire going in the (your) north bedroom, for Olivia's and Peter's arrival, then leaving it on subsequent days for him to organize. I gather he was never too successful. Fire has always fascinated me. I nearly set the house on fire, when I was twelve, but I do also understand how to get the best out of it. I completely remade the parlour fire today (where we were at work on the catalogue), after Fergus's efforts, which resulted in mutinous sulks (from the fire, not him).

However, dear Beth, you'll do better to delay a visit for six weeks or so. Come with the crocuses. Do you remember when we sat in the garden, for coffee after lunch, with a rug on top of your slithery ground sheet, and overlooking a sheet of purple, mauve and white Dutch crocuses, in the drained upper moat and the orchard, where daffodils later take over? But the two bulbs can intermingle, as there is a gap between their flowerings. Well, the winter crocuses, concentrated either side of the front path, should peak in the second half of February (they did last year), followed by the Dutchies, in March. One is always at the mercy of the weather, of course, and if overcast or chilly, the crocuses show their displeasure. But how I love them for the way they respond when the weather relents.

Repair work on the house has still not begun, though preparations have been going forward for several weeks, now, and the scaffolding is in place. But can they possibly, as planned, be through with this stage by the time we open for Easter? No, is the answer, and I shall be greatly inconvenienced, having nowhere to put myself when the show rooms, which I normally use, as now, are debarred to me.

One example of how progress has been delayed involved the plumbing. The radiators against the outside wall, where new timbers have to go in, needed to be removed. Instead of the old method of draining the whole system, so that the operation could

165

go forward, there is a brave new method, which allows water to remain in most of the system, by freezing the pipes, just behind the radiators that need to be removed. I said I was sure that with an old system like ours, this would be found to be inoperable. It was. Not discouraged, several days later, they came along with a more powerful freezing machine. That, also, was too weak to cope with our diameter of pipe. Eventually, still more days later, the system was drained and refilled, after all. Which actually worked. Meantime I had had three days without central heating instead of one.

The vegetables I am getting from the garden are pretty limited. So far, we have prevented the celeriac from being spoilt by freezing, by laying a double layer of hessian over them. I made an excellent fish soup today, using potato, celeriac and garlic, precooked in olive oil, as a matrix, before adding the fish stock and cubes of fresh (frozen) haddock.

Fergus or Perry still manage to excavate leeks for me, as required, though the green part is clogged with ice. We ate masses of sprouts over Christmas, but since the frosts have become really hard, I have thought it best for them to defreeze naturally, before I resume consumption. Just before the hardest frosts, I picked a huge head of 'Sugar Loaf' chicory, which I am still eating in stages. It keeps beautifully, in a plastic bag in the larder. I have to say, my normal enthusiasm for salads is slightly reduced in this weather. If I leave olive oil in the kitchen, it is all solid within the day. It must be the coldest room in the house.

Looking back on 1996, it was a good year for me and Dixter. Visitor numbers were up by 3,000, which was reflected in increased sales, for which we managed to produce more plants. Thanks to the increased sales, we were able to put a new wing on the old greenhouse, to be run at a slightly higher temperature. This will enable us, I hope, to keep our Egyptian papyrus from year to year, rather than having to treat it as an annual.

Any strangeness in the weather has compensating values, which are often forgotten in people's anxiety to express what a battle their lives have been. The spring garden was the best ever. Fergus says he didn't feel happy about the summer and that there was a lack of achievement in certain areas. I suppose there will always be an element of robbing Peter to pay Paul. New enterprises or renovations may subtract time from other aspects of our work. He reckons we came up trumps by and large, but that one should always be aware of the failures and not become complacent. But when we look back, by means of Jonathan Buckley's photographs, taken throughout the season, there are some wonderful images. With the help of a bit of creative accounting, we might even break even this year! Who knows?

My best wishes to you for 1997, dear Beth. To wish people of our age a happy new year is to be a bit blinkered, I suppose. Andrew's frailty cannot be expected to improve. The nursery's fortunes? You tell me. But at the least, I hope you will keep well. So much hangs on our good health.

Much love, Christo

– ❊ –

Wednesday 15 January

Hello Christo,

I am sitting on the raised hearth close to my wood-burning stove, thankful to feel the comforting warmth thaw out my bones! Several layers of clothing don't seem able to keep out the penetrating cold of freezing fog. Isn't it strange how cold we still are in the south-east? Possibly, being so close to the continent we share their climate. (At the opposite extreme, a friend in the Isle of Man rang me last evening, saying he had spent the day outside in his shirt sleeves!) The snow has gone, all but a few persistent humps, but the ponds are totally iced over, the roadways around the nursery rutted like corrugated iron and hard on my feet. The soil is still too rigid to kick into the holes and scrape marks made by the wretched rabbits.

Yet on a morning such as this, deadly for travellers, the garden looks beautiful, cruelly beautiful. Everything stands silent and still, veiled in shrouds of frozen mist. As I walked (guiltily) across the frozen grass into the Reservoir Garden, silhouettes of *Pinus radiata* and *Eucalyptus pauciflora* subsp. *niphophila* loomed ahead of me, contrasting darkly with the silver birches encrusted with ice, drooping like frozen waterfalls. Heavy hoar-frost creates beauty where there was none before, emphasizing structure among the deciduous shrubs and remains of herbaceous plants. I found myself stopping to enjoy anonymous bundles of curving stems or angular leafless structures I hadn't troubled to pause by before.

I enjoyed this monochromatic screen, in detail, and as a landscape effect, slowly back-lit by the cold, yellow light of the sun. Distance was blotted out, tree outlines disappearing like faint pencil sketches off the edge of the page. Perhaps the essence of enjoyment is variation (or do I have a short attention span?). Out of this grey and white scene a patch of the variegated *Yucca filamentosa* caught my eye, its low tuffets of yellow sword-like leaves faintly veined with green, surrounded by rosettes of bergenia with reddened top and undersides, yet still undamaged. Even brighter, shining lipstick-red, are the year-old stems of *Cornus alba* 'Sibirica', the Westonbirt dogwood and the brightest of all forms. It's lovely to come across it out of the mist, with the low sun behind you.

From my kitchen window I look across to the little nursery reservoir where I can see a well-placed *Salix alba* 'Britzensis', its long, young, bare stems aflame, when the sun strikes them. Later, when the sun has gone round to the west, this feature disappears into the background, leaving the whitened trunk and branches of the Himalayan birch, *Betula jacquemontii* to dominate the view.

Do you remember we were driving back from shopping in Hastings one day, and we spotted across the fields *Salix alba* 'Britzensis', isolated in a farm hedge? Presumably from neglect rather than design, it consisted of several storeys of young shoots, making it a tall vertical feature ablaze with orange-red osiers. It made me think we should not cut ours down to a basic stump, but allow a few central stems to stay, and then when they are stout, prune them at a higher level – this we have done. I would like to do more like this, since coloured stems are so cheering in winter, and their narrow silvery-grey leaves make a pleasant background in summer. Further along, a bank of olive green *Cornus sericea* 'Flaviramea' is caught in the spotlight.

Another winter feature along the bank of the small nursery reservoir is the ghost bramble, *Rubus cockburnianus*. The first year it makes stout stems 2m (6½ft) tall, and sometimes more. The second year these elongate and arch over long, trailing stems which touch the ground, where they root, extending the group. The mature stems look as if we had white-washed them, being overlaid with powdery bloom, while the young shoots are polished and plum-coloured. Ours haven't been cut down for a couple of years or so, so they now form a tangled bird-cage surrounded by ivy-clad willows and the red and green stemmed dogwoods.

The ashen colour of still-frozen ponds is relieved by the warm russet carpets of fallen swamp cypress needles; chestnut piles of the ostrich plume fern (*Osmunda regalis*) and bleached stems of the dainty grass, *Molinia caerulea* 'Variegata'. Weeping willows are already yellowing as the sap rises, their string-like branchlets falling straight as a girl's blond hair on to the frozen pond. Against the mown grass edge another good grass, *Pennisetum alopecuroides* f. *viridescens*, forms a bouquet of fluffy flower heads, soft brown like sandalwood now. Earlier, the large green, brown and black bottle-brush-shaped flowers were impressive; twice as fat when the long, fine hairs at the tip of every seed were outlined with dew, or hoar-frost.

Looking around in mid-January it is interesting to see how few good shapes and textures, both large and small, are needed to make a satisfying landscape in winter, all held together with smooth expanses of mown grass.

These icy mornings I dash out to see the Gravel Garden before
the sun peels away the frost. The remaining seed heads – including
flat-topped sedums, bobbly stems of caryopteris, *Phlomis tuberosa*
'Amazone' and *Verbena bonariensis*, among many others – create
sparkling borders of ice crystal 'flowers'. Leathery-leaved cistuses,
vertical conifers and variegated forms of privet provide a backcloth
to these ephemeral pleasures while the bushy greys – santolina,
ballota, lavender and low sprawls of helianthemum – make sharp
contrast, whitened with ice crystals trapped in fuzzy felt. One of
the prettiest effects is *Gypsophila* 'Rosy Veil' ('Rosenschleier'); not
yet cut down, last summer's growth forms large cumulus-cloud
shapes along the edge of the gravel walk. Bending to see, you can
enjoy the complicated interweaving of wire-thin stems and tiny
flower stalks carrying complicated patterns of ice, beautiful as any
silversmith's art.

So far I cannot tell if there is much damage. Very little so far
appears to be hurt. *Melianthus major* looks a bit bedraggled; I
would have expected it to have collapsed in a mushy heap. By
springtime we will have cut it down to the ground, and then it will
return vigorously from underground buds, as it has done in this
well-drained soil for the 20 or so years I have been growing it. The
empty space left after it has been cut down will allow bulbs and
creeping thymes to fill the gap in spring.

In bold contrast to the filigree effect of many tiny leaves in the
Gravel Garden, I love to come across the great leaf rosettes of
Verbascum pulverulentum. (I'm not certain of that name. I used to
call it *Verbascum olympicum*, as I had been given to understand
by my old friend, the late Sir Cedric Morris. But your *Verbascum
olympicum* is very different, having greyer leaves with wavy edges.
Our form has white, felted, wide, petal-shaped leaves lying flat
against the frozen soil like a great dahlia head, sometimes almost 1m
(3ft) across. Smaller ones make very effective punctuation marks.)

It is time I 'came in' from the garden and re-read your letter.
I enjoyed it first time round. I would love to join your party for

Janáček's opera *The Makropulos Case*. Many thanks for inviting me. Do let me know the date, so hopefully I will not be obliged to back out. You know I would hate to do that – it would only be if something dire and unavoidable turned up.

Concerning the future of good or interesting gardens (whether they are either is very much a matter of personal opinion!) I think we both feel much the same. It all depends on the ability and inspiration of the man or woman responsible. And, of course, gardens themselves need to change, to go forward, to evolve. They cannot be encapsulated in time like a fly in amber. Some could well fade away, and another picture could be painted on the old canvas.

I'm glad Dixter had a good year. There is always so much unseen expense in running any enterprise. We have increasing competition as the leisure industry thrives, and new nurseries emerge up and down the country, like mushrooms overnight. Although we are blessed with good staff and have delegated responsibility to provide backstops where possible, much still does depend, whether we always feel like it or not, on our ability to steer the ship. And as you say, that depends very much on our state of health. On the whole, I think we do pretty well for our age! Much to be thankful for, as my mother would say. My tiresome shoulders are much better. I have infinitely less pain than a year ago, helped, I think, by various means – going to a good chiropractor, having a massage at home on a regular basis and exercises to help keep the joints free and mobile. You know my views on healthy food, but you also know that I love preparing and eating food for pleasure, not merely because it is 'good for me'!

Winter is not my best time. Nor is it for most people, I would guess: too little sunlight, not enough physical exercise out-of-doors. Even outdoor people like us spend many more hours on administration or writing in winter – jobs we put off in summer when we are actively involved outside.

Anxiety sometimes clogs up my mind, if it can't be cleared with physical effort. The normal stress of everyday events is something else. It can be a challenge to put something in motion; decide, yes we will, or no, we will not. Such pressures, provided I feel well, I find exhilarating – indeed I often think I need them in order to stay well! But sometimes there are anxieties which have no simple solution. Sometimes we just have to be patient; not always easy.

One evening recently, before going to bed, I turned off all the lights, put a candle inside a ceramic fretted shade (shaped like a Turkish dome), and watched the petal-shaped patterns of light and shadow cast over the white painted wall and Parana pine ceiling. Suddenly my eye was caught by another light, that of Sirius, the Dog Star, high up in one of the tall windows, at roof level I watched it move slowly across the window until it was caught in the grey branches of the big magnolia tree outside the sitting-room doors. I unlocked the door and stood outside to find Orion's belt above me, and multitudes of stars in the dark cold sky. Aren't we lucky to be able to stand in starlit gardens, away from the glare of city lights? Only moorhens and a cock pheasant to disturb the silence.

Time I made my hot-water bottle and went to bed.

Goodnight Christo, love to everyone, Beth

– ❦ –

Monday 3 February

Dear Beth,

It is 3.00pm and sunny and I have just visited Fergus, working in the Barn Garden. He is doing the borders very thoroughly and says he is enjoying the work a lot. It gives him time to look at things closely; to see how plants have progressed since a year ago and to assess new seedlings, as of the variegated honesty, the one with the mauve flowers. We shall pot some of those for later sales.

He reckons that winter is over, and I can see what he means. There are frosts at night – the ponds had a skin of new ice over them this morning and the ground was crusty – but the sun is now warm enough (when we see it) to melt that ice in the course of the day.

And the first crocuses are out – late, but there they are. There was a pale blue form of *Crocus chrysanthus* wide open to the sun, this morning. Later, Fergus found two orange *C. chrysanthus* and two mauve *C. tommasinianus*. The snowdrops are backward, too; even the early 'Atkinsii' is still only gathering its strength. But what satisfyingly fat clumps it makes. And it was growing under the snow. When that melted, after a couple of weeks, the progress was notable.

We greatly savoured that hoar-frosty, foggy morning on 15 January, too. Were greatly excited, in fact, and as well as rushing around with our own cameras, Andrew summoned Jonathan Buckley down from London. He came straightaway, bless him, and wished he'd been earlier, though he was here soon after 10.00am. The sun was winning through, which was beautiful in itself, but death to the rime.

As you remarked in your last, recent, letter, quite ordinary plants were transformed. The old tamarisk and Japanese anemone stems, side by side at the top of the Long Border, were unrecognizable, clothed with ice prickles all along their stems. Behind them, my golden king holly (which supplied me with berries for Christmas decorations but was by then stripped) looked its normal self and provided a handsome contrasting background.

I doubt if the winter, so far, has done much damage, though some (not all) of the astelias are looking rather unhappy. I have little experience of them, as hardy garden plants, so it will be interesting to see. I love their grey spear leaves, clustered in spiky rosettes, if you can speak of a rosette in a plant that is all points.

Fergus will next descend into the Sunk Garden, which needs a lot of tidying up. We examined that, minutely. So much self-sows and spreads, down there. The huge mat of biddy-biddy, *Acaena novae-zelandiae*, must be reduced. Its burrs, so bright a carmine, in July, then tiresome in your socks where they make clusters, are now quite pale fawny grey and perfectly soft – no longer burry. A mat-forming plant like that is never dead flat. In winter sunshine, particularly, you are conscious of its undulations, as in a landscape. Even more so where we have an ancient colony of white-flowered thrift, *Armeria maritima*. From its original hump, big as the biggest anthill, it has spread into a family of junior hillocks. The acaena invades them and must be pulled out.

Work on the house restoration is at last in progress, full swing. They seem a good team and work well. Fergus likes having them around. There were huge bangings with sledge-hammers going on one day when I met a workman walking away with a bag of rubble clasped to his bosom. 'Knocking the place down?' I asked him. 'Yes,' said he gloomily, 'I never did like it.' A couple of inquisitive but lively youths, aged 17 and 20, have been employed to carry in bags of ballast, to set at the foot of the scaffolding, so that it can't sway over from the top, which is heavy with a roof of corrugated iron – the sides are enclosed in plastic; all this so that work can go on in adverse weather. The younger of these two asked Fergus about me. 'Does he live in the house, then?' 'Yes, he's there all the time.' 'He writes books, don't he?' 'Yes, all sorts of articles and books.' 'He must be really intelligent then. What's he like to work for?' 'He's really good.' 'Treat you well at Christmas, did he?' 'Yes. I was working Christmas Day morning.' 'You were working Christmas Day?', incredulously. 'Then I went in and had lunch with him.'

Actually, the weather, even with all their protection, does make a difference and, although the work is on the weather side, which is where the rain blows against the building, normally, in the past two months, all the weather has been on the opposite, north-east side.

We measured 484mm (23in) of rain at the end of the year, which is 179mm (7in) below our average. Can you work out what yours was, January to December? I know you normally reckon October to September, but I suppose you have the monthly figures. The last two months have been very dry – 32mm (1¼in) in December, 18mm (¾in) for January. Although we need winter rain to top up much depleted reserves, I must say it is extremely convenient not to be plagued by it. We have had to cart a lot of composted long grass (from the meadow areas), that was heaped down by the potting shed, up to the vegetable plots, which are now being dug. There is a steep, grass slope, near the Horse Pond, which can get hopelessly slithery, but although it is looking a bit worn, it has held out, so far. Also, digging itself, in the wet, is so unpleasant. Everything gets gummed up, including your spade. Furthermore, our heavy ground is so much easier to turn over, like it is now. So I must try to remember that when I am moaning about the drought, next summer. I don't want a wet summer, either!

I'm right back into salads, again. My 'Sugar Loaf' chicory looks terrible from the outside, but that has given protection to the heart, which is perfect. Pak choi is making new shoots – those that will run up to flower; you can see the flower buds already. The shoots are tender as could be and have the characteristic, strong mustard oil flavour. Lacy young leaves of mizuna made headway, only days after the snow's disappearance. Rocket is still rather depressed, but alive. I've had my first cuts of corn salad, a large-leaved kind from Chiltern Seeds. I'm not too proud to top up with lettuce from Sainsbury's. They haven't offered 'Witloof' chicory for months, but I'm culling that from the cellar stairs. People keep on turning the light on, there – to do with scaffolding in the foundations – so I've thrown an old blanket over their big pot (one I use in summer on the terrace for tender 'geraniums' and the like). The blanket is really destined for the dogs' bedding. As you know, I find them cheapest to buy in Scotland, and stuff the boot of my car with them. The dogs devour so many. I told the woman this, in the shop where I was buying them, in Cupar. 'Could you no give them a tin of meat?' she asked, with a perfectly straight face.

There's a pigeon – just one, a bastard which doesn't even bother to fly away when I approach – eating my greens. I've not been visited by the usual half-dozen wild wood pigeons, for the past two winter/springs. I wonder if the returned sparrow hawks have been eating them. My books tell me they are favourite food.

My bergenias look as awful as ever. Even 'Ballawley' is a depressing sight. You mention your Westonbirt dogwood. What about the *Cornus sanguinea* cultivar – 'Midwinter Fire', was it called? – that you wrote about a year ago. Is it good again? I haven't seen it in its season.

Since the beginning of the year, our seared grasses, which were such a standby up till then, have gradually been going off. The miscanthus have had a huge moult, but their flowering stems are still well worth seeing. I love the bare stems – just pale rods – of *Calamagrostis* 'Karl Foerster'. But others we are cutting or have cut down. The molinias don't last, chasmanthium has lost its flattened seed heads and the giant reed grasses might scare the crows, but could serve no other purpose. So, the slow transition from autumn to spring is being made.

The last batch of photos that I recently had back from processing includes the second half of my day with you, in October, and a nice one of the lovely spread you made us – so very much a Beth spread – for lunch. I am having a print made to send. I have an excellent recipe which you'd like, for using some of my huge crop of shallots. Perhaps I'll send it, if not too late, to Erica, to include in my *Gardener Cook* book. You cook quite a lot of shallots, roughly chopped, very slowly (half an hour) in olive oil and the moisture they generate themselves – that's all. Add quite a lot of balsamic vinegar and allow to get cold (seasoning, of course). Then serve with slices of Parma ham and thin shavings of a cheese like Parmesan. Quite enough for a meal, when I'm alone, but more suitable as a first course, with guests. Why do I always over-eat, in company? I've been doing so well on half as much, lately, while on my own. Sheer greed, of course.

I had Howard Sooley (my photographer for *Gardener Cook*) and Keith Collins, who was left Prospect Cottage at Dungeness by

Derek Jarman, to dinner, recently. Keith goes sea fishing, with three
or four others, nowadays, much of it at night. That varies with
the tide, but they always need to land their catch in daylight. He
brought a most wonderfully fresh turbot. I have that in the deep
freeze, but mustn't keep it too long. He does the garden at Prospect
Cottage now, and very well. I think it has improved since we first
accidentally came across it, that June day when we had picnicked
on the shore. We must do that again. Canna would like it.

Don't forget, while they're about, to put some Seville oranges
in your freezer, Beth. They are so useful during the year, for
flavouring sauces.

I'm sorry I forgot to tell you the date for Glyndebourne: it's
Thursday 7 August.

Now the light is going; I'll pop out to see how Fergus is
getting along.

Much love, Christo

— 🦋 —

Saturday 15 February

Dear Christo,

After weeks it seems of dreary weather, overcast and gloomy
as the bottom of the sea, despite lengthening hours of daylight,
this morning suddenly is wonderful, the lid taken off. There was
early frost (my nose was cold when I woke), thick and white on
the green moss of the roof tiles beneath Andrew's eyrie window,
forming a thin skin of glass over the ponds. But now we have deep
blue sky, bright sunshine, and no wind, thank God!

I had forgotten to take bread out of the freezer last night, so
I put a flat round loaf into the oven while I carted logs into the
house for the wood-burning stove. Coming in from the cold air I
found the smell of warm bread and wood smoke comforting. After
breakfast I went out to empty the sink bucket, feed the birds and
collect fresh vegetables, intending to take only a few minutes, but

177

an hour easily slips by on such a rare morning. Near the compost heap, where I empty the waste-bucket, I spotted a fine plant of *Euphorbia wulfenii*, seeded into a narrow crack in the concrete floor at the foot of a south-facing wall. It looks better, if anything, than many I have in cultivated borders, possibly benefiting by having its back to the warm wall. After all it comes from the southern Mediterranean countries. I shall be watching it carefully – there are a few down-turned flower heads – to see if it will be a specially good form, preferably a good yellow-green. I bent to look for the flower buds and found clusters of ladybirds, tucked close to the stems, protected among tight whorls of leaves, waiting, ready for their first meal of aphids when they arrive.

On my way back to the house (intending to start writing to you), I found Andrew sunning himself in the Gravel Garden. I was so pleased to see him there: his breathlessness now makes a walk into the garden a rare event. But I wanted him to see how well the colony of *Galanthus* 'Atkinsii' has increased, how, warmed by the sun, they lift their narrow 'petals' horizontally like little helicopters hovering over the stones. I wanted him to see much more, yet knew he could not walk far in the cold air. Around the corner I had parked our little electric buggy, hoping such a beautiful morning might tempt him outside. The initial response to the ride was, of course, no, but watching my face he relented. To please me he would ride to the Wood Garden. (Perhaps if *we* live to be 88 years old we too will rebel at the thought of losing our independence!) But all went well; it was a treat for us both to share the yellow drifts of aconites mingling with opening bunches of snowdrops. We saw how the aconites have increased in just three or four years. Around the flowering clumps was a scattering of one-year-old seedlings making their first ruffs while last year's fallen seed was germinating like cress. I can see how, in unwise planting, they might become an invasive weed, but how heart-stirring it is, so early in the year, to see these early patches of gold stretching into the distance between the tree trunks.

This is the place, too, for *Narcissus* 'Cedric Morris', protected by shade from attack by the narcissus fly. They are late this year. This little wild daffodil from northern Spain does not increase very rapidly so you can't expect to see drifts of it, but to come across the odd clump with a dozen or so beautifully formed lemon-yellow trumpets is always a thrill. Elsewhere, beneath the big oak, among dwarf cyclamens another early daffodil flowering now. I think it is *Narcissus asturiensis*, even smaller than Cedric's form with slightly 'waisted' trumpets.

I showed Andrew how well *Cornus mas* has budded up at last in the Wood Garden. This shrub is slow to come into flower, using all its energy to make new wood. One bush we moved about three years after planting, hoping the shock would delay this headlong rush into growth. It worked. The year following we had quite a sprinkling of flower buds; this year it is crowded, the buds just opening now to release clusters of tiny, starry yellow flowers. Although individually they are less significant than *Hamamelis mollis*, I enjoy the effect much more. A well-flowered bush, or small tree, creates a gauzy haze of yellow among bare tree trunks, against winter evergreens, and best of all for me, the flowers are not damaged by frost. This year we have a sparse showing of flowers on both *Hamamelis* and *Garrya elliptica*, a result I imagine of last summer's drought. There are just half-a-dozen long silvery-green catkins on the garrya, I can see them from my kitchen window. I confess I will be relieved not to see the big bush laden with withered catkins for months to come. Pity they hang on to them, like the messy brown bundles of double camellias, or the chamois leather-brown of *Fremontodendron californicum*, left behind when the large saucer-shaped yellow flowers have faded – all asking to be picked off (who has the time?). There's a job for the breeders, to invent a gene which would neatly detach all these inelegant remains.

Leaving the Wood Garden we passed a group of *Cornus sanguinea* 'Midwinter Fire'. You asked how it was in your last letter. Well, I haven't changed my mind from last year when I wrote about it. If I had room for only one coloured-stem cornus, it might well be this. Just one bush is attractive. A group seen with the sun behind you draws you like a warm fire towards the glowing effect of bare yellow basal stems topped with coral-red shoots. You should plant half a dozen in the area of the Horse Pond. The habit of growth is much less coarse and shorter than *C. stolonifera* – which I love too, in a different situation. Ultimately, this cornus could be 2m (6½ft) tall in good soil. Mine, so far, are only 1–1.25m (3–4ft).

After stopping to put away the buggy and have a cup of coffee with Andrew – both of us pleased with the success of our adventure – I went back to look round the nursery, since we shall be open again on Saturdays from the beginning of March. Although I am not always involved with visitors (my staff cope very well without me), I relish, as they do, having a two-day weekend throughout the winter months. Not a very business-like attitude for these modern times! Of course we are all cheered up to see our early visitors arriving during weekdays to see the snowdrops and aconites. Some come throughout the winter, just to see what it is like 'out of season', and are surprised how much there is still to enjoy.

It was good to see all the repair jobs the men have been doing over the past weeks when the weather has been wretched, no sun, messy drizzle, but no real rain. They have laid new Mypex on the nursery pot-standing area. Mypex is a kind of perforated plastic sheeting whose purpose is to prevent the germination of weed seedlings, thus doing away with the need to spray with herbicides. Laid over smoothly raked sand it provides a clean base for pots of plants for sale which can soak up moisture through the matting after rain or irrigation. It is a big job moving all the pots and replacing them, but as the girls clean and groom the pots during January and February they cooperate with the men to do a section at a time. The Mypex lasts about four or five years, largely, I think, because throughout the year, when handling stock, the girls are careful to sweep up spilt compost which would encourage weed seed blown in to germinate, thrust roots through the matting and create holes in this protective cover.

You asked me about last year's rainfall here. From January to December '96 we had 420mm (16½in) in total. This figure differs slightly from the way we measure the year in the garden. We take the winter months October '95 to March '96, 200mm (8in), plus the summer months April to September '96, 165mm (6½in), a total of 356mm (14in). Our average rainfall is 500mm (20in). Like anyone else whose work is primarily out-of-doors, we too find wet weather bothersome. We cannot spend all day under cover. There have to be comings and goings as trolleys of plants are brought in or taken out. Trouser legs get wet and cold even in a drizzle. But so far we have had worryingly little rain this winter. Apart from 115mm (4½in) in November we have had 25mm (1in) in December including snow, 18mm (¾in) in January and 13mm (½in) so far this month. What has happened to 'February-fill-dyke'? No doubt you have read reports that this current year, April '96 to April '97, has had the lowest rainfall over the country for 250 years. The pattern of rain sweeping from the south-west across the Midlands to Scotland leaving the south-east with little or nothing, looks like becoming a set piece. With envy we heard this week of somewhere in Wales having 180mm (7in) in a few days, yet we wouldn't know how or what to grow in such wet conditions! Not all is glum. There are exciting signs of life coming fast everywhere, buds breaking, hazel bushes a-fluttering. They are a comparatively rare sight in roadside hedges up here, unlike your lovely deep lanes where I'm always impressed by such vigorous bushes laden with catkins.

It cheers me up to see new shoots coming in the nursery pots. Suddenly there are rigid little buds, crumpled, pink-stained leaves, sudden splodges of green where only yesterday there was nothing. We start packing orders the first week in March. I prefer the spring pack, glad to see both top-growth and new root action before the plants go away. I'm especially glad to see good stocks of *Euphorbia griffithii* 'Dixter'. In the autumn we were not sure if all the pots had viable plants in them, but now they nearly all show strong basal buds.

In the propagating house there is already an inviting green smell as the sun quickly warms up this double-skinned building. Trays of root cuttings, including *Papaver orientale*, eryngiums, verbascums, cichorium and *Anchusa* 'Loddon Royalist' have been on-going since autumn, so show various stages of development. We have to be careful how we handle them. If lifted and potted too soon they can collapse and die. Large leaf-rosettes are formed well before the new roots are established as they can live for a while on the original inch or so of old root. Usually the top-growth has to be trimmed back to wait for the new root systems to catch up.

Tucked away in the corner of a bench are my seed pans of new salads: various old packets of lettuce needing to be used up, even old vegetable seed in little pots being tested for viability. All will be pricked out shortly into little pots, to go later into the vegetable garden tunnels, before the tomatoes, or outside if conditions are right. Keith put a fence of temporary netting round my winter greens the other weekend; apparently pigeons don't like being confined – there's no need to have netting over the top. Just as I was about to grouse because I couldn't fly over the wire, I spotted the cunning little sliding gate he had made to let me in. Sorry Keith! I'm picking and enjoying the 'Pentland Brig' curly kale. The new shoots are so tender. Last night I shredded some finely, sweated them for a few minutes in hot steam, then added them, brilliant green, to a vegetable stew of red beans, golden corn, pearl barley et al! The colour scheme was brilliant, and the taste good.

Seakale pots and straw are heaped over the rhubarb. I must remember to use up last year's. I have put some Seville oranges, as you reminded me, into the freezer. When I next come to Dixter I will ask to be reminded of the special recipes you have for using them, apart from marmalade. I recently ate marmalade made by Mary, my younger daughter – who also makes it for one of her charity stalls – so the tradition goes on even though I no longer have the house filled with the scent of boiling marmalade.

When I started to write this, warm sun had opened *Crocus tommasinianus* where it has seeded over the bed filled later with the Californian tree poppy, *Romneya coulteri*, at the bottom of steps leading to our outdoor sitting area. I watched the patch of bright mauve stars from the table where I sit. Now as the setting sun is already travelling further west along the farm boundary hedge they are left in shadow, and have folded themselves up for the night, slender pallid buds like sad little ghosts. And so they will remain, almost invisible I fear, since the forecast is for more days of unsettled weather. That wouldn't be so bad if it would really rain!

Last year at this time I wrote about picking branches of twisty willow to watch the tiny ribbon leaves opening, long before they are showing outside. This year I have a big jugful of flowering currant standing on the hall box where it looks down the open staircase into our living room below. To add substance and join the bare branches to the rim of the jug I used sprays of the cream and green large-leaved ivy, *Hedera colchica* 'Sulphur Heart' (we used to call it 'Paddy's Pride'), and two or three dark rosettes of *Euphorbia amygdaloides* var. *robbiae*. Now, after only a few days, the fat flower buds are lengthening, their delicate pale green colour matching the pale centres of the ivy leaves. Each day I look for the change and development in this living picture. Most of our flower arrangements can only fade and deteriorate after the first few days, but it will be some days yet before these pendulous buds open pure white flowers, white because of the lack of light indoors. In the garden, in the weeks to come they will be pink. Some people detest the smell, of cats they say – maybe – but I enjoy these strong foetid scents early in the year: the bruised leaves of *Iris foetidissima*, the first foxy whiff of *Fritillaria imperialis* as it pushes its snout through the soil, even before you can see it. They indicate the strong surge of growth waiting to erupt all around us. When it comes there is suddenly too much to observe individual effects as we can now.

Monday tomorrow, the week filled already with people and things happening. And it's not March yet.

This letter is running away with itself, but I can't wait till the next one to tell you we have at last put up the two owl boxes David Ward made last winter. Gerard had hired a hoist – a marvellous Meccano-like contraption which has a little platform attached to a long arm on which he stands to remove dead or unwanted branches from the tops of tall trees. While doing this it seemed a good opportunity to find suitable sites for the owl boxes. Moira, who works in my propagating team, and is a good friend of Fergus, came out to look, and told us a white barn owl is using her box this year, the first time since it was put up three years ago. We may have a long wait. I am so glad to hear the owls again at night, hunting over the surrounding farmland. Today I think there are fewer suitable nesting sites for them; farm buildings and church towers are in better repair maybe, but often owners object to the mess made by nesting birds.

Every day now the green woodpecker is yaffling in the garden, another evocative sound . . .

Goodnight Christo, love from Beth

– ✿ –

Wednesday 5 March

Dear Beth,

My father would have been 130 today! He was 54 when I was born.

Well, I'm in the solar, with a fire, left, and dogs alongside my right leg on the sofa (feet up). The usual pattern, in fact. I was in the garden for quite a while, morning and afternoon. Fergus and I have started work on the Long Border. Naturally, the dogs were out with us and they are consequently soporific (like the flopsy bunnies) now.

Canna gets wildly excited when I am preparing their meals, and turns in rapid circles, before barking. The circles are always performed clockwise. Do you think they'd be anticlockwise if we were in the southern hemisphere, like bath water going down the waste pipe?

Talking of that hemisphere, we had a volunteer New Zealander arrive today. A nice lad, aged 22, BUT his visa was not correct. It was a holiday visa, and I suppose if he'd filled in the forms accordingly, no questions would have been asked, but he admitted to being a volunteer WORKER. As a consequence, he has to fly back to NZ on Sunday and can only return when his visa is corrected (perhaps a month later). The flight back there will be free, as the airline should have spotted the error before he left, but he will have to (if he can afford it) stump up for the second flight out. Isn't that sort of bureaucratic inflexibility maddening?

Some friend has sent me an article by Julia Clements, about you, showing you posed in front of a *Garrya elliptica*, full of catkins, so that wasn't taken this year. And I was amused, after your comments in your last letter, what high praise garrya was accorded. I got so bored with mine – ugly for 11 months out of 12 – that I 'lost' it. You mention several shrubs that are tiresome for not shedding their dead blooms, but what about roses? Considering their prevalence, they must be the most obtrusive of all – the double-flowered kinds, that is. This seems to be a point that the breeders have never considered and the gardener, so it seems, turns a blind eye. This one doesn't!

So we both have ladybirds on the tips of our euphorbia shoots, when the sun comes out in late winter. You say they are waiting for the arrival of the first aphids. I wonder. Can they really be so prescient? If so, they make a poor job of mopping the aphids up, as we generally have to take steps to wipe them out ourselves. Luckily the populations of ladybirds seem to be as prolific as ever.

Our method of dealing with pigeons eating our greens in spring
is to stretch string, supported by short pieces of stick, around
the greens at a height of 15cm (6in) or less. It really does work.
Pigeons like to walk into their food, hopping up on to the Brussels
sprouts, or whatever, at the last moment. The string thwarts
this intention.

Wonderful how the garden is burgeoning. Last time I wrote, the
winter crocuses were only just beginning. Now, they are finished
but there is a great tide of Dutch polyploid *Crocus vernus* surging
forwards. Fergus is as thrilled by them as I. They are thickest on
the south side of the house, in the orchard and the drained upper
moat, and they keep on increasing. But the repair works in progress
somewhat spoil the setting. I am getting really anxious about the
apricot, which badly needs to be untied, to be allowed to flower and
be pollinated. It is always the earliest blossom out, here. The builders
and architects must be fed up with my constant nagging.

The ponds are looking particularly clear and clean, just now.
That in the Sunk Garden is full of great crested newts, and one of
last weekend's guests asked to be allowed to remove a couple for
his own pond. In the Horse Pond, where it has been missing for
several months, there is at last a sign of the water violet, *Hottonia
palustris*, returning. I thought it had vanished for ever.

You write of *Narcissus asturiensis* and that is the earliest with
me ('Cedric Morris' seems to have faded out), but it has been
closely followed by an only marginally larger, mini-trumpet species,
N. minor. That copes perfectly with rough grass turf. Meantime,
the dog's-tooth violets, *Erythronium dens-canis*, have made
their usual sudden appearance. I think they should open wide,
tomorrow, if this weather continues.

Didn't you weary of all that wind? I didn't bother to visit my
favourite fishmonger, in Old Hastings, but I might, on Friday.
Given the right conditions, this is an excellent season for many fish.

Thank you for remembering my birthday, Beth. As it came on
a Sunday, Fergus organized quite a party for me. We were sleeping

eight in the house on Saturday night and there were four more for dinner. So, for a change, we ate and drank in the Great Hall, with a huge fire blazing. So nice to use that room as it should be used, and the weather was quite mild enough to make it easily heated. I have to say, I spent a lot of time in the kitchen, but not so much that I couldn't enjoy my friends.

Our rainfall in February was about average. My grandfather always said that February-fill-dyke is a misrepresentation of F.-full-dyke. It is not a wet month but inherits a legacy of rain.

My love, Christo

– ✾ –

Friday 28 March

Dear Beth,

It's Good Friday and we've just been open for the first time. I think we had some 120 visitors in all, which is a good start. I hid myself away until near the end, when there were only a few left in the garden. Among them, a German couple who are living in Northiam and were neighbours to Andrew and Fergus during the winter. They became friends towards the end and Fergus thoroughly enjoyed a dinner with them.

They were most appreciative, but while we were talking near to the house repairs, Dahlia appeared looking very self-conscious, not to say guilty, with a packet in her mouth. Assuming the worst, I said 'drop it', very firmly several times, and she did. There was hardly time for everyone to be impressed by her obedience. I turned aside and in no time she'd snatched the packet from my hand; it fell open to reveal some meat sandwiches. The old German lady, mother of the wife I've been talking about, was hugely delighted and couldn't stop chortling.

In retrospect, I was so sorry not to have seen you off properly on your departure last Saturday, Beth, but I was feeling really exhausted, at that moment, having just given the volunteers from

Wisley their lunch and then peeled the potatoes for the evening. It was so good to be able to stretch myself out on a rug, with the girls, in the sun. You did say not to move, but I should have. Anyway, it was lovely to have you for a few days and you were most helpful in getting things ready for the gang's first meal. There were 15 of them.

The weekend went excellently and I only felt the backlash on the Monday, when it was all over. Kept falling asleep while writing my weekly piece for *The Guardian*. I hope it won't be noticeable in the result! As you know, we had a big fire in the Great Hall. Perry was there, Saturday evening, and his boy, Joe. Really, we were too big a party to be able to be together in a single group. I suspect that things livened up after I went to bed, as the others didn't retire (into their sleeping bags, on the floor) until 2.30am, Fergus among them.

I was at Wisley, yesterday, judging the pulmonaria and polyanthus trials (the pulmonarias were hating the combination of an exposed site, warm sunshine and a strong wind), and bumped into no fewer than five of the students who had been here. They are a good batch.

Kate – one of them – was working among shrubs in an informal planting on Weather Hill. I pointed out to her how meaningless and fidgety the wiggles in the paths were, and how all you needed was for the path to take one bold, sweeping curve. 'Do you see what I mean?' I asked. 'I see exactly what you mean,' said she. (Intelligent girl!) For the most part, the soil between shrubs is bare, apart from mulches. Where there is ground-level planting, it is in tight groups. Nothing flows. Of course the entire area between and underneath the shrubs should be planted with erythroniums, anemones, snowdrops, Solomon's seal, lilies-of-the-valley, pulmonarias, navel-wort (*Omphalodes*), tiarellas, dicentras, ferns and the like, but it never will be. Their thinking is utterly sterile when it comes to creating a pleasing scene.

188

It is the same in the double herbaceous borders. These never settle down, because they have a rotation which demands the complete upheaval of a section every year. It would be so much more intelligent, if a little harder to organize, if renewal was on a piecemeal basis, replanting when and where it was desirable, not just because it was the turn of that section. In this way, renewals can be absorbed over the whole border and it will never look unsettled.

I met another of the students who was at Dixter, working there. I told him that two things had just been making me fume. In a piece of border that does not appear to be in line for disturbance this year, there is an enormous patch of a 2.7m (9ft), perennial helianthus, one of the invasive kinds of no great distinction. It didn't flower till October and there was absolutely no supporting cast. It just rose from nothing. Now that is thoughtless and so is it to let it go on increasing its range, which is now well into some of its neighbours. Of course, I know that in a deep border you need tall plants at the back, but there are so many interesting ways of doing these things and better material to do it with.

The other thing was to see the hardened stems of plants that had been cut back last autumn leaving 30cm (1ft) or more at the base. If we cut back in autumn at all (often there is no need; you can leave it till spring, especially easy at Wisley, where they close the borders to the public from October to March), I insist (whatever the season) that no stumps should be left. For several reasons: they get in the way when making low cuts in subsequent years; they are hibernating opportunities for slugs and earwigs (and ladybirds!); but, most important, they deal vicious wounds, from the top of each stiff stem, to anyone cutting at a low level in the future.

'Who is overseeing this job?' I asked Alastair, the lad I was speaking to. 'She's pruning that buddleia,' said he, pointing to a bush at the back of the border, that was shaking (probably with rage) as its invisible pruner worked from behind. 'I'd better get out before I'm lynched,' I said and did.

I'll leave it at that for now, Beth, and light a fire in the solar. The house is quite warm, after absorbing the day's sunshine and anyway the heating is on – perhaps rather too high. The daffodils in the orchard are just at their peak – two to three weeks ahead of average.

Much love, from Christo

—❀—

Sunday 13 April

Dear Beth,

Start with the present. 10.05pm; cold night without; comforting fire in the solar. Dogs alongside my right leg. Well . . . Nothing unusual about all that.

I wrote an article this morning. Then a Wye student dropped in just as I was preparing to drop off, lunchtime. Today, Sunday, we were open for free to the Northiam parishioners, as for as many years as I can remember. Daffodils are supposed to be the occasion, but with everything being three weeks ahead of normal, it was tulip time and we have more of them than ever. I do love them, and so, thank goodness, does Fergus. I went into the garden and exchanged pleasantries with a number of nice people. It was our local spring flower show yesterday, so I'd seen a number of them then. Fergus had been asked to give the prizes at the end of the show. I wasn't there, but he evidently enjoyed the experience.

Back to today: it was the celebration of Betty Hussey's 90th birthday – a tea party at Scotney Castle. I arrived there rather later than most of the guests (it was organized by the Kent group of the National Gardens Scheme). Christopher Hussey, Betty's late husband, was one of those men who couldn't open his mouth without saying something interesting. He knew and worked on books with Gertrude Jekyll; was editor of *Country Life* (not his happiest assignation); and was such an erudite man on buildings, art, gardens . . . Betty is indomitable, still full of energy and so lively. I always enjoy her company immensely, and I think she does mine. We spark on the same fuse. John Ward was there. He must be a pretty great age himself. A marvellous portrait painter; including a portrait of Christopher Hussey. I asked him if he was still painting. 'Of course I am,' said he. 'You're still gardening, aren't you?' He has such a forthright way.

So it was a good party. Quite a time was taken up by a young(ish) soprano, singing lightweight stuff. Lovely voice, but she took everything at much the same tempo and somehow all the music ended up by sounding much the same, too.

Then, at home, I went on going through proofs of *Gardener Cook*. This was my first experience of Jo Christian, who is editing it. Editing, these days, is apt to be so sloppy that the final publication is no different from what the (fallible) author sent in. Not in this case. Jo Christian has put a great deal of helpful effort into her task, which necessitates, on my part, a good deal of careful re-reading and response. This has gone slowly, as I have so many other distractions. (Tomorrow, Richard Ingrams, who started *Private Eye* and now edits the *Oldie*, is coming to lunch with his son, and son's girlfriend.) Certain editorial policies annoy me. For instance, with sales in the southern hemisphere in mind, they do not want me to mention months (or aspects) by name. Instead of May to early June, they want late spring . . . That sort of thing. Well, I want to say late spring myself, on occasions, but May to early June on others. They, with their well-meaning intention, wish to restrict me in my use of the English language. I like the names of the months, but they only want them if specifically applied to a Dixter situation. I shall fight that, as I had to with Dorling Kindersley, but it is a bore.

Beth, I have deferred mention of you and your health till now. Of course you cannot write while you are in such an exhausted condition and with so many anxieties. I shall phone you, but I wish I could help. Anyway, we are frequently in touch.

We had a marvellous Easter. An early Easter is usually disastrous, in terms of trade, but each of the four days was full of sunshine and without serious wind – something rare in any Easter, let alone an early one. So we have had lots of public visiting, then and now. It is good to see them enjoying themselves, with the weather cooperating.

The drought, of course, becomes increasingly serious, and we have been doing some irrigation, and not merely on newly planted stuff. Much that was planted last autumn is suffering. The tulips, however, are a revelation, and I never cease to want to go out and enjoy them, whether closed, or open to the sun. Everywhere, with or without tulips, there are forget-me-nots, running through the borders as a continuing theme. Particularly charming, at one point, where, self-sown in paving cracks, they intermingle with the young, palest yellow shoots of *Euonymus fortunei* 'Silver Queen', itself leaning across a fair portion of the path.

Phase Two of the work on the house is almost complete, thank goodness. When I can use the Yeoman's Hall in the house added from Benenden again, there'll be somewhere to put myself and guests when we are open to the public but still want somewhere to enjoy our coffee after lunch. To date, we have been so lucky with the weather that we have been able to take rugs out into the garden and have our coffee, basking, there.

How do you like this, as a description of a plant (perhaps a camellia): 'so pretty, you wouldn't know it's not artificial'. Another social comment: I find that 'see you later' actually means 'goodbye; I shan't see you later', but it's an easy way out of the rigours of a definite farewell.

Very much love, Christo

PS Sharp frost in the night.

—❁—

THE BETH CHATTO GARDENS

Dappled shade in Beth Chatto's Wood Garden in early May with ground-covering forget-me-nots and *Hosta* 'Krossa Regal'.

Below: Snowy mespilus, *Amelanchier lamarckii* in spring. Bottom: In the Long Shady Walk, chestnut *Aesculus indica*, with mixed underplanting.

The Kashmir birch, *Betula utilis* var. *jacquemontii*, with blossoming cherry *Prunus* 'Shirofugen', underplanted with forget-me-nots.

Far left: Planting in Beth Chatto's Damp Garden includes *Primula bulleyana*, *Iris sibirica* form and *Onoclea sensibilis*. Below: Pink spikes of *Persicaria bistorta* 'Superba' face *Carex elata* 'Aurea' across the stream. Bottom: *Primula bulleyana* among hostas.

Top: Midsummer in the Gravel Garden with mauve *Phlomis tuberosa* 'Amazone', purple *Nepeta* 'Six Hills Giant' and the succulent spikes of *Agave americana* 'Variegata'. Below: *Nigella damascena* fills the gaps between *Allium nigrum*, *A. cristophii* and tall yellow *Verbascum bombyciferum*.

Top: Late summer with *Verbascum bombyciferum, Eremurus* Shelford
hybrids, *Anthemis* and *Gypsophila repens* 'Rosa Schonheit'.
Below: *Sedum 'Herbstfreude'* and *Stipa calamagrostis* in autumn.

Top: Dogwoods add fireworks in winter: red *Cornus alba* 'Sibirica' and yellow *Cornus sericea* 'Flaviramea'. Below: Billowing pampas grass, *Cortaderia selloana* 'Sunningdale Silver'.

Thursday 8 May

Dear Christo,

After more than a month of empty silence, I must write to say how heartwarming it has been to have your letters and especially your phone calls. Andrew feels the same; we are both very touched by your concern for us. It cheers me up no end to hear your voice. I am at last beginning to feel more myself, but cannot sustain the effort needed to sort out my jumbled thoughts. At this wonderful time of year so much is happening daily around me, but I cannot grasp it in my hands to give you – it only remains in my mind.

For once Beth hasn't the energy to talk much! But it will come back. Meantime it comforts me to think of the warm welcome always given me by you and Fergus – and the little dogs – and of my space at Dixter. Bless you for keeping in touch.

Much love, Beth

— ❧ —

Tuesday 20 May

Dear Beth,

It is today 95 years since my parents were married. 'Our day', my mother always referred to it.

I was so pleased to get your note. You are pulling slowly out of the trough. At least the doctors have confirmed that there's nothing inside you that's physically wrong. Fergus tells me that he wrote to you and said he'd be delighted to fetch you over to Dixter, whenever you thought you could spare yourself. Come when you can, but it's little more than a fortnight that I plan to be off to Scotland for three weeks. The amount of writing I need to get done before that appals me – as usual.

The garden is in a transitional stage, as is the way with gardens that indulge in a lot of bedding out. There is a gap between the spring displays and the planting up for summer. However, the division isn't hard and fast. Just now, the lupins that we treat as bedding are at their peak. We sowed two strains, in April last year; a blue-and-white one and a red. Then, after they'd been growing on all summer, mixed them evenly when planting them into the Long Border. A big, informal swathe of them. I love the arrangement of their spikes, in tiered whorls. Sometimes the whorls are on a slant, and then they look like spirals.

In a few weeks they'll be over and replaced with various summer goodies. I haven't been in the garden as much as I should wish – you know how it is. I had a little more than an hour in the Exotic Garden, this afternoon, which Fergus and I will be planting up in the next ten days. But there's preparatory work, first: weeding, pruning *Artemisia* 'Powis Castle' (it doesn't always respond to a straightforward cutback), tidying up the phormiums, still shabby after winter. You can't just cut back their dying leaves – that looks awful. If possible, I like to wrench out old leaves so that they part company with the plant at their base, but they are tough and don't always come, in which case a temporizing shortening may be the only answer. The leaves grow in bundles – or fans, rather. If you pull too roughly, the whole fan could come away, good and bad foliage together.

I have been looking at a lot of bearded irises in other people's gardens, lately. I deliberately refrain from growing any but forms of *Iris pallida* myself. This is not a good iris year (last year was exceptionally good), probably because last summer was quite cool. But varietal factors also come into the picture, and it struck me that now would be a good time for iris enthusiasts to decide which varieties – those that have a shy-flowering tendency, for example – to throw out, making space for others that might perform better (or for something else entirely). Of course, another common reason for shy-flowering is that the colony is starved through overcrowding. One way or another I think these irises are generally better admired off one's own property, as they make a lot of work, cannot be disguised much out of their flowering season and have quite a brief season, finished by mid- or late-June, just at the time

when most of us want our borders to be reaching their zenith.
I can't remember whether you have them in your Gravel Garden.
They would certainly love the conditions.

I do remember that you told me how *Tulipa sprengeri*, latest
flowering of all tulips and abundant now, sowed itself right
through the irises in Cedric Morris's garden. They must have
looked wonderful together, the tulip such a pure shade of red, yet
quite dusky on the outside of its outer segments.

Mine get more every year, I'm glad to say. They are generous
self-seeders and often turn up on fresh sites. Only today I noticed
four or five of them in my huge colony of *Epimedium pinnatum*
subsp. *colchicum*. I should have thought that had made too dense
a network of rhizomes for any interloper to get a toehold, but
apparently not. I find that sort of self-sowing quite exciting. This
tulip is generally expensive to buy and not always easy to find, as
its small bulbs and stoloniferous habit make it unsuitable for the
big bulb firms to handle; but once you have it established, it never
looks back.

I was at the Chelsea Flower Show yesterday. So many friends
there, I didn't feel like getting down to the business of making
notes. This year, the resident blackbird has made its nest in an ivy
on Fibrex Nurseries' stand. One loves to see and hear it, while
appreciating that when the party's over, its nest will have to be
dismantled with all the other apparatus.

Lots (all, in fact) of students from Wisley who have been to
Dixter for working weekends. It was so good to see them all; a
really good bunch, this year. Sad that one has to lose touch with
some, but others will come back.

At the President's lunch, there are all sorts, who have served
the RHS in one way or another through the year, unpaid. Many
are journalists, as well as committee members. The President, Sir
Simon Hornby, in his opening speech, told us that there was no
guest, this year. Something of a cheer went up; we have had such
rotten speeches from Ministers of Agriculture and from Mr Major

himself, who said absolutely nothing of interest but pumped it all
out with an enthusiastic emphasis on every other meaningless word.

However, the President took this as a vote of no confidence
in the new government, forgetting or ignoring the fact that it
had had a landslide victory in the general anxiety to replace a
worn-out, 18-year-old government. Sir Simon hoped that the
new government's strictures on blood sports, particularly fox-
hunting, would not be extended to an embargo on the growing of
carnivorous plants. There was a groan and I made my escape.

Wednesday 21 May
You were much missed at the holders of the Victoria Medal
of Honour centenary celebration lunch. As you know, our full
complement is 63, the number of years of Victoria's reign, but I
believe there were nine absentees, including Tony Schilling. He and
Vicky are just establishing themselves in north-west Scotland, and
have quickly found a house on the outskirts of Ullapool. They are
over the moon about that. I shall see them on my northern journey
next month.

At the lunch, each of us was allowed to bring a guest
(I brought Sonia Coode-Adams, who lives quite near to you;
she's so dynamic and receptive). All RHS Council, including our
non-VMH President, were there – I can't think why. It was a most
enjoyable occasion, my only regret being that it was impossible to
talk to nearly as many as I should have liked to. Dame Elizabeth
Murdoch was there, as full of vitality as ever, and I shall see her
again at dinner at mutual friends, next week. You remember
our visit in 1989 to Cruden Farm, where she lives in Victoria.
She says it's looking better than ever.

I got a word in with dear old Prof. Willie Stearn, and asked
him why we'd been forced into using the suffix 'aceae' for all
plant families, thereby impoverishing the English language,
which has taken onboard words such as composites, umbellifers,
crucifers, legumes (*Leguminosae*), labiates and so forth. *Apiaceae*

for *Umbelliferae*, *Poaceae* for *Gramineae*, are not nearly so user-friendly, in any case.

He took my point but said that we were going back to what Lindley had decreed. Lindley was a great man and his dictum should be followed. Not much comfort there. The RHS are so arrogant that in the latest tome of the *Plant Finder*, which they have taken over, they have even dropped all the old familiar family names given as the (to most people) recognizable alternatives. What's more, the new volume does not stay open where you want it to, as did the old, leaving your hands free to read or copy, but has to be held open at the required place with both hands. Cheaper for the publisher, of course, but what a backward step!

We were assigned places, at the lunch, and I was next to Penny Hobhouse, which was nice. I'd just been reading parts of her latest book, *Garden Designs*. I take off my hat to her for becoming involved in some pretty daunting design work, often for business tycoons, who want to splash about a bit but, being self-made, they are depressingly conformist outside their own professions. Where there is money for exciting experimentation, it has to go into, let us say, an English garden in a (for most of the year) hot, desert area. Where you'd love to be playing around with dramatic, sub-tropical foliage plants, succulents and swathes of bougainvilleas, there has to be an English rose garden or lawn (re-sown annually) or herbaceous border, at its best in April, before the heat is turned full on; later, perforce, abandoned for a second (or third or fourth) home in a cooler area. Lip service has to be paid to the shibboleth of time-consuming flower gardening needing to be kept to a minimum, yet what is thought to be acceptable in terms of design and features is often extremely costly.

Well, it was, as I said, a good party. I got rather excited at one point, telling a gentleman who is moving from a garden that I had visited (with Fergus) to another home that I hoped he wouldn't be making the same mistakes again. As his style is ultra-pretentious, I felt he could take the criticism.

The other recent event was a weekend visit, with Fergus and Brent McKenzie (whom you met in New Zealand and who is over from there), to Paris. We travelled by rail and tunnel, which is extremely convenient for us. Returning on Sunday morning, the door-to-door journey, leaving our hotel at 7.30am, was only 3½ hours. We had left my car at Ashford, where the train stops *en route* for Waterloo, and that is only 20 miles from Dixter.

We wanted to see the open-air flower show, principally for on-the-spot plant sales, at the château of Courson, perhaps 30 miles outside Paris and taking place now and in autumn, every year. There are several others like it. The grounds are spacious yet there's a kind of intimate, family atmosphere, far more relaxed than our equivalent at Hampton Court.

We were met in Paris and escorted to Courson, by an old friend, Alain Woisson, who is the park and garden director at Bagatelle, the highly organized gardens in the Bois de Boulogne. I think you may have been there. My previous visit was some ten years ago.

Alain took us there the next day, and spent the whole day with us, over what should have been his weekend respite; cooked an excellent lunch for us, too, his charming little house being in the middle of the gardens. These are impressively organized. He has a team of 40 gardeners, and the justly famous rose garden (laid out by Forrestier in the early years of this century), an acre in extent, has ten gardeners permanently at work in it. The ghastly system of putting work out to competitive tender has luckily not reached here, so there are the opportunities for detailed planning, planting and maintaining which are quickly lost by the cut-price work-hiring system which we have adopted. Bagatelle is considered a vital jewel in the crown of Paris's image, and it lives up to every expectation. I do wish you'd been there.

So much is happening. The rose breeders test their new varieties, here, against others of their kind and there are various juries which regularly meet to assess and award. Whether you're a rose person or not, you cannot but help be fascinated by what you see. It's the same with other flowers: irises, for instance, and peonies.

I see I'm into a new page but I must stop. I can hear Edward (Flint) taking a party round the garden. This afternoon, I'm taking another, of Australians. This evening, two American friends of Fergus, from *Horticulture* magazine, will be here and we'll visit Derek Jarman's, now Keith Collins', shingle garden at Dungeness, followed by an evening meal at the Pilot Inn.

Tomorrow, Sean Hogan, a young American whom I've met more than once in the Berkeley Botanic Garden, near San Francisco, is coming for the night. TV for *Gardeners' World* (next year), on Friday, and so it goes on.

Love from Christo

— 🪢 —

Saturday 24 May

Dear Christo,

It seems, it *is* AGES – two months – since I have felt able to write to you. During all that time your letters and phone calls have been so very supportive, even if they did make me feel sad because I could not respond. Throughout the winter we had a series of anxieties, problems and difficult decisions to make. The gloomy weather didn't help. Come spring, I thought, I would bounce back with the daffodils. But not so. My eyes could see, but my heart skipped no beats. It felt as if the light bulb inside me had fused, the batteries were dead. Once before, in my early forties, a few years after I began the nursery, I had similar symptoms of nervous exhaustion, and had to keep away from the nursery and garden for several months. This time the condition affected my digestive system; I've lost a lot of weight, so suddenly I knew I had to seek help. Initially my doctor prescribed sedatives, but also arranged for me to be seen by a specialist in gastric problems. So far my X-ray examinations and gastroscopy (where a camera looks round the inside of your tummy!) have revealed nothing obviously worrying, but we still await the result of the biopsy.

After six weeks of sedatives and anti-depressants, cancelling all my outside commitments for three months, and delegating more responsibility all round, I am feeling much better, but still shy away at times from really awkward decisions, and don't feel strong enough to be away from home.

It was a shame to miss April. I mostly saw it from my bed, watching the candle-smooth buds of *Magnolia* x *soulangeana* opening day by day, and beyond, the great white cherry, *Prunus* 'Taihaku', afroth with bunches of paper-white flowers set among tender bronze-tinted leaves. I could see, framed between the magnolia branches, across to the ponds where borders of large-flowered marsh marigolds, *Caltha polypetala*, leant out from freshly emerging rafts of great round leaves, their golden faces repeated in mirror-clear water. They reminded me of the wild daffodil, *Narcissus pseudonarcissus*, I saw in March (first planted by your mother) and now seeded all around the Horse Pond at Dixter, in among the huge rough crowns of gunnera, even seeded and flowering right to the water's edge.

For the first few weeks I couldn't face the garden or nursery but did value my team leaders coming to my bedside for us to reassure each other that all was going well, to discuss planting plans with David, and the vegetable garden with Keith. (During February I had managed to start early salads and vegetables in pots and trays.) Bless them, they brought in little vases of early spring flowers which warmed my heart, so I could turn over, leave things to them and go to sleep!

Gradually the tension and panic feelings are abating. The light bulb switches on when I walk in the garden and see dear familiar plants flooding the garden once more. In winter I fear the garden can never be as last season, yet when spring comes I marvel at the maturity each year brings. We can easily become over-anxious about damage from frost, drought or whatever else may be waiting to attack, but now I am trying to remember one of my American friends' exhortations, 'Beth you must think paasitively!' So I am trying to enjoy this moment, this day, and not to 'spoil today's blue skies with tomorrow's clouds' as I read and re-read around one of my mother's cream jugs when I was a small child. I am not always successful!

Whit Sunday 25 May

I am re-reading your most recent letter, and of course it was sweet of Fergus to write and tell me how you would both be glad if he could come and fetch me for a little break. You know I would love that too, but I could not feel at ease to leave Andrew: he has had several bad times over these past two weeks, and is physically very frail, although his mind is still clear. The time may yet come when I shall need someone in the house with me to help with him, but so far I can manage well. It is good for me still to be able to talk with him, share so many things and put by his chair little pots of flowers which he cannot walk out to the garden to see. His memory for plants is going, but it helps to see them. And although he eats so little, it is a pleasure to make tempting little dishes we can share. There is already so much in the vegetable garden: young carrots from the tunnel (I sowed them 3 March), and broad bean tops, asparagus and true spinach – all are treats. The spinach is early because we tested an old packet of seed for viability weeks ago. It germinated, was potted up and later planted out under a big cloche frame. Now there is enough to share with my students, and there are young seedlings coming on in succession. I have to concede that it is superior to spinach beet, being more delicate, but I still grow the beet to take us through the autumns and into next spring. The cool weather just now is preventing the true spinach from bolting too fast.

Like you I have lived through my iris phase (almost). For years I admired Cedric Morris's introductions, lovely delicate creatures, often heavily veined on a pale ground, like moths or butterflies wings. But 30 years ago or more, new American hybrids were coming in, with much bolder, brighter colours and much larger, sometimes over-ruffled petals. As my collection of species plants grew, and with them perhaps a different approach to garden design, I found I could not cope with them. They need space and sunlight to ripen their rhizomes – this meant a boring job with a vegetable knife to tease out the weeds which easily seeded among them. I do have two of Cedric's varieties, restored to me by Tony Venison, planted in the Gravel Garden where they do well, and look handsome. But in the nursery stock beds I see David has been tempted to try some of the newer introductions. Among several, two are outstanding. *Iris* 'Pearly Dawn' will seduce most women, I suspect, with translucent chiffon-textured petals faintly coloured like a peach water-ice, deepening into the centre. On shortish stems (64–76cm/25–30in) and free-flowering it is quite enchanting. Very different is *I.* 'Black Swan'. On taller stems, up to 1m (3ft), it has black-velvet-textured falls, the colour proven and enhanced by glistening dark purple standards. Somehow I think these two will find their way into the Gravel Garden, probably with *I.* 'Jane Phillips', for her large well-formed azure-blue flowers with creamy beards.

Peonies and oriental poppies come into a similar category, I think. I love them for their exotic beauty and bold effect, but have learnt not to rely on them. Their days of glory are brief. I appreciate their more modest neighbours, many of which keep me very pleasant company throughout the year.

I was very disappointed to miss the VMH lunch and the opportunity to meet old friends. Unless one goes to the the RHS shows there is very little opportunity to meet the many and varied horticulturists whose friendship and helpfulness I enjoyed in the years when I was an exhibitor. We mostly have too many responsibilities at home to go wandering, but I am aware that I miss opportunities of gaining new experience and knowledge if I never leave home.

I'm glad you teased Dr Stearn about some of the name changes which plague us all. But I have fond memories of him visiting the garden here in its early days, and we all value highly *A Gardener's Dictionary of Plant Names* begun by Isadora Leighton Luce Smith, and revised and enlarged by William T. Stearn. Did you know that *arietinus* means 'like the horns of a ram'? I looked it up this week when I was making a label for *Paeonia mascula* subsp. *arietina*. This plant is wonderful now with large, cherry-red buds incurved to look like huge bubbles floating above a base of finely cut leaves. Its single flowers open to show a mass of orange stamens; they are fleeting, but the effect of a mass of them on the nursery stock beds was delightful.

Monday 26 May
You have puzzled both David and me, referring to *Tulipa sprengeri* as stoloniferous. Certainly it seeds freely (you just have to be patient for it to make flowering-sized bulbs), but we've never noticed that it made stolons and don't dare dig up a clump now to find out since they're in full bloom. *Tulipa saxatilis* is stoloniferous – that has covered yards under the pines in the reservoir garden. It needs light, well-drained soil and plenty of heat to get it to flower well, and then it makes wide carpets of short-stemmed, pointed pink petals with large yellow eyes. It was one of the few things Cedric envied me. In his good loam it rarely flowered.

Next week Susanne Weber, companion and right hand of the late Helen von Stein Zeppelin, celebrated recently for having been for 50 years such a support to the nursery, is coming to stay for a couple of nights. She has just published a really beautiful (and I'm sure most knowledgeable) book on the genus *Iris*. It is in German of course so unfortunately I can't appreciate the writing. She has been over for Chelsea and meetings with all the iris enthusiasts (one of the meetings at Hadlow College I think) and is coming here on her way back to Germany.

I was especially glad to read of your visit to Paris, and meeting with Alain Woisson. When I was invited several years ago to give a talk to the Horticultural Society in Paris I was entertained for a week by a charming Englishwoman, Pamela Currie, who has lived in France since the end of the Second World War. She showed me the countryside of Normandy, and good gardens, including Bagatelle, where we were shown around by Alain, and given tea in his unusual and attractive house. I was particularly impressed by the architectural framework of the huge rose garden – all in full bloom, but the wash of colour I could overlook, so fascinated was I by the Victorian basic planting: many kinds of beautifully clipped hedges forming the outside boundary, one hedge set against another, like the modelling you sometimes see around picture frames, contrasting with scalloped ropes of climbers, and the whole scene linked by the perfectly clipped pyramidal shapes of evergreens, spaced among the draughtboard effect of the rose beds. And the eye was led, I remember, to a high vantage point topped by a pavilion, where no doubt august persons sat in tight clothes with high collars to view the scene.

I can't begin now to tell you about the garden, except that it is lovely! The Gravel Garden so full of colour and still everywhere fresh and green despite only 87.4mm (3.44in) of rain since January. Outside the dining-room window *Abutilon vitifolium*, grown from seed we collected in Alan Roger's garden in Scotland, has been in flower for weeks. It is possibly a hybrid, or could be the wild form I remember in Cedric's garden, with large pale violet flowers opening wider than the darker form *A.* x *suntense* 'Jermyns' which is in flower in the Gravel Garden. The first flower of Alan's very pale grey-blue *Iris sibirica* has already opened. Together with his large celandine, *Ranunculus ficaria* subsp. *chrysocephalus*. I shall always have these to remind me of his charm and warm hospitality. It is sad to think of such an articulate, entertaining man confined now to a hospital ward. I'm so glad you have visited him. I am enclosing the obituary of his brother, Bunny Roger, whom I never met, but whose influence I felt in the interior design of Dundonnell.

We now have two cats. Fudge came as a refugee last autumn, a neutered female. In mottled tones of sand she almost vanishes, sprawled, sunbathing, on the gravel paths. Another stray has been named Humbug by the nursery girls, because she is a prettily striped, grey and white tabby. Today David took me to my Chelsea house, the small potting shed, where I prepared plants for Chelsea. There, hidden behind boxes, Humbug produced kittens yesterday. Already there are takers, even though we haven't yet seen them. Just now we could do with a team of cats; the rabbit problem is still a great worry.

Most people are complaining, understandably, about the cold north-east wind bringing such low temperatures almost at the beginning of June, but I know the garden cannot last so well as it is now, with so little moisture, if we have sudden heat. There is still such freshness everywhere, so many thousand shades of green. I love that, and share it with you and Fergus.

With all my heart, Beth

— ❧ —

Thursday 5 June

Dear Christo,

I can't wait to tell you – at last it's raining here, real rain! Water is flowing across the paved area beneath the magnolia tree, drumming on the roof, flowing over the guttering. Thunder rolls promisingly in the distance; not too distant I hope. After more than five months with only 90mm (3½in) of rain, with frosts, gales and heatwaves in between, I can hardly stop myself from going outside and getting soaked through. As it is, I am in the middle of washing up bread tins before going to bed, but can't resist running round the house to open doors and windows to watch and smell the rain, 'the soft, silver passion of the rain . . .', soaking into the thirsty garden.

Beth

—❧—

Monday 9 June

Dear Christo,

We caught only the perimeter of the storms on Thursday
and Friday nights, but although each burst of rain was of short
duration their circling around amounted to almost an inch
(25mm). Already the garden looks more relaxed. And so do we!
All the staff came in smiling this morning, all thankful for some
real rain at last.

'This is the Garden of Eden!' said Diana, my normally
unsentimental elder daughter, who had arrived for the weekend.
We sat outside having Sunday morning breakfast, overlooking the
house pond, the sun behind us highlighting the living theatre we
were facing: feathery bamboo; huge thrusting leaves of gunnera;
foamy masses of pea-green *Alchemilla mollis*; great sheaves of that
splendid dark-stemmed iris, *I.* x *robusta* 'Gerald Derby', as well
as the rich, soft falls of *I. laevigata*. The caltha I wrote about last
time has finished, but on the house side of the pond appears almost
a 'meadow' of *Ranunculus lingua*, large, yellow cups in their
hundreds, standing above rafts of the broad-bean-like leaves of
Melianthus major. Together these two plants form a wide, irregular
border creating a very natural effect, contrasting with the round
waterlily pads just opening their first flowers, but they could, and
will, invade too much of the water surface left to themselves, so
I think someone will be required to wade in, after flowering has
finished, to restrain them.

As we sat absorbing the scene, listening to a concert of bird
song, orchestrated near and far, the cast arrived: Diana suddenly
spotted a cluster of brown and yellow baby mallards, warming
themselves on the opposite bank, beneath the parasols of gunnera.
Mother duck had heard us, and was making low, throaty noises
to warn her babies. We dashed indoors for more bread, and soon
nine little balls of fluff were hoovering up the soggy pieces, while

mother, head held high and alert, held back, waiting for the bigger pieces we tossed to her. Ever-hungry red-finned rudd surged just beneath the surface, knocking the ducklings off balance. A huge, dark shape, streamlined like a submarine, glided towards us. It was a carp. He circled round, while we held our breath in wonder, then silently disappeared. We rarely see them so close. I was glad to have Diana with me to share this treat, but too often the story ends like the song 'Ten Green Bottles . . .': 'nothing but the smell left hanging on the wall'. Often by the end of the first week all the ducklings have vanished. How? Probably the heron picks off an early morning straggler, but I think the moorhens are responsible. They also breed on the house ponds, both father and mother ceaselessly guarding their offspring; while the husband of the duck is skulking away somewhere, useless to his family as he loses the fine plumage of his courting days. Being a single parent is a tough job for mallard mothers.

Saturday evening 14 June

During these last few days the garden has erupted into a carnival of flowers, a luxuriousness of growth such as I've never seen here before. It is both breathtaking and frightening. Frightening, because in no way can I take it all in, the overwhelming emotional effect it has on me, as well as the simple fact I cannot get round in time to see it all! I feel I should be outside all the hours of daylight to absorb the changing magical effect of plants at their peak in mid-June, but that would be like sitting all day eating your favourite food – simply indigestible. I just have to come inside and lie on the floor for a bit, to calm down.

There are other excitements. We have had several parties this week; an early morning visit from New Zealand, organized by Beth Leydon, who regularly brings visitors here. I always enjoy meeting her and the people she brings are both knowledgeable and appreciative. I have at last, firmly instructed by Diana, asked David to join me when I give talks in the garden so that he can take my place when I'm not able to do it. We should (and will) be training more members of staff to help David with this. The problem is, having so much work needing to be done at this time of year, we could cut everyone in two and still find enough jobs. It is already a great help to me to have David on these occasions, and gives more to the visitors when two can answer queries.

On the same beautiful summer's day as that of the New Zealanders' visit, Dame Elizabeth Murdoch came to lunch, with Michael, her head gardener. They are both so keen and knowledgeable, it is a relief, when names have dropped out of my head, to have them found for me. As you know, Elizabeth, 88 years 'young' now, has been over here for five weeks, looking up family and friends, visiting gardens all over the country. Here, after lunch, she and Michael studied the garden in such depth, I thought we would never get round the half of it. We didn't, of course, and were both quite thankful to sink on a seat in the Wood Garden. We have kept in touch by letter since we met in Melbourne, when you and I had lunch with her, when we gave talks there several years ago. She is a dear person.

The next day David and I had a day school, another of our yearly events. We woke to rain, grey clouds brushing the treetops. And so it continued steadily as it has not done for months, until almost half past eleven. Before then our party had arrived, so we welcomed them with coffee, sitting them on dry straw bales in the potting shed, while I explained the hows and whys of the garden. Then, the rain easing a little (and the 'foolish virgins' provided with the odd pair of wellies and 'left behind' umbrellas), we wandered through the Gravel Garden, transformed by rain. It astounds me the way plants have taken off in such a short time, when little more than a week ago I was saying we would soon be obliged to cut back certain plants to reduce evaporation. Hot winds had been tearing through the garden, as damaging as a hair drier. In the past ten days we have had over 70mm (2½in) of rain, almost as much as in the previous five months.

The warm wet air brought the scent of philadelphus and old roses drifting towards us from the long curving entrance border, planted in the early days of making the garden, where a sloping bed of soil is more moisture retentive than that of the Gravel Garden. Much that looks good there now has made itself by increase or self-seeding. In some parts of the Gravel Garden the effect, at this peak of the year, is almost meadow-like. *Tanacetum niveum* attracts everyone with large mounds of tiny grey leaves completely whitened now with clusters of small, yellow-eyed daisies. It seeds freely, so we met it in unexpected places, sometimes better than I would have thought of, but in some cases needing swift removal, to rescue what was suffocating beneath. White-flowered love-in-a-mist, Cedric Morris's rainbow forms of *Papaver rhoeas* and *Omphalodes linifolia* (called the broderie anglaise plant by my small daughters many years ago because it looked rather like the lace edging on their cotton petticoats) – all these flowing in drifts, highlighted with self-sown opium poppies, sometimes single, some incredibly double.

A good form of golden-leaved marjoram makes a bright curving border against the gravel path, backed by *Euphorbia polychroma*, covered now with furry coral-red seed pods. When they are ripe and collected for sowing we shall cut the euphorbia to the ground to encourage new growth, and maybe see a second crop of flowers in late summer. If left it will become mildewed in dry conditions and look unsightly.

The cistuses are at their best, new buds opening each morning, dropping by the afternoon (helianthemums drop before lunch). Before breakfast is the best time to see both of these, the cistus petals creased and crinkled before being smoothed flat by the sun. *Cistus* 'Peggy Sammons' has come through several severe droughts. I was surprised in the hot summer of '95 to see cistus shedding their leaves, but this year the bushes are large and handsome, crowded with large rose-like flowers in light and dark tones of pink. They make a backcloth for a clover-red penstemon,

P. 'Andenken an Friedrich Hahn' (who needs a name like that?), velvety grey ballota and *Salvia tesquicola*, a brilliant plant with long tapers of pink flowers in dark purple bracts.

Huge bouquets of *Crambe cordifolia*, a Spanish broom and *Abutilon vitifolium* var. *album*, crowded now with large white blooms, back the landscape effect formed by a deep planting of *Santolina virens*, just opening primrose-yellow buttons, and soft purple mounds of fresh-leaved *Salvia officinalis* 'Purpurascens' – all interspersed with drifts of pale greenish-yellow spires of *Ornithogalum pyrenaicum*, while onopordums and verbascums stand out like carved statues above the many softly rounded shapes.

But for all the importance of these strong verticals, I find myself stopping by two grasses, *Helictotrichon sempervirens* and *Stipa splendens*. Their tall, needle-like flower stems create delicate screens through which to view the intense blue of *Linum narbonense*, fragile against the stout waxed leaves of *Sedum telephium maximum* 'Atropurpureum', mingling with the metallic silver-veined *Eryngium giganteum*, Miss Willmott's Ghost.

After lunch we went to the Wood Garden, saw the new plantings in the Reservoir Garden, and finally, 'Could we see the vegetable garden?' So we ended there.

And there I remained, to stay and thin the latest emerging crop of carrots, glad to be quiet and still in my private place.

Sunday morning 15 June
Goodness me! Another change in the weather! Yesterday hot and humid, while this morning I woke early, shivering under one blanket. I turned on the radio and heard there was frost in northern and central Scotland. Thought of you with Colin and Kulgin, and hoped you had packed a few winter woollies! I got up quickly, wanting to share with you the Wood Garden while it still has colour. Outside was overcast, drizzly and uncomfortably cold. I needed a coat, and a pencil instead of a biro to make a few notes on wet paper.

On the way to the wood, I passed a plant of *Phlomis russeliana* in the Reservoir Garden. We had to remove it from the Gravel Garden – it was just too dry for it there. I love the effect of crowds of vertical stems carrying primrose-yellow, parrot-beak-shaped flowers held in clusters of tubular green bracts. They are spaced all along the upper part of the stems, each surrounded by long pointed 'collars', formed by pairs of leaves set alternately up the stem. These add considerably to the effect. For the rest of the season, and into winter, the whorls of calyces make good seed heads.

In the wood I was met by the sweet clean scent of the rose 'Paul's Himalayan Musk'. I can also enjoy it across the little yard, outside my kitchen window. Here it is a delight to be washing up and see the first rosy buds open, and then, almost by the hour, more and more appear, until now it is a vast fountain of flowers cascading from the top of a young oak (50 years old), simply thousands of clusters of small, double shell-pink roses. More scent in the Wood Garden comes from two different selections of our native woodbine, *Lonicera periclymenum*. One named after Graham S. Thomas has clusters of large flowers the colour of clotted cream. The other, of equal size and vigour, has pink-flushed buds opening ivory-white, fading to rich cream. Both plants have enveloped the trunks of two oaks, completely encircling each with wide columns of flower. An amazing sight.

I love white foxgloves, lighting up the garden like church candelabras, carrying the eye deep into dim recesses, self-sown, in drifts or singly. Each year I fret when they are in flower – should I be planting more in strategic places for next year? Sometimes we get round to it, but more often than not, left to themselves, they make a better job than we might have done. But, using heavy mulches, we could be caught out sometimes where seedlings fail to germinate. Last year I planted *Digitalis ambigua* and *D. lutea*, both perennials. *D. ambigua* is flowering now on shorter stems, about 61–76cm (24–30in) with close-set spires of chubby yellow flowers.

D. lutea, still to come, is taller, up to l.2m (48in), with very narrow pale yellow flowers – making interesting verticals. So, too, do the thalictrums: *T. aquilegiifolium* rises well above the surrounding greenery, flaunting clusters of white or mauve fluffy flowers, reminiscent of candyfloss.

Some of the dicentras were demolished by frosts in April, but have recovered themselves, and now both pink and white forms of *D. spectabilis* are dripping with lady's lockets. The smaller-flowered *D. formosa*, in several forms, I value most for the contrasting effect of its finely cut leaves, but just now all the variants of Dutchman's breeches are attractive. Especially admired is a wine-red form called *D.* 'Bacchanal'.

The graceful little horned pansy, *Viola cornuta*, in shades of blue and white, has wound its way obligingly, and the astrantias have survived attack by rabbits (last year they were munched to ground level). We are obliged to put wire netting round some of the new plantings – but often find the same plants are left alone once established.

Heucheras are fashionable – they could be overdone. Like hostas they are being selected for leaf variation in a big way in the States. But who has room for hundreds of new introductions, especially when the variations are slight? We have a few of the more distinct forms coming along. One, much commented on, *H.* 'Ruby Veil', has large basal leaves exquisitely marbled deep purple and silver with the fine silken texture of its parent, *H. americana*. The dark beetroot-red leaves, diminishing in size, as they continue up the stem, creating more interesting effect than the spindly spires of dark buds which open to insignificant greenish flowers. Other heucheras have very effective foaming spires of flower, including 'Green Ruffles' – good clumps of frilly green leaves with handsome whorls of pale green flowers.

There is much more, but I will spare you!

In passing the little ditch bed on the edge of the wood, I wished you could stand with me and see the *Ranunculus acris* 'Stevenii' you gave me, making a shower of yellow saucers hanging over the water. I think it deserves to be more widely grown in semi-wild places. Although heavy rain or strong wind does tumble some of its tall, 1.25m- (4ft-) plus stems, it is not a plant to be corseted with stakes and string. To come unexpectedly across these huge bouquets of glistening buttercups, so light and airy, always thrills me. Beneath them is the water fern, *Onoclea sensibilis*, its broadly segmented leaves running round a huge blue-leaved hosta, while the ditch bottom is filled with the water forget-me-not, *Myosotis scorpioides* 'Mermaid'.

In Scotland I am sure you will be seeing all these delights and more, and everywhere looking as beautiful as the gardens and countryside are here now after the incomparable blessing of rain. We are all making the most of such fresh beauty while it lasts. (Perhaps the essence of our delight is that it is ephemeral.)

I hope I haven't exhausted you! Somehow I have to write when I can make the time and find the energy needed to put down the wealth of impressions crowding into my mind every time I set foot out of the door.

Have a wonderful holiday. I send much love to all my dear gardening friends in Scotland – and a big hug for you.

from Beth

PS David says philosophically when all this fecundity collapses, due to drought returning, there will be plenty of green remains to activate the compost heaps!

– ❧ –

Monday 30 June

Dear Christo,

Every time I hear the weather reports I think of you in Orkney and hope it is not so bad for you as it sounds, both cold and wet, with gale-force wind, day after day. On the rare occasions when the forecasts describe torrential thunderstorms in south-east England, Diana rings me from the Midlands, hoping it is true. More often than not, we are still waiting for something noticeable to fall. But at this moment there can be no moans from me! We have had 140mm (5¾in) of rain since 11 June. I don't think we have ever recorded so much in one summer month in all the years we have kept records.

Friday 27 June was the special birthday I share with my twin brother, Seley. Usually we spend it here, having lunch and opening our cards together outside, sitting beneath the shade of the big magnolia tree. This year we planned to go out to lunch, to a small restaurant he knows well in Stoke-by-Nayland, less than an hour's drive away. The day began with steady rain, and continued all day until late afternoon. Everyone said, 'What a pity for your birthday outing', but it wasn't! It was so beautiful, driving slowly through the Suffolk lanes, the trees heavy with foliage, banksides sprinkled with flowers, hedges full of wild honeysuckle, and the last flowers of wild rose and elderflower. Flowering grasses arched over streams of water, rushing ahead of us, creating deep pools in the low ways where we had to drive even more slowly in case water stopped the engine. In one place we had to be diverted because of flooding.

The village of Stoke is clustered on a low hill overlooking the surrounding farmlands. Its fine perpendicular church is a landmark, seen from afar, with the village of Nayland settled along the banks of the river below. We arrived at the Angel by midday, in good time to choose both a table and the menu in peace. We made a dash through the rain from the car, glad for the shelter of the pub's welcoming interior. I had been led to expect something special and was not disappointed. The atmosphere is at once comfortable and relaxed, not too smart, with no hint of London interior decorators. The customers, some local and some obviously holidaymakers, are mostly elderly at that time of day, but there was a cheerful sprinkling of mini-skirts and long bare legs, once the long macs were removed. Everyone was friendly, coming in, shaking umbrellas and grousing about the rain, while I couldn't resist startling them by saying how much I enjoyed it. (No, I didn't let on I was Beth Chatto.)

The food was delicious. We were offered a wide choice of dishes which were not striving hard to be different or clever. But different the food was, in its presentation so fresh and colourful, we felt as if we were guests in a friend's house.

We were away by 1.30pm. Still clutching umbrellas, we negotiated deep puddles to reach the church, and paused there awhile, admiring its surprisingly tall nave. Then several miles of tortuous lanes, uphill and down, past little gardens spilling flowers and vegetables almost into the road, took us to the small town of Hadleigh, where I stopped to buy wholemeal flour ground locally. I like to buy it fresh, then put it in plastic bags into the freezer, since I cannot buy it fresh each week as you do. In this shop I am always tempted by other irresistible dried goodies, both fruit and nuts, for my store cupboard.

At 3.00pm, after more rain-washed winding lanes we arrived at a tiny hamlet, Kettlebaston, where an old Suffolk farmhouse, the Hall, is the home of my friend Janet, the potter. There she had lit her wood-burning stove and we were glad to sit beside it, drink tea and eat a delicious cake she had made for us, decorated with heads of marigolds (we avoided puddings at the Angel to leave room for tea!). Janet recently went to Nepal for three weeks with a party of Buddhists, so it was interesting (and peaceful) for me to listen to her and my brother discussing matters Indian (Seley was in India for four years during the war and retains a great interest and love of the country). Then, leaving Seley indoors to browse through Janet's books (her first husband was an antiquarian bookseller), we put on our wellies and traipsed through the wet garden.

Janet was despondent about the roses, old roses from Cedric's garden, huge bushes now, but all bowed down, with soggy bundles of silk and velvet petals reduced to brown tissue paper. They just don't take wet weather. Slugs, too, were devastating the vegetable garden, clearing off rows of young seedlings overnight.

215

We changed tack and made for the pottery where she is preparing for a sale. This place always fascinates me, both the smells and the sights: the wheel and table of dampened clay; mysterious jars and bottles filled with materials used in glazing; shelves of unglazed pots. Sometimes I find these more effective than the finished result, perhaps because I can appreciate the pure shapes with nothing else to distract. The firing process always seems to me like awaiting a birth, exciting and uncertain – so much depends on unforeseeable happenings. This can't be the case with commercial pottery, but dear Janet is an artist-craftsman, always experimenting, not with gimmicky ideas, but with subtle colour and forms.

The rain stopped in time for the drive home. It had been a lovely gentle day, shared completely with my brother. We both felt it had been a true holiday, while Andrew was relieved to see us both safe and sound.

On Sunday morning I drove to Wormingford (also in Suffolk) to see the specialist, Dr Cowan, who has conducted the investigations of my digestive system. Now I am writing quickly to tell you of the results of all the testings, including the biopsy. Dr Cowan said nothing seriously wrong had been revealed. Such a relief. I am still unable to improve my weight, but Dr Cowan thinks my situation may have something to do with it, and somehow I have to adjust my mind so that I do not burn up more than I can retain. I am sure that this is the case. So much is happening here all the time.

Sometimes I wish I could switch off my mind as easily as I did the deep freeze recently to defrost it. This is possibly the most detested job in housekeeping. Yet there I was with the vegetable garden bursting its sides after such good growing weather and nowhere to put anything. Who defrosts your freezer? I wondered. I know how well filled you keep it. Like mine, it is never at a sensible low level. But if someone else defrosted my freezer, how would I find anything again? It's bad enough with my own system. And how would anyone else decide what to keep, or what to throw away?

This time I tackled it differently. I switched the freezer off, opened the lid, and left it intact for about two hours while I had lunch and tried to rest under the magnolia tree. Then, longing to get the job done, I collected large pot-trays from the nursery, filled them with frozen food and covered the heap with a big duvet. Using a flat wooden spatula, I was easily able to dislodge the frost thick on the sides of the cabinet, and sweep up the dry ice with a dustpan and brush, instead of mopping and squeezing buckets of icy water. After a quick wipe with warm water, everything needed was back in a more orderly fashion in an hour and a half. I was tired, but oh-so-smug to have it all done.

Today Steffi, my dear German student from Laufen, helped me pick and shell peas and broad beans. Once again we have all been amazed at the crop of 'Hurst's Greenshaft' peas. They hang in clusters, so prolific – and sweet, just so long as the pods remain squeaky fresh. Steffi had lunch with me and we discussed a few of the differences in the way we run our nurseries. Some systems cannot be translated from one environment to another, but it is always thought-provoking to hear how we appear to fresh eyes and minds. Some of her observations were very sound. Later I discussed our conversation with David, and he agreed, especially on the potting side. Although several people pot throughout the year, we do rely too much on one girl who, throughout the summer months, does nothing else. What would happen if Ann broke her arm, asked Steffi, and wouldn't Ann sometimes like a change? Both obvious questions.

David will arrange for everyone possible to spend an hour with Steffi before she leaves, to learn from her the German method of potting. This will not only save us time, but be less physically demanding.

Much love, Beth

– ❦ –

Thursday 3 July

Dear Beth,

I hardly know where to begin; it's been so long. Start with the weather, perhaps; that's in a good English tradition. Pip drove me home from Orkney, and as we swooshed through Essex, it rained harder than in the whole of the previous three weeks in the north. I thought of you. That was on 27 June. For the month, we've recorded 155.5mm – more than six inches, which is half an inch more than last November, our most recent, previous wet month.

Main victims have been the old, once-flowering roses (of which I grow virtually none), what they now like to call heritage roses. I asked some American visitors, who were at Mottisfont Abbey, the National Trust heritage rose garden, the day before (26 June), how it had been there. Good, they said, automatically (Americans never bad-mouth anything or anyone). The roses must have been at their peak, I suggested, mischievously. They then had to admit that they were a disaster. If it isn't the wet, it's heat or drought that ruins them, again and again.

Here, it was the flowers of the last, late-flowering, bulbous, 'English' irises, *Iris latifolia*, that suffered, before the buds had even opened. I have ribbons of them between the double aster hedges (*Aster lateriflorus* var. *horizontalis*) that link the topiary pieces in the Peacock Garden, as it has now come to be known. Otherwise, the rain seems to have been entirely beneficial, but I do now want warmth, to promote growth in the Exotic Garden, where such as bananas and castor oil, daturas, begonias and streptocarpus would immediately respond with a great surge of growth.

However, the garden as a whole looks marvellous and there are lots of happy cameras clicking away. There are some pretty striking colour contrasts; I don't know how you would respond to them. I think you would approve of most, while holding reservations about using them yourself. You have always been very generous about my handling of colour. And that isn't all hectic, by any means.

In a stock bed, I have adjacent patches of purple *Salvia* x *superba* and *Penstemon* 'Drinkstone', bright cherry red, and I like that very much. But it so happens that they have a patch of *Achillea* 'Moonshine' in front of them, and I hate that. It is only a comparatively soft shade of yellow but much too bright in this situation. In fact, I'm fed up with it and have got Fergus to agree to its being eliminated from our nursery list and from the garden altogether.

I have a robust form of the really cool yellow *A.* 'Taygetea', which I really do like. It is in the trial of achilleas that is now starting at Wisley. Oh, I must tell you. I was on the trial ground yesterday and Wendy Bowie (Carlile) snorted that some of the entries should never have been allowed. It appeared that she was referring to single-flowered forms of *A. ptarmica*, which are quite close to the wild plant and have just the one framing row of rays, with no doubling. 'They have their charm,' I ventured to say; 'So has the Devil,' was Wendy's riposte.

A trial of annual poppies has been planted up but it is woefully uneven, there having been failures at the seedling stage. Some will clearly not do justice to themselves. It was suggested that they should have been direct-sown, but I think that makes for unpredictable results. Sowing direct into modules had apparently not worked well, and the received wisdom that poppy seedlings won't transplant, because of their fragile tap roots, was given an airing. But received wisdom is seldom put to the test and Fergus, coming to the subject uninhibited, has proved it wrong, here. He sows poppies in a pot then pricks them off individually into modules at a very early stage. This is perfectly successful, as can currently be evidenced by a planting, just coming into flower, of Thompson & Morgan's 'Angels' Choir' strain of *Papaver rhoeas* and by fat plants, not yet flowering, of *P. commutatum*, deep red with a large black spot at the base of each petal, which sells as 'Lady Bird'.

From T & M and admired on their trial ground two years ago, we have flowering *Nepeta transcaucasica* and *Penstemon barbatus*, both up to 1.2m (4ft) high. Both are of good upright habit and sufficiently self-supporting (though we took no risks with the nepeta). The blue of the one with the coral of the other would go excellently together, I believe. The penstemon seems unlikely to be a sound perennial, however. We might have to give it biennial treatment.

There are some strong yellows that I greatly appreciate and one of them now flowering is *Anthemis* 'Grallagh Gold', which is in the stock bed with the double-rosette cranesbill, *Geranium pratense* 'Plenum Violaceum'. In front of them, the prolific *Hemerocallis* 'Corky', which is a softer shade of yellow than 'Golden Chimes' and longer flowering; the deep blue *Campanula lactiflora* 'Prichard's Variety'; and, for height and a different habit, candelabrums of a yellow, biennial verbascum.

A point I noticed at Wisley, yesterday, is that many of their plantings are boringly level. In the double herbaceous borders, for instance. Pam Schwerdt remarked of these: 'They're always pulling them apart. They never settle down to anything.'

There's a good area at the back of the Long Border, just now, where *Clematis* 'Jackmanii Superba', trained up a 3m (10ft) pole and just becoming a column of purple, has an airy bush of *Hoheria glabrata*, with snow-white, cherry-like blossom on one side and 1.8m (6ft) *Senecio doria*, with panicles of yellow daisies; candelabrums of yellow *Verbascum olympicum* in front.

Well, about my northern trip. Frank Ronan, for the third year running, volunteered to drive me to Scotland at the start, which is a great help, as I'm increasingly bad on long drives by myself. Instead of 1,100km (700 miles), as last year to Dundonnell, it was 600km (400 miles), to Kirkcudbright, in the south-west. The draw in that area is Michael Wickenden, who runs a nursery in a big old walled garden, a few miles away. I can't remember if you came here with me. He is an intrepid man and last winter was in north Uganda and Ruwenzori, the so-called Mountains of the Moon. He always likes to travel on his own and finds it far easier to slip into and out of awkward territories this way, without attracting the attention of corrupt and uncooperative authority.

He has a lot of the latest geranium hybrids that keep on being named. Frank suggested that 'Latent Charm' would be a good name for one (almost anyone) of them. Michael has some new raised beds, giving best drainage to alpine plants requiring it. One of these had grey, succulent leaves lying close against the very pale grit surfacing the bed. Frank thought that a piece on 'the Invisible Garden' would be good. I might work on that one. You could take a visitor into it and be asked when it would be in flower. 'It's in full bloom now,' you would reply, but with such as *Paris polyphylla*, *Bupleurum lancifolium* and *Zantedeschia* 'Green Goddess', whose flowering is so subtle that you don't notice it. Would it win a Gold at Chelsea, do you think?

Frank and I visited the Edinburgh Botanic's outpost at Logan, near Stranraer. The gardens are under the excellent stewardship of Barry Unwin and he is always having fresh ideas. This time, it was a pebble garden, with mounded beds of pale beach pebbles from the nearby shore. They are grey and some larger boulders had been included. Plantings included *Parahebe perfoliata*, which enjoys the drainage, and others that like to filter sideways through an open medium. I hadn't realized that the parahebe could have a suckering habit. It looked extremely happy and was covered with spikes of blue veronica blossom. They cut it almost right back, early in the year.

From the next day, I drove around solo and lots of old friends asked after you and sent best wishes. Will tell you when I see you. Tony and Vicky Schilling (he was curator at Wakehurst Place) have moved from Sussex to the north-west and have just bought a very suitable home overlooking Ullapool. They are thrilled to be in that part of the world. We spent a whole day and two evenings together; the weather was pretty foul but they are very happy and so was I.

On my way to Gairloch, I looked in on Dundonnell, hoping perhaps to get a glimpse of Johnny and Cathy McSporran, but they were not around either there or in their cottage. It was pouring, and with the place deserted, the scene was sad indeed, all the rooms emptied (as I could see through the windows), Sotheby's having removed the furniture for security. That's the end of a long chapter, starting with my first visit in 1963. Alan (Roger) was the most generous of hosts. He has been moved to a hospital in Berkshire.

Next I visited Ruth and Robin Crawford, at Balcarres. She is justly proud of her garden, which is a picture, but they should have more help. There is so much work. Then to Colin and Kulgin at Frenich, where there was a sea of poppies. After a long tour of the garden I said I thought I'd sit and do some reading (I always read from his set of Chekhov short stories, when there). 'Yes,' said Colin eagerly, 'shall I get you a basket?' He had misheard reading for weeding!

Now Pip joined us from Edinburgh and he drove me to Orkney, first to their Mainland and then, by ferry, to Westray, where there are marvellous bird colonies on the cliffs. You'd love all that. Crossings were all smooth and the ground was dry, but it was grey and chilly. Unfortunately I had contracted a cold-cum-hacking-cough by then (still recovering from that) and ran a temperature, keeping to my bed for a whole day. I couldn't have been more comfortable, however. Still, the last week was somewhat marred. Pip drove me home in three hops.

So here I am and very glad to have your news in your long letters. The date for Glyndebourne is Thursday 7 August. The others can do the picnic: Fergus and Amanda, Stephen and Judy Anderton, so don't worry about that. I'm so anxious for you to see *The Makropulos Case*. Don't let anything (within reason) stop you coming. You must make provision for being away from home with someone to caretake, sooner or later. Perhaps you already have.

Could you bear a day visit from Fergus and me before that? We should love it.

I could use your cat, Fudge, in my Invisible Garden.

I do hope you're really near to well, dear Beth,
Love from Christo

– ✻ –

Sunday 6 July

Dear Christo,

I was so glad to see your spidery handwriting among the envelopes on my desk. I set it aside, to have the luxury of your typed sheets later in the day when I had time to relax and enjoy them. So, you and Pip were swooshing through the same rainstorms we were negotiating on my birthday, as he drove you home through Essex. As you point out, there has been a downside to such an amount of unaccustomed rain, more generally Wimbledon, the Test Matches – and the unfortunate growers of soft fruit. In our own sphere, I agree, the delicate-textured flowers, especially old cultivars of rose, bearded iris and oriental poppies and peonies all suffered, some more than others. But although we may have missed their glory this year, I would not be without a few of all of them. I used to have a big collection of old roses, but our light soil is not ideal for them. Those that I have retained remind me of Cedric, and my young days of learning to be a gardener, learning through him to look and really see.

It was good of you so soon after coming home, faced with a mass of writing commitments, to find time and energy to write me such a long and absorbing letter. I am glad you had Frank for a companion and driver. (I recently had a concerned letter from him and wondered how he had found out I had not been well.) Like me, you are forgetting quite recent events while no doubt able to recall in detail things we did much longer ago! You took me to Logan about three or four years ago, and we visited Michael Wickenden too. After a fascinating and exhaustive afternoon studying his intensive plant collection, we took him out to supper when he regaled us with blood-chilling tales of slipping into New Guinea, finding contacts, making friends, living as one of the tribe in the jungle, in constant danger of ambush by the opposing government forces. A rare young man I think.

I share your sad thoughts at closing the chapter on Dundonnell. For you, more like closing a much loved book. I would not have cared to look into the empty shell of the house which had been such a warm and welcoming retreat for so many of Alan's friends. But hopefully a new family will recreate a life there, and the fine old house in its beautiful setting will be happy again.

I think maybe last year I wrote to you about the pink notholirion given me by the gardener of your late cousin. David has gradually built up the stock on one of the raised beds in our Maternity Shade House. Recently I had the luck to walk in just at the right moment to see a row of plants in full flower. Such a strange shade of pink bells on tall stems.

Christo – I have been feeling anxious for some weeks about Glyndebourne. The thought of it is worrying me, which is not what you would want I know, But still, I do not feel strong enough to take all the excitement of coming to Dixter, and being able to give myself fully to the special treat I know it would be to share Janáček again with you. Added to this feeling is my concern for Andrew. I cannot have peace of mind to leave him even for one night. It is not simply a matter of finding someone to care for him. Although he is still able to be up and dressed, it all takes such an exhausting effort. Even to walk about the house entails several rests to reach from one end to the other. And 7 August will be our 54th wedding anniversary. Like many married couples there have been times when the anniversary has slipped by without our noticing and we have laughed at our forgetfulness, but not now. There will be no big party as there was for our Golden Wedding when family and staff gave us a wonderful surprise evening, but Diana and Mary will come, my brother too. So Christo, please forgive me this time for disappointing us both, but understand I am not sorry for myself. I could not be happy doing anything else.

But come yourself to see us please do, with Fergus as soon as we both can manage it. There is so much to see (before the drought arrives!), and all too much happening. The plans for the new Tea House are not yet set down in detail, but the project is on course; the old Pratten greenhouse will be taken down soon, and re-erected alongside the shade sales area. Already part of the little Mediterranean garden has been dismantled, precious fritillaries, anemones and species tulips lifted as well as plenty of cuttings taken. This morning Keith, who knows about such things, has hired the correct tools (at the right price!) and with two of his sons, Gerard and Simeon, his youngest (now about to go to university to study Law), together with David Plummer our handyman, and Chris, the schoolmaster who joined us last winter – they are all dismantling the wall, cleaning old cement off the blocks and stacking them on a sackbarrow to wheel to the tractor where Gerard carts them away for future use.

Such upheaval with all the decisions involved has affected me deeply. But we have thought about it for many months, planning the practicalities as well as adjusting, these past few weeks, to the prospect of tearing the existing picture apart.

There are many possibilities as to how we shall design the new area. Although ideas gestate in my mind, I cannot make decisions until the present picture is wiped out and I face a new canvas, with a fresh palette of plants and ideas. Why don't you come soon, you and Fergus, to help stir the pot?

For moments of sheer relaxation, best of all in early morning, before breakfast, I go to the pond side and call my ducks. There are only five now, but with their mother still, already half grown, with absurd little flaps for wings, which they use to lift themselves out of the water and on to the mown grass dam where I feed them. One has lost a leg. I picked it up to see if it needed attention, but there was no dangling foot, just a bit of bare bone hidden among the fluff and feathers. Yet it felt plump and strong in my hand and swims as efficiently as the rest. I feared it might go round and round in circles like a broken toy.

On the nursery, Humbug's two remaining kittens, both fat and black, are tumbling about near the vegetable garden. The staff are concerned they might be caught under a tractor but they will have to take their chance, like the ducklings.

Do you remember I mentioned a *Euphorbia wulfenii* had seeded tight against the base of a wall by the compost heaps? This year it has flowered, magnificent rounded heads, similar to one I used to envy against the Suffolk-pink walls of Cedric's old house, but from which I never managed to strike a cutting. Perhaps Debbie will be more successful with this one! I hope so.

Suddenly the weather changes again, the temperature soars into the upper 20s°C (lower 80s°F), the drying season is here once more. Emily is busy collecting, both seeds for sowing and flowers for drieds and potpourri. Somehow she manages to fit this in with her work in the propagating house. She has taken this over from me, as she and Debbie have also planted the pot gardens this year, with very little meddling from me. Each season's tasks come round again so quickly now. Such a short while ago it seems I wrote to you about the rose petals covering the spare-room beds. They are there again now. But my routine has changed a lot. Many things I enjoyed doing I miss, but to be able to teach and see the young people carrying on our disciplines and traditions – as well as introducing some of their own ideas is very reassuring. I am proud of them – and feel happy at the thought of sharing it all with you and Fergus soon.

Love from Beth

- ❀ -

Tuesday 19 August

Dear Beth,

It is a sweltering afternoon – nothing unusual about that, this summer – and I am in the Yeoman's Hall with the door into the garden wide open, but the curtains half closed, to cut down on the glare. The noise of our long-grass mower comforts me in the background, as we are only just getting to grips with the orchard. I have enjoyed the grass enormously, these past four months; it never got laid because the earlier drought kept it short. The pink haze of common bent in flower was a joy for many recent weeks. On the topiary lawn, which I have allowed to grow long for the past three years, pink smoke on the smoke bushes, *Cotinus coggygria*, seems like a sublimation of the flowering bents beneath, each belonging to the other and particularly beautiful on dewy mornings – which every morning is.

It has been a wonderful year in the garden, for us, who like to grow many plants which revel in heat and humidity. Whenever there seems the threat of another drought, relief arrives, after which the sun and heat start up again. Last Tuesday night, after an ideal picnic at Glyndebourne, there was lightning in the sky as we returned home. When I went to bed, after midnight, the temperature in the porch was still 72°F (22°C, but my old thermometer, which has served me well for many years, has not learned to read Celsius). Everyone I subsequently spoke to was awake for a considerable part of that night, with continuous thunder and lightning, though it never sounded dangerous.

Next morning, Fergus started up the sprinklers as usual, not trusting the weather gods to have done their job properly, but the rain-gauge measurement taken at 10.00am, registered 42.7mm (1¾in). I got hopelessly muddy, clearing up and removing 1.8m (6ft) plants of self-sown, purple orach, *Atriplex hortensis*, which had collapsed on top of their neighbours.

The old rose garden – the Exotic Garden – is brilliant, although I say it. The only failures are some of the begonias, normally grown as conservatory plants for their foliage, but which we wanted to try (as also much else) in the garden, for a spell, to see how they enjoyed a breath of fresh air. Many of them haven't. Some have, however; enough of them to encourage us in our stupidity.

Among our greatest successes has been a grass, *Setaria palmifolia*, which both Fergus and I have admired in America. It is unashamedly tender, but grows at a great pace in the summer months, entirely as a foliage plant. Fergus says it flowers early in the year. The leaves are broad, of hard texture and with dauntingly sharp margins. They are deeply ribbed and ridged, the venation running parallel with the main vein.

Then, *Colocasia esculenta*, an aroid, which you normally only meet in conservatories, but it should be widely adopted for summer bedding to give a tropical touch. It has magnificent leaves – about 45cm (18in) long, heart-shaped but each drawn to a point. The feathery venation, albeit on a smooth surface, is entrancingly delicate. This leaf blade is held aloft, to 60cm (2ft) or more, on a stout stalk, and it swings from side to side, when there is a breeze. One of the extraordinary things about these leaves is that from about 6 in the evening until 8 the next morning, they are wet. This is partly condensation but they also seem to generate their own water droplets, which are channelled to the leaf tip and drop to the ground. Under each leaf that happens to be overhanging stone paving, there forms a puddle. This morning, I had to be up early to say goodbye to Anne Wambach (whom we met up with in Vancouver, some years ago). We visited the *Colocasia esculenta* and there was a toad sitting motionless underneath a leaf tip, enjoying the overhead drip shower! Such experiences are precious. We walked away on tiptoe.

The *Yucca gloriosa*, which last flowered in August two years ago and have been building up their strength since then, have two thick buds thrusting upwards, like giant asparagus points. I am so glad that they have not waited till the end of September, as is often their irritating habit, by which time it is too late for them to flower properly before frost arrives.

The dahlias are a delight, all in bloom before the end of July, which is easily achieved if old tubers are used. We also take cuttings, which come into their own later. Cannas are revelling in the sub-tropical weather and there is a fine group of *Lobelia* 'Queen Victoria', closely planted (and carefully staked by me!); their rich red, 1m (3½ft) spikes set off by the white-variegated reed grass, *Arundo donax versicolor*, behind them. We never let up on running repairs in this garden, but Fergus cleverly makes them not seem apparent. It is a most labour-intensive form of gardening, but such a lot of fun and visitors do appreciate it. So many gardens are going downhill, by now, but ours only very slightly.

You know the kind of voluptuous perennials we depend upon, elsewhere. The rich purple eupatorium, which you gave me; the creamy plumes of *Artemisia lactiflora*, so well suited to our heavy soil; the strongly, upward-thrusting orange pokers of *Kniphofia uvaria* 'Nobilis', which I have had since I was on the staff at Wye College, in the early 1950s; the graceful, light blue spikes of 1.8m (6ft) *Salvia uliginosa*; big white corymbs of Canadian elder, *Sambucus canadensis* 'Maxima' (I tried making elderflower cordial with these, and it was a success, though slightly different in flavour from *S. nigra*, two months earlier); and the proudly upright (because carefully supported) lemon-yellow, green-coned *Rudbeckia* 'Herbstsonne', which goes up to 2m (7ft) on Fergus's lavishly nourished soil. There are also the upright columns of willowy foliage on *Helianthus salicifolius*, at various levels. If the wind knocks them sideways, their tips immediately resume an upright position, albeit at a lower level. But those that have remained vertical throughout are up to 2.7m (9ft) tall – still a foliage feature, pure and simple, although by the end of next month, they will be carrying their branched antlers of yellow daisies.

It is now 3.30pm and stifling, but I still love it! Those who are working outside, physically, probably do not, but there is a breeze, out there, stirring the wisteria foliage.

We were all very sad that you could not join us at Glyndebourne, but all send their love: Anne, Colin and Kulgin (who wanted you to have a spare ticket they were landed with), Ken Rawson, Russell Pascoe (from Cornwall – breezy as ever) and others. Graham Gough, who used to be in partnership at Washfield Nurseries with Elizabeth Strangman, but now no longer, has been to all the Glyndebourne productions this year, taking tickets in the gods at £10 a time. Although officially standing room, there is space for your own, small, folding chair. He says the sight lines are excellent and reckons the sound to be better than in the stalls. Even if that's an exaggeration, pretty good value, don't you think? Not much elitism about that.

The Makropulos Case, which you should have seen, was most moving, with a wonderful star in Anja Silja. If you analyse her character, it is not at all sympathetic, yet she commands total sympathy. Fergus couldn't wait for the long interval to end; he was so anxious for the final climax, and it did not disappoint. I really should get the music on compact disc, now that I have a CD player. There is so much in it to learn. Stephen Anderton, who was there with Judith, is doing that.

Beth, Fergus, Ken and I greatly enjoyed our day with you in July, and it has taken me nearly a month to say so. The Gravel Garden, in particular, was looking super. It was good to see Andrew and he took part in our visit for quite a lot of the time, which was so nice, though exhausting for him. I can see how frail he is and well understand why you feel you cannot leave him for a night. He looked quite wistful, at our parting, as though he did not expect us to meet again. I hope he's wrong.

I went to Alan Roger's cremation, which was at Golders Green. What a fine bunch the To's, for whose education he was responsible, are, I thought, seeing them all together, and what a credit to him and to themselves. They were all in deepest black (I was not), evidently having hired the necessary clothing. Alan wasn't a Christian, but it was a Christian service. Easiest that way, no doubt, making the believers comfortable.

When I told my Anne about how good you'd been, turning out your deep freeze, she was fired to do the same for ours. But, to my shame (and relief), I was not present to say what could be thrown out. Consequently, after bumper crops of peas and two kinds of beans, before you reach the peaches and plums, with tomatoes on the way, there is far too little space for new entrants. Serves me right.

It was funny seeing Michael Wickenden with you, when we visited. He's never been to Dixter. Says it'll have to be the winter, but it would be so much more fun now. Ah well. I can see how he's tied. So was I, at his age, when I was doing most of the propagating.

My South African trip is off. No sponsor forthcoming to get me there and back business class, and I do, at my age and liable to cramp as I am, insist on that. It is a disappointment, especially as the wild flowers in Namaqualand are said to be especially plentiful, after good rains, this year. I was prepared to give my lectures for free and to write in three much-read publications about the trip, but the South African tourist board seems to be less well organized than most and there is no tradition of visiting lecturers, as in the USA, New Zealand and Australia. I shall not get bored, here, you may be sure.

Christo

PS I nearly forgot to tell you that on the *Makropulos* evening at Glyndebourne, we found ourselves picnicking next to Germaine Greer and a friend, who were next to the ha-ha. I wouldn't have known her but my young friends, who see TV, spotted her, so I went over and introduced myself, and was myself introduced to the friend as 'the greatest gardener in the world after Beth Chatto'. Of course I graciously accepted my position but couldn't, as on many other occasions, help wondering at the way people regard life as a sort of competition. Understandable when you're young, perhaps, but after that . . .

The friend was wearing a flashy necklace that appealed to me; I think she would like our Exotic Garden. I invited them to Dixter and Ms Greer suggested that they bring you over to lunch, which sounded an excellent plan, to me. I do hope she will follow it through, and soon. She has fine eyes, which it was a pleasure to meet.

An hour ago – it is now 7.30am – I went into the old rose garden and my attention was called to a nuthatch, calling from the hovel roof. It then flew down on to the stem of one of our tallest cannas, where it fidgeted around as nuthatches do, before heading for the orchard. I liked the linking of home (nuthatch) and abroad (canna).

I prop open the door on to the terrace, early, these days, and the smells of cut grass and of the myrtle waft through the house. The myrtle is flowering extremely well, this year. I fear for it when Phase Three of the building works starts, once we're closed to the public. The scene of operations will be the Great Hall, and poor myrtle is bang in front of it.

– ❦ –

Sunday 17 (not sent till Thursday 21) August

Dear Christo,

It is early Sunday morning, the air cool and fresh on the terrace beneath the magnolia tree where I sit, the grass below me still wet with dew. Soon the sun will have sucked dry every thirsty leaf, and the garden will endure another day of great heat. I have just eaten a bowl of fresh raspberries, picked half an hour ago. It felt like going into a cool shower as I pushed among the canes heavy with dew, my arms and legs drenched as I filled a bowl with 'Autumn Bliss'. I am attempting to write this outside, but there are so many irresistible distractions I shall probably have to go back to my table indoors where I can see but shut my ears to the wildlife. Blackbirds and thrushes are silent now, but several little birds, including wrens, still twitter ecstatically from among the trees and shrubs which screen us from the visitors passing by the ponds. The sleepy sound of pigeons and doves can be very evocative of lazy summer afternoons, but there are times when we could shoot them! We have had several pairs nesting around the garden. We know all their themes and variations by heart. The pretty white collared dove (which arrived from the Continent several years ago and now is an all-year-round resident) sits on the roof above us calling out 'For God's sake, for God's sake', three flute-like notes rising and falling, before fluttering down agitatedly, because we are sitting there, to sip water delicately from the large pottery saucer I bought at a roadside garden shop when last I stayed with you at Dixter.

My last letter to you was written 6 July. Shame on me to have let most of July and half of August slip away so quickly! But these weeks have been so full of happenings I have difficulty in keeping up. The whole summer has felt like that. No sooner do we start a new month than we are writing the date in double figures – and next day is the end of the month! Sometimes I am glad to take round a party to discover a new scene, which has suddenly come into bloom, which I might well have missed. I am thankful to be taken away from my desk, or general administration of house and garden.

All of which must tell you I am much more myself, for time hangs heavily on those who are imprisoned or sick. I have much more energy, and have even put on a few pounds' weight after sticking at 7.5 stone (47.6kg) for weeks. That was the best anniversary present I could have had, to find I was not still getting scraggier; 7 August was our 54th wedding anniversary (and the day you had invited me to Glyndebourne). We celebrated quietly with Diana and Mary, Andrew now very exhausted by his condition which is aggravated during the very humid days so he can hardly speak. He is a little better when the air is fresher. But only this week he was suddenly taken by surprise. Coming across a visitor in the house, he could not get his breath to utter a word and was very embarrassed, poor dear, by his apparent lack of good manners.

But anyone can see his predicament – and I soon had him resting on his bed.

Well now, what happened in July? Oh yes, three friends from East Sussex came for the day. They arrived just as I had finished taking a party through the garden. Although it seems ages ago now, it was a treat to have you, Fergus and Ken Rawson, and a relief for me to see the garden still benefited from the rain we had in June. Including the first week of July we had 155mm (6in), the most ever for that vital time of year. It fell in gentle stages, so much of it benefited the plants. The results have been extraordinary, combined with high temperatures, the growth on most plants, trees and shrubs has been remarkable.

Wasn't it a strange coincidence that Michael Wickenden was here the same day as you? He had arrived unexpectedly with one of his students the night before. Sally kindly invited them to share the caravan with her. Last year she spent a few weeks in Michael's nursery in Scotland, so they are good friends. It was a pleasure to have you all sitting together under the magnolia tree, with Andrew too for a short while, but I was having too many treats on the same day! – and was grateful Sally was able to show Michael the garden as well as I could, since she has come to know it very well.

It is always fun to see the garden through your eyes, being teased as ever, over some of my plantings. I don't mind that. Sometimes I agree with you – sometimes I don't. That's OK. But we both know so well that what we do, or haven't done, could be improved if we could make time, at the right time, to plan even minor alterations, not to mention major ones. David and I have been saying for weeks we must spend a day together with notepads and pens, while we can still see the faults. It hasn't happened yet!

We have had several day schools, who stay all day. David, Debbie and Emily are now taking part in these events, helping to give everyone more attention while they absorb some of my tales of how and why we have made the garden, so they will be able to carry on when I am unable to do so. I have to admit, so long as I am fit and well, I enjoy my visitors, and often feel revitalized by a group who I can quickly tell are genuine gardeners. As they file off the coach in their sunhats, you might sometimes think they had come for the ride and a nice sit down, with a good cup of tea, but within a few minutes I can pick out the lively faces and am happy to invite them to entertain me with their questions and comments.

Steffi, our German student, left at the end of July to go back to Laufen and replant a field of peonies. We all became very fond of her. Before she left she had several members of staff potting alongside her, for an hour at a time, to get the feel and rhythm of potting the way I was first shown by Helen von Stein Zeppelin. It is not only quicker, it is less tiring, since you learn to reduce the number of movements to a minimum. 'She was so nice, she didn't show us up, make us feel small,' I was told. High praise from East Anglians who are as a race, to this day, nervous of invaders.

3.00pm Sunday afternoon
At this point I am feeling distinctly nervous and cross with our neighbouring farmer, who, having been bought out of fruit by Brussels, now has his land managed by someone else. Together they have, unfortunately, a right of way through my Wood Garden, to reach 10 acres of land which originally belonged to Andrew. We have erected rabbit netting and gates bearing notices 'To be kept closed at all times'. Hearing harvesting machines I have just been out to find all gates wide open on to my land, knowing there are at least 50 rabbits in their field. My staff comment every day as they drive to and from work, seeing the rabbits rush ahead of them across the road leading to our nursery and garden gates. This has happened so many times. I feel like Canute, trying to stem the flood of rabbits surging into the garden. What to do? Sell up in despair! I think not, although sometimes I feel that way. But I think I need to consult my solicitor in the morning to see if there is any way I can be protected from this kind of problem. Meanwhile I must calm down, think of Dixter, and try to finish this letter. (I've just

remembered, tomorrow Rosie Atkins is coming to lunch to write a profile of me. Which me?)

Let's go to the vegetable garden for a bit of peace. There is still the most wonderful scent of sweet peas on one side and 'Baron Solemacher' strawberries smelling like strawberry jam on this hot, humid air. There is less green salad to give away now, but loads of cucumbers and courgettes. Some cucumbers I juice to make a very pleasant chilled drink. After a slow start when it was so cold in June, the tomato house now looks and feels like a tropical jungle, loaded with trusses of 'Gardener's Delight' and 'Sungold'. Soon we shall be freezing them, as raw pulp. We had enough last year to use potfuls freely until the new crop was ripening. Peas and beans were frozen in July. Runner beans just taste of water, I think, after freezing, so I don't bother, but last evening we ate the first pick of the violet-coloured, silky textured runner beans. They are my favourites, just need topping and tailing, and are steamed whole.

Last week Michael Burge (Australian) and his team, Alan, the cameraman (English) and Susan (American), came to finish the last pictures and recordings for the video they have been filming since last September, showing how the nursery and garden are vital to each other throughout the year. It was a day's work for me this time, to sit talking to the camera, to provide voice-overs for any of the activities filmed without speech being recorded at the time. It was a nerve-racking day, since, as so often, it was a tiresomely windy day, lots of noise of leaves rattling – as well as stopping for planes going over, or lorries reversing far away and making that horrible warning shriek. However Susan knew how to cope with all this, and had appropriate equipment to cut out the wind, so they appeared satisfied with the day's work. David and I have been left with a video machine, to stop and start the tapes, so we can provide Latin names – and correct spelling.

My other big project is planning our new Tea House. Many years ago Graham S. Thomas, while staying here for the night, begged me not to consider such a thing. 'You will change the whole atmosphere, the type of people who come here,' he said. He was probably right at the time, while I certainly was not in any way able to consider the matter seriously. But times and circumstances change. Many more people new to gardening, yet keen to learn, now expect some comfort and hospitality, since it is what they find in most garden centres, stately homes and at other rural activities. Although not overwhelmed by complaints, I do take note of those who write glowingly about the gardens, but are scathing about our lack of civilized facilities. I know we need more loos – it is horrible to have to queue after a long coach trip, and a decent cup of tea would be welcome. This subject has been the topic of long and heart-searching discussion between myself and staff now for more than a year. It would, they say, be very helpful if visitors had somewhere comfortable to sit, out of the cold, the heat, or the rain, to spend a little longer here and be able to glance through their catalogues before a long journey home.

Last winter, through various channels, I met some architects, and finally chose one to develop some ideas further. He is Brian Haward, from Southwold, who with his son Nick, a trained architect but a practical man on site as well, will together be responsible for this scheme which I still find awesome, but begins to excite me with possibilities. Brian and Nick are both very aware of the surroundings here, of the need for the building to keep a low profile, yet at the same time the need to create something which will improve our setting, as well as diving into all the practical pros and cons of our daily activities. We have had several meetings after David, Keith and I had submitted our ideas of what we needed. The initial routine plans were surprisingly close to our requirements, but some simplification was needed and more wall space than glass, for plants and people to shelter – although it is important to have enough windows to be able to view the Gravel Garden on one side, the nursery on the other.

This coming week I go to Southwold to meet Mary and together discuss the newly drawn plans which should arrive here any day now.

Overall the plans will include, for planning permission, a new layout of our working premises so that eventually present wasted space can be used more efficiently. If it all sounds alarming I can tell you it is, but I often think of you responsible for the upkeep of the fabric of a great historic building – and know I must have the courage to go on, to take my nursery and garden as a viable whole into the 21st century.

I've hardly written a word about the plants and there is enough to fill a book out there in the garden; yet what visitors see, here, or at Dixter, is only a fragment of the organization and effort needed throughout a lifetime to keep it going. In one year, in six months even, my garden and nursery could become a wilderness again.

After four weeks now with no measurable rain, and temperatures between 25–30°C (77–86°F) – much more in the sun – the Gravel Garden has not collapsed but I almost spat blood to hear of places scarcely a mile away having a downpour one late evening recently, while we received the dregs of the storm. Large drops fell on the paving below my bedroom window where I could count them like spots on a Dalmatian dog. Nothing more. Every day we might have a thunderstorm.

As I walk across the gravel, the air all around me is still and heavy, colours fading. Outstanding are the straw-coloured plumes of *Stipa tenuissima*, while tall and impressive clumps of the golden oat grass, *Stipa gigantea*, catch the light, especially when seen in a void, illuminating the scene like tall standard lamps, as the colour of verbenas, origanums and catmint slowly drains away in the scorching heat. *Calamagrostis* 'Karl Foerster' makes elegant columns of leaf and stems bearing buff, slender heads while the arching plumes of *Stipa* (or is it *Achnatherum?*) *calamagrostis* intertwine with the lavender-coloured flowering shoots of Russian sage. Early morning or late evening is best to see the light shining through the transparent sickle-shaped pods of *Colutea arborescens*, the bladder senna, still carrying small burnt-orange pea flowers on its tip shoots. Branches of these seed pods picked now and dried make very attractive and unusual additions to dried arrangements.

Ballotas and santolinas were cut back in July – a painful job when they are only just past their best, but it needs to be done to encourage them to make close-knit mounds for the winter. Helianthemums hard pruned just before you came have, with the June rain, put on plenty of fresh growth, and now almost cover their allotted spaces. There should be signs of stress – some plants do wilt in self-defence in the hottest part of the day, but early morning, dew-covered now, they recover amazingly well. The only thoroughly 'dead-looking' plant, totally brown now, is the carpeting *Leptinella potentillina*, but we know that will return. Coming through it is a low-sprawling campion, *Silene* 'Max Frei', with angular, branching stems holding large trusses of rose-pink flowers. It looks as fresh as paint, but cannot be sent through the post, such brittle stems easily break, and although we know the plant itself will survive, the recipient can't believe that, and demands a refund, or replacement.

Now can you help me? How is your *Cotinus coggygria* from Pamela Milburne? Does it get a wilting disease? Part of mine is dying back badly from the tips – it could be drought, but it hasn't happened before, and nothing else around it appears distressed. David and I are both concerned, but have cut the worst bits back and hope it will go no further.

Thursday 21 August
Your letter, dated 19th August has just arrived. Already another week almost gone, accelerated by meeting our solicitor to see if there is any amicable way, as neighbours, the rabbit problem could be tackled, visiting my architect in Southwold and passing his plans for our Tea House preparatory to getting planning permission (we might not – what then?), and finding this morning I could now pick a bushel of slender purple beans, all at their best! Shall I freeze some, give the rest away?

I have just taken a break and enjoyed your letter, especially the bit about the toad. I've never seen one here (there are thousands in the marshland around Southwold, Mary always had them in her garden), but we do see frogs in the garden, especially now in the Sales Area where the pots are irrigated every night.

If only I could stay now, to reply to your letter, and tell you of some of the good things I had to leave out in this letter, though for us and the garden this long period, a month now, of dust and heat, has become very wearing.

With love to you all, Beth.

—⚘—

Friday 29 August

Dear Christo,

At last, a month of drought has been broken by ragged fringes of storm skirting around us. Andrew and I sat by the glass doors of our sitting room, looking on to the south-facing terrace, hoping the damp patches on the paving would become shallow, plopping puddles and then rivulets running down the steps on to the grass below. Then without warning, a heavy downpour fell out of the black sky and rattled hard on the roof long enough to cascade over the gutters like waterfalls, lasting perhaps a quarter of an hour. It was wonderful to open the doors, hear the clatter on the magnolia leaves, touch and smell the wet. To our relief the rain clouds hung around for a further 24 hours, releasing gentle steady rain amounting to 40mm (1½in). As it fell on to toast-warm soil the atmosphere outside suddenly became like the inside of a mist-propagation unit, you could almost watch new growth emerging. The dried-up *Leptinella potentillina* I wrote about in my last letter produced fresh fern-like leaves pressed flat to the gravel within a couple of days.

Have I mentioned before another carpeting plant, *Phyla nodiflora*? It behaves so well in the Gravel Garden, never showing distress in dry times. For weeks now it has sparkled with life, despite the dry heat, its carpets of prostrate stems smothered in tight clusters of little pink flower heads above grey-green leaves. It is related to the woody shrub *Aloysia triphylla* (known as lemon verbena). The individual flower shapes of the phylla are identical to those of aloysia, although on the shrub the flowers are carried in long, rat-tail racemes.

Before I start rambling round the garden with you in mind I must take a look at your last letter (we crossed in the post). Ah yes, the encounter at Glyndebourne with Dr Greer. Dear me, I thought, here is my dear Germaine, putting her foot in with both hands, but then laughed with relief at your 'gracious acceptance' of her *faux pas*. I love the idea of having lunch with you and Germaine if she would not mind picking me up – but on second thoughts I'm very uncertain just now if I could manage to come. Andrew has been very poorly this week, much more breathless than usual. It is with difficulty now that he can cross the room. The least effort leaves him gasping for breath, although when he is settled again in his chair he becomes easier. I will telephone you later to tell you if he recovers from this phase. Going back to comparisons which we both find embarrassing, I too have no wish to be weighed in the balance. Why bother to compare gardeners any more than musicians or painters? I think visiting good gardens, large or small, could be on a par with looking round an art gallery. Some works you like, some you may heartily dislike. Sometimes works you could not immediately relate to, stay with you and later, much later perhaps, you become aware that your focus has shifted, you have a fresh point of view. Recently I listened to and watched a Promenade Concert on the television. During the interval after Rachmaninov's 2nd Piano Concerto, played by a square-faced young Russian who looked more like a rugger player than the supremely musical pianist he is, we were given a talk on Bartók's *The Miraculous Mandarin*. I don't always find Bartók comfortable to listen to but was held by the interpretation of this extraordinary decadent work, illustrated by Simon Boughton with piano and cartoons. So I stayed to listen to the performance, played by the Concertgebouw Orchestra graphically conducted by Riccardo Chailly, and became absorbed by the strangely colourful sound. It helps me with such music to have some visual aid, to watch the different instruments – or to see the opera, as I have seen and enjoyed Janáček previously with you. I hope that most visitors to our gardens, yours and mine, enjoy them because they are different. As my old friend (and least competitive of men) the late Sir Cedric Morris said here one day, we may all use the same palette, but we all paint different pictures.

Incidentally I loved your picture of the toad sitting under the drip from the leaf-tip of an aroid – something magical that happens perhaps once in a lifetime, like the evening Andrew and I stood on one of the nursery paths, and a baby hedgehog came purposefully towards us and, finding my feet in the way, stumbled unconsciously over them. Like you and Anne Wambach we held our breath.

Before the drought was broken I drove one morning to Southwold to meet Mary at our architect's office, to see and approve the final outline plan for our new building project. Although we do not yet have planning permission, or any costing(!) I am already becoming excited at the prospect of planting, both inside and around it. The south-facing wall will be home for *Solanum crispum* 'Glasnevin' and *Solanum jasminoides* 'Album', with *Tropaeolum tricolorum* swimming among the blue flowers of *Teucrium fruticans*, as I used to have years ago, and a woody zauschneria, new to me, growing now in the propagating house. It was sent me from Los Gatos, California, by Ed Carman. Some years ago I stayed with him and his wife Jean after giving a talk in San Francisco. Practically single-handed he runs a fascinating nursery full of unusual plants. He made time to take me out to see hummingbirds feeding and later encouraged me to make a pig of myself in a real ice-cream parlour. To go back to Ed's zauschneria, still in a one-litre (2-pint) pot, it now hangs like a shawl from bench to floor. It is a woody plant, smothered in felty leaves, and large, light orange, trumpet-shaped flowers, paler than *Z. californica* which is a much smaller plant. I am going round the nursery collecting up newcomers which need re-potting ready for the new plantings we have in mind.

Before meeting Mary in Southwold, I delivered to her house about eight bin liners filled with bits and pieces for two large church window-sills she had been asked to decorate with green arrangements. I stretched that definition a bit as Emily and I, the day before, had picked and soaked well in large buckets as varied a mix of shapes and shades as we could find. After four weeks without rain, and temperatures of 25–30°C (77–86°F), we were thankful to find tall, pleated leaves of *Crocosmia* 'Lucifer' together with its curving green seed heads, arching stems of Solomon's seal, still good in the Wood Garden, tall flowering stems of silver-grey *Artemisia ludoviciana* var. *incompta*, and metallic, spiky stems of *Eryngium variifolium*. For background cover there were branches of fresh laurel and large bergenia leaves. To pull it all together and provide lighter colour we picked lime-green heads of *Euphorbia seguieriana* subsp. *niciciana*, apple-green mop caps of *Hydrangea arborescens* subsp. *discolor* 'Sterilis', transparent pods of senna (*Colutea arborescens*), and finally, greenish-white heads of *Sedum spectabile* 'Iceberg'. I think Mary had fun using these. It was interesting too, to see Emily and Moira pick and arrange quite a different range of plant material than they usually choose, to decorate the packing house for the day school which came later in the week.

The sweetcorn has not been so impressive as last year, damaged earlier in the season I think, by the mulch of straw I put round the plants. I was puzzled by the unhealthy look of the leaves, striped yellow; then suddenly it came to me, the straw was probably sprayed before cutting with something disagreeable. Keith raked it off and spread a layer of compost instead, which encouraged fresh green foliage, but the plants never made the growth of last year. However, I have been able to freeze about 30 well-filled cobs; frozen immediately after picking they retain a honey sweetness. Another blunder has been the leeks. I sowed them too early, so they stayed too long in the seed row before transplanting because there was no empty space to plant them. Now many are throwing a flower stem. I cut them off as soon as I spot them, hoping a long, damp autumn might encourage a second 'tiller'. I wonder! Unlikely, I fear.

Saturday evening 30 August

I have just been walking in the Wood Garden. You might not expect there to be much interest there at this time of year, a fairly monotonous tapestry of green once the overhead canopy has cast shade over much of the area. Yet I am always pleasantly surprised by the various effects I find there, quite apart from the tranquil atmosphere. I came across the lovely white-flowered *Fuchsia* 'Hawkshead'. Do you remember the eye-catching plants we saw of it in the Logan Gardens, Scotland, several years ago? My young plants are established now in partly shaded places in the Wood Garden, the narrow, pointed sepals tipped with green, making me think of elegant, painted fingernails. Elsewhere we have a form we originally named a *Fuchsia magellanica* var. *molinae* 'Alba'. It must be 20 years ago now, forming an important feature this time of the year, on the corner of a mixed border, about 1.5m (5ft) tall and 2m (6½ft) across, arching over with thousands of slender, shell-pink flower sepals, enclosing faintly lilac 'petticoats' from which protrude long cream anthers and stamens. I love several other varieties of this fuchsia, among them the yellow-leaved forms, and especially *F. m.* 'Versicolor'. Last year I planted this on the south wall of the house (partially shaded by the big magnolia), at the foot of *Clematis* 'Prince Charles', which I'd forgotten and you named for me a few weeks ago when you saw it in full flower. I enjoy this clematis for its long flowering season and for its nodding light blue flowers. This summer the fuchsia has reached almost 2.5m (8ft) tangling among the last flowers and seed heads of the clematis. It cascades away from the white painted wall, its slender, arching stems covered with pretty, pointed leaves suffused with pink and cream on grey-green, dripping with long tassels of cherry-coloured flowers revealing a glimpse of violet 'petticoats'.

Back to the Wood Garden, *Heuchera villosa* usefully creates a spring-like effect now with fresh green, maple-shaped leaves setting off long, narrow heads of greenish-white flowers held in tiers, creating a lacy effect, good contrast for the dark, holly-green leaves of *Helleborus foetidus* seeded near by. Scarlet bunches of *Arum italicum* berries catch my eye, until the ducks find them, growing through green carpets of *Tiarella cordifolia*, the small-leaved periwinkles, or the white-flowered form of herb Robert, *Geranium robertianum* 'Album' which still has a sprinkling of little white stars. Fat clumps of *Cyclamen hederifolium*, in shades of pink and white, repeat at ground level, tall colonies of Japanese anemones disappearing among the tree trunks, in company with ferns and hostas. Early evening sunlight slants through some plants, leaving others in dim shadow. Too much spotlighting in August, when the temperatures read in the 30s°C (high 80s°F) in the shade burnt brown some of the beautiful green heads of *Hydrangea arborescens* subsp. *discolor* 'Sterilis'. Fortunately most were shaded so we can still enjoy them, and have hung up others for dried arrangements.

Apart from these precious plants flowering now at the back end of the season, I enjoy all the contrasting shapes and shades of leaves which cover the soil in shady areas. Among several ferns, including the simple, shapely hart's tongue, probably the most long-suffering and enduring is *Dryopteris filix-mas*, the male fern, while *Dryopteris wallichiana* could be one of the the most elegant, contrasting with a colony of specially bold-leaved lily-of-the-valley (*Convallaria majalis* 'Hardwick Hall'), with silver- and gold-leaved forms of *Lamium maculatum*, slate-purple leaves of *Viola riviniana* Purpurea Group and trails of yellow-leaved creeping Jenny.

As I turned to look back into the wood before leaving, I could not help giving a gasp of delight, as I do every year at this time, to see the drifts and bunches of colchicum, edging the winding walkways, half hiding beneath shrubs. There are now so many to choose from, giving us a season of many weeks, from August well into October. They come in varying shades of rosy-mauve, in various sizes, from the tiny species *Colchicum corsicum*, which we collected in Corsica 40 years ago and have only recently lost through renovations I'm ashamed to say, to large-cupped blossoms which could hold half a pint if you stuck their petals together! One of the showiest just now is *Colchicum byzantinum*. When established it produces clusters of light cyclamen-pink, narrow-petalled flowers which open flat, like stars. *C. parnassicum* (ex *laetum*) and C. 'Lilac Wonder' are similar in shape but with deeper colouring. These have been out for some time. Just emerging now is *Colchicum* 'Rosy Dawn', with large goblet-shaped flowers composed of faintly tessellated segments, chequered colouring, as in *Fritillaria meleagris*, rich, purplish-pink bleaching into a white throat. Several years ago I rescued a tray of remnants, all tiny or broken bulbs from the nursery potting shed, which now are creating brilliant patches of colour, planted among carpets of *Geranium macrorrhizum*, in bays between the shrubs, along the car park entrance, having made up well with a little care and even less attention.

This year, thanks to the rain in June, *Rosa rugosa*, along this car park border, has produced good-quality hips, shining scarlet and round like small tomatoes. I hope to find time to pick some to make rosehip syrup, flavoured perhaps with elderflower syrup already in the freezer.

Last Sunday I woke early as usual, but snuggled down again to plan my day, this special day of the week, when the garden and nursery are silent and still. I looked forward to picking raspberries and freezing them; perhaps putting purple basil leaves into jars of oil to steep in the sun, ready for winter salads. I turned on my bedside radio expecting to hear the weather report. Instead the newsreader was speaking in the past tense of a princess. Who was she? What had happened? My mind spun round until it had to accept he was speaking of Princess Diana. She had been killed with her friend, Dodi Fayed, and driver in a car accident in Paris. I felt stunned.

Why such a strong reaction, you might be asking. How many other young people were killed in car accidents alone that same day, leaving desolate families and friends? I shall get bogged down with platitudes if I'm not careful. So much has been written and said over the past week, and will go on it seems, *ad infinitum*, but beneath it all there is, I believe, a genuine feeling of loss, of great sadness for the waste of all bright young lives prematurely cut down, but saddest of all this week has been the inevitability of a tragic ending.

Goodnight dear Christo, Beth

— ❧ —

Monday 8 September

Dear Beth,

Our last letters pretty well collided, so here goes with another. Lovely, lovely weather and I can still have the door open into the garden and feel really warm, though it is near to sunset.

We have had a TV team here all today, as part of a series. This must be the sixth time, or so. They're very conscientious and are coming again in a week's time just to catch up on plants mentioned in the interview. It's a mini-series for *Gardeners' World*, to go out next year, either with a series of small slots in that programme or (and this is our hope) in one whole programme, with all the items used to show how we change during the growing season.

Stephen Lacey was the interviewer and stayed here last night. His ideas on colour combinations are very subtle – so much so that when he appreciates the juxtaposition of two plants in the garden,

I not only haven't planned it but can't even appreciate the merit of what he's seen when it's pointed out to me.

I said how seldom you see blue agapanthus effectively used in gardens. It's usually an unsupported feature. I'm trying to grow a late-flowering one with a late, orange crocosmia. I think it'll work when the agapanthus are a bit more numerous. I asked him how he would use them. With the Russian sage, *Perovskia atriplicifolia*, he said. Well, that's blue itself and wouldn't highlight the agapanthus in any way. It seems to me that a companion of almost any other colour would be preferable.

Now, it is early autumn at its best and we (Fergie and I) are proud of the way we're looking. I just hope the Indian summer will last a little longer. It is quite an amazing season, with so many perennials flowering freely a second time. Border phloxes are particularly generous. *Buddleja* 'Dartmoor' is having a second go, too. The old trusses have blackened but don't look too bad at all and the new blossom is among them.

In the Exotic Garden, we now have three *Yucca gloriosa* candelabra, in various stages of flowering or being about to flower. The plants that invariably appeal to the public's fancy, more than any other, are the two *Paulownia tomentosa* that you gave me as seedlings. I regularly stool them, almost to the ground, each spring, so they produce enormous leaves (now already withering from the bottom up). I tell the enquirers how easy this is to do, that they are hardy and that they, the enquirers, could perfectly well grow them in their own front gardens, but they seem uninterested in that possibility.

We've done a piece of bedding that is experimental, so I'm watching it to see whether the effect will be as I imagined it. Although *Limonium sinuatum*, known as statice, is commonly grown for drying, it is a good border annual if you choose varieties that are not too coarse, with overblown, winged stems. Such is 'Pastel Shades', but the shades are all pink and mauve. So we've added into this mixture another of similar habit, called

'Moonlight', which is pale yellow. The result still looks a little flat and weak to me, so we have interplanted with all the spare stock we could muster of the South African bulb, *Nerine bowdenii*, which is a very strong shade of pink! The nerines are just throwing up their flower buds.

The autumn-flowering bulbs are early, incidentally, and I'm sure this is because of the rains we've had, breaking their dormancy and starting them (and the little *Cyclamen hederifolium*) off. We already have some *Crocus speciosus* in flower by the Horse Pond, and before we have cut the long grass there. We're at that, now.

Going back to limoniums, for a moment, their white, funnel-shaped corollas, which are not everlasting or papery at all, are charming, it seems to me, and at the stage when they are flowering, popular with butterflies.

Fergus is very tied up with preparations for a course we are running all next week for a dozen Americans (advertised in their magazine, *Horticulture*), who are coming over to do and learn about hands-on gardening and how things are organized in a garden such as this. Each day will be spent in a different part of the garden. There are ten women and two men. They'll be staying in Rye and have a minibus to ferry them. I do hope it goes well and that the weather holds. I shall back Fergus up all I can, but he's at the heart of it all. It's difficult to get practical training, in America, and becoming less easy even here, with many young horticulturists wanting administrative or design jobs, which are comfortable and well paid. That's not Fergus's form, at all.

Thank you for your long and meaty letter. I appreciate your apprehension over the approaching building works. Also the necessity of various rather boring but necessary extras like loos. We are planning to add to our quota of these too and it will necessitate keying into the public sewerage system at some distance, as the present loos belong to my sister-in-law (they are leased to us) and she doesn't want any extras in her sewerage system. There is also the question of whether we should go on to the public water supply, while we are about it, and have an open trench that could take both. Personally, I like our own water, pumped up from our own deep bore and free of chlorine, but it is too rich in manganese, which isn't harmful but tends to cloud the supply and we're not allowed to use it to make tea for the public (nor even to wash up in it, for them). All very tedious, expensive but non-ignorable.

Talking of tomatoes, which you grow under cover but we grow only outside, we face different problems. You put me on to 'Sungold', which is the best flavoured I have met in this country. It may not be quite as free as 'Gardener's Delight'; this you also grow but I have given up, because 'Sungold', albeit a little less prolific, has a slightly larger fruit, which means a better ratio of pulp to skin and also less skin to scald off, if you need to. And there is the flavour. I'm growing two larger-fruited varieties, but the bane of our life (which doesn't affect you under polythene) has arrived – blight, caught from the potatoes. This despite our having sprayed weekly with a copper fungicide. We shall have to go over to a systemic fungicide and hope to do better with that next year.

Re *Cotinus* and die-back: this genus is well known to be subject to verticillium wilt. We lost one to it in the Long Border, the year before last. So I hope you have a spare to grow in soil elsewhere.

My business manager, Andrew Trump, left at the end of last month after three months' notice. I told him he must find his replacement and he narrowed the applicants down to four. We have now appointed an excellent young woman, Elaine Francis. One of our guides – all female – expressed surprise that I had appointed a woman. I couldn't see that sex should have anything to do with this. Andrew has been with us for three years and clearly wants a change to chime in with his forthcoming marriage next year, and to allow him to be, if possible, closer to his fiancée. I don't know that he has found anything yet.

He had three farewell parties, the last of them given by himself from Dixter. Clearly, he had planned this while thinking I should be in South Africa. Well, I was at the party instead! But I retired to bed long before it was over.

Enough for now, dear Beth. I am being visited by Rosemary Verey and Rupert Golby (who won the gold medal for his garden design for *Country Life* at Chelsea) tomorrow morning. The next two days are being more or less disrupted by more TV for the programme called *Garden Party*. I never see these things unless I've taken part in them and then I go down to Perry's cottage to look in on their set.

— ❧ —

Monday 22 September

Dear Christo,

Despite no measurable rain since the end of August, the garden has come to life in these past three weeks of warm sun, heavy dews and heavenly skies, often deep blue filled with mountainous white clouds. Too much wind as usual of course, but little damage done as yet. Wait for the equinoctial gales, when we expect to see brittle-boned trees like paulownia shedding great limbs.

Re-reading your last letter reminds me I wanted to ask if you had either *Agapanthus* 'Albatross' or *A.* 'Blue Moon'. As you say agapanthus need careful placing: to stand well clear so their whole form, head, stems and leaf clusters can be appreciated. James Russell gave me *A.* 'Albatross' when he was growing it outside under a wall at Castle Howard, York, so I think it would survive at Dixter. Ours are still in large tubs, placed between a row of seats on the nursery backing on to the Shade House. This year they flowered well, huge, globular heads, almost 30cm (1ft) across, of large, white, funnel-shaped flowers, each globe made of differing length stems, giving a lighter, more lacy effect. When they were at their best I happened to see the seats filled with elderly visitors whose white cropped or curly heads, poised on the same level as the agapanthus, contrasted, to my mind, in an amusingly endearing way. *A.* 'Blue Moon' (an old hybrid I had originally from Eric Smith), has the advantage of being latest to flower and is still showing a little of its pale-blue flowers, but it forms the normal solid head of flower, impressively large on stout stems 60cm (2ft) high, and quite hardy with us – might be good in your Exotic Garden.

I sympathize with your sewerage problem, and all the worry and cost involved. Several years ago we were obliged to install machinery and all the underground pipework necessary to pump our effluent about half a mile back towards the village pumping station. So far we have had no serious troubles, but the underground pumps have to be regularly checked by Keith, and every six months by Anglian Pumping Services.

Much more fun to read was the news that you and Dixter will be shown on TV on *Garden Party*. Seeing it advertised for last Friday I sat all excited to watch it, but found myself puzzled by something very different, another garden based on inanimate design, without, I felt, either the plants or the sculptures feeling comfortable together. Separately, I think, there were some interesting ideas, but one needs to consider the effect of man-made objects all the year round. Some of this designer's garden might look better in winter – who knows? It would be unfair to make a judgement without seeing the actual garden for oneself.

Here at the moment, grasses are as eye-catching as any sculpture in my opinion, despite jewels of colour dotted about everywhere; either true autumn flowerers, or second crops of mid-summer flowerers, like the hardy geraniums, catmints and *Gaura lindheimeri*, a star in the Gravel Garden with its never-ending flights of white flowers. It has taken several years for me to build up my collection of grasses, to place them in the garden to their advantage and then wait for them to bulk up, to show themselves at their best.

In the Gravel Garden *Stipa* (*Achnatherum*) *calamagrostis* has arching, feathery heads, shining green when fresh, fading to soft-fawn as they dry. Since they continuously send up new flower stems, all stages contribute to the overall effect of light and warmth as the massed stems gently sway above the carpet of bergenia leaves beneath them, contrasting with deep rose heads of *Sedum* 'Matrona', all backed by the rich plum foliage of *Berberis* x *ottawensis*.

Poa labillardierei is also well designed for dry conditions. It makes a neat tussock of tough, grey-green leaves which roll into thin wires to conserve moisture. Above them a shower of filmy flower heads are produced indefatigably throughout summer so that now we have a fan-shaped haze composed of countless stems, and delicate flower heads, all bleached straw-coloured; they shimmer in low sunlight above drifts of purple colchicums nestling in carpets of *Geranium macrorrhizum*. Elsewhere in the garden, this diaphanous shape is outlined against a huge *Phormium tenax*, both similar in outline, fan-shaped, but diametrically opposed in texture.

This spring David planted *Oryzopsis miliacea* in the Gravel Garden. I wish it had a less awkward name because it has made such a lovely feature on a corner that I go out to look at it at all times of the day but still can't remember the name! Like most grasses it looks best in a void, surrounded by plants lower than itself so its exquisitely dainty heads on 1–1.5m (3–5ft) stems have no interruption. Our plant is surrounded by thymes and low mounds of santolina while green seed heads of an agapanthus add a suitable touch of solidarity.

Nearby a good 'lemon peel' form of *Clematis orientalis* (*C. tibetana vernayi*) has seeded itself, now clambering over a large cistus, its second crop of flowers picking up the colour of late-flowering *Spartium junceum*. Have you noticed how strongly perfumed is this Spanish broom? Such a rich, heady scent on a still, warm morning. I can't say I had noticed it before. Too often we travel too fast, too busy to make time to stop and stare and sniff.

The caryopteris bushes have put their feet well down into the gravel soil, finding enough moisture to have made huge billowing shrubs now, loaded with blue blossom, lovely with tall, purple wands of *Verbena bonariensis*, all fringed at the gravel path edge with low-growing *Calamintha nepetoides* humming with bees.

We seem to be making a collection of different forms of achnatherum or stipa. I came recently across a batch of newcomers on the nursery stock bed, obviously being tried out by David. I look forward to writing them up when they are more mature, but among others we grow in the garden, one of the most attractive just now is *Stipa (Achnatherum) brachytricha*. Still with fresh green basal leaves it has stiffly upright flower stems 1–1.5m (3–5ft) carrying narrow, pyramidal flower heads, like refined bottle-brushes, somewhat pewter-coloured when fresh, grey-green with a touch of mauve; a shape inviting you to enclose it with your hand, to feel its soft texture. Throughout autumn it makes a good vertical above carpets of grey helianthemum or *Stachys byzantina*.

I can't leave out *Pennisetum viridescens*. David has planted this in a 'waste' area where he was determined to try out plants normally verboten in sensible gardens. Backed by the view of the reservoir, framed by oaks, he put in a 'river' of variegated ground elder together with the white-flowered rosebay willowherb. The ground elder still looks dewy fresh, light green leaves boldly edged cream, the rosebay still producing late flowers. To stabilize these rampers David planted among them a group of *Pennisetum viridescens*, so this area which had been poor and neglected now looks attractive, backed with the large-fruited *Euonymus alatus* and the silver filigree leaves of *Rubus thibetanus*. The flower heads of the grass are almost black, dark, caterpillar-like heads, with closely set, green seed cases enclosed in long, almost black hairs which protrude like cats' whiskers, forming a filmy brush or tail more than 5cm (2in) across. Against a mown grass edge these elegant bouquets catch every low shaft of light while their silhouettes are repeated as shadows on the grass carpet.

Stopping to look at the collection of grasses for sale in pots on the nursery I wonder why I haven't yet planted them together as a grass garden, or meadow. Partly because I haven't thought of a suitable place, largely because they can look a mess if not well and carefully groomed. But today my nursery collection looks very attractive all together, tall miscanthus waving shimmering, silky feather dusters, green-and-white striped *Miscanthus sinensis* 'Variegatus' contrasting with the yellow-banded *Miscanthus sinensis* 'Zebrinus', brown and purple rice-like seed cases of *Melica altissima*, pale veils of *Deschampsia cespitosa* 'Goldschleier', dry now, but still effective, tall and short molinias, all attractive in flower, even more so when bleached ivory or gold. Perhaps I should plant them together one day.

Do you have *Lavatera* 'Lilac Lady'? If you feel some of the rosy-pink lavateras a bit overdone – poor plants, it's our fault if we feel that way – then you might like to try it. Just now with renewed growth with cooler weather, all my lavatera make a most welcoming entrance to the garden – as do several bushes I enjoy when I drive through the village. But *Lavatera* 'Lilac Lady' is more upright, with less vigorous growth. Its narrow, maple-shaped leaves are felted grey-green, with smaller, flat-faced flowers about 5cm (2in) across, are translucent, silk-textured and pale lilac-blue, held in upright spires. Last year I was not too impressed, but this second year they have made handsome, shapely bushes, and are still in flower long after the colony of purple atriplex seeded beside them has gone. But I can still watch one here from my window, placed against the pale green 'flames' of a tree heather, *Erica arborea*, whose acid-green young growth will delight us all winter. The effect is cool, restrained.

Thursday 2 September at 8.30am, I made sure to be outside in time to see eight of my men including students transport the framework of my 30-year-old Pratten greenhouse to its new foundations alongside the old Mediterranean Garden, displacing the wall and original little gravel garden I had made there about

15 years ago. Keith and David Plummer had taken out the glass, strengthened the woodwork where necessary and released it from its original base. Supported on four strong wooden poles I watched as the men, well rehearsed beforehand, slowly lifted, moved, backed and forwarded towards the new base, with Emily helping to direct. The operation went perfectly, all men straining with the weight, but they made it without a quiver. I was proud of them.

Now it has all been reassembled, freshly painted and the glass restored. It looks as if it had always stood there, as we were able to retain both ends of the original wall, furnished with vines, cistus and clematis. There is still much to be done and plan. Emily's raised bed of sempervivums which you enjoyed last time had to be taken down in order to move the greenhouse. We need to design a new area to provide accommodation for such plants: plants which can be lost in more general planting. My daughter Diana, whose work involves providing help for handicapped or elderly people suggested more raised beds, in place of the old Mediterranean garden, where people in wheelchairs could more comfortably look round. I like the idea but am not at all certain how to carry it out so that it would integrate with the rest of that part of the garden. This winter we will strip out the centre of the old Med. garden, then perhaps I will be able to visualize how it might look.

Throughout this beautiful month I have been busy preserving fruits, herbs and vegetables. I do enjoy harvesting when there is such a bounty of good things, the sun warm on my back, the scent of late-flowering honeysuckle and roses adding to my pleasure. The *Rosa rugosa* hips have been very good this year, in spite of another dry summer. I suppose they now have their roots well down along the car park boundary border, and the thick mulch of straw must help a bit. Big as small tomatoes, juicy and red – I'm not generous enough to leave them all to the birds, especially as my tomato crop is poor owing to potato blight (ugh!). So I have simmered bowlsful (first cutting off the calyces), then strained through a muslin cloth, sweetened with honey and flavoured with rose-geranium leaves steeped in the syrup overnight. Packed into small plastic pots (crème fraîche holds half a pint or a third of a litre), and stacked in the freezer, it will be delicious in winter in fruit drinks, specially nice in white grape juice, and in fruit salads.

I have also preserved elderberries. As children we had to drink elderberry syrup for colds. So disappointing, not a bit like blackberries. Yet there they hang in such profusion (and blackberries are not good around me this year, the farm hedges slashed to keep headlands free for tractors). Tempted by heavy clusters of elderberries in my little conservation area, I picked a basketful, pulled off all the berries with a fork, pressed them raw through a mouli-sieve, sweetened again with honey and flavoured with rose-geranium. It is quite delicious, a wonderful colour, lots of vitamins for dreary winter evenings! In large coffee jars I packed, washed and dried leaves of basil, covered them with sunflower oil and stood them in the sun for two weeks. Some were also put into white wine vinegar. Both are now strained into bottles, the vinegar which had purple basil leaves is faintly pink, the oils are pale green; all taste strongly of basil. You can buy this ready-made in supermarkets but it is so much more fun to grow the plants and make your own.

Emily and Chrissy have harvested all the gourds and winter squash, some edible, many ornamental, which smother our large compost heaps all summer. They look so attractive, all shapes and sizes, striped, speckled and plain, drying now on pallets placed in the sun. They need several weeks to dry well enough to survive all winter. One variety I have, the fig-leaved gourd, *Curcubita ficifolia*, I grew three years ago, and it still is a perfect specimen, like a fine ceramic. Its dark green skin is marbled with irregular white spots running in vertical lines from stem to base. Inside it has white tasteless flesh and large black seeds. This year I cut open another three-year-old. Its flesh was still fresh and the seeds germinated well.

Moving the greenhouse meant we had to move the pot plants grouped around it, including the nerines. We have a small

collection of these established in pots since they are not all hardy.
There are several shades of pink and white *N. bowdenii* forms,
some tiny, *N. filifolia* and scarlet *N. sarniensis*. Together with pans
of the scarlet-trumpeted *Cyrtanthus* (*Vallota*) *elatus*. Emily grouped
all these under the birch, *Betula pendula* 'Laciniata', which stands
on a little island at the entrance to the house. I can see this gay
group from my kitchen window, and how often visitors stop to
look at it, unexpected as it is to find such a group there! When
the beds around the greenhouse are prepared we will have a long,
warm, west-facing border for such treasures, for eucomis and
tulbaghias and late-flowering *Amaryllis belladonna*, and doubtless
more than enough tender treasures to fit into the space! It's time for
bed. Another day tomorrow, not yet creased.

Much love, Beth

PS I am sorry to tell you Sally left us in Sept. We were all sad
to lose her, and it was a difficult decision for her, but she was not
ready yet to put down roots into the profession. She has almost
too many talents to make decisions easily. She is very intelligent
– considered doing a classics degree or African studies – but has
finally taken a foundation art course. She paints and draws flowers
very well. So we wished her well, hoping the garden may continue
to be a help to her.

Wednesday 8 October

Dear Beth,

It is a very dark morning and the wind blows at gale force when
we are overtaken by the next squally shower. The long Indian
summer came to an end the day before yesterday, but what a
wonderful spell that was. The heavy rains of August that we were
lucky enough to receive were ideal preparation for a mere 3mm
(⅛in) in September. Day after day of halcyon weather.

The garden has been full of flowers and it is an oasis set in
the parched countryside, which has to look tired at this time
of the year. A garden does not have to, which is why I think it
so important to keep up the pressure and to make sure that it
is a rewarding place to be in, given the delightful weather that
lures us into it. So unlike shivery spring, beautiful though that is.

Some American guests, who had been travelling around,
amused me by saying that my roses were by far the best furnished
with healthy foliage of any they'd been seeing, most of which
were already stripped. Well, as you know, I have pared down the
garden's rose component to perhaps less than 100 bushes, in a wide
range of types. They are none of them gathered together, which is
the way to encourage the spread of rust, black spot and mildew,
but are scattered all over the garden among mixed plantings, where
diseases do not find them out. They are never sprayed but are
still full of leaves (*Rosa glauca* excepted, I have to admit; I have
that underplanted with the pink 'Hadspen Abundance' Japanese
anemone, and do enjoy the way it combines with the sulky orange
of the rose's hips).

During a week in late September, I escaped with Pip Morrison
for company, and to drive me, to the west country, eventually
reaching Cornwall. As countryside, that unfortunately exposed
duchy looks hideous, in autumn. All the trees and shrubs are
brown and battered. No warm autumn colour could develop from
them. Ah, but those wonderful coasts, I am told to remember.
True, the National Trust has saved bits of them but, on the whole,
mankind has done his utmost to ruin them. Even a charming
coastal town like St Ives, which I had not visited before (and I
was certainly impressed by the new Tate Gallery), is so seething
with humanity and the gimcrack trappings that are laid out to
attract tourists in any holiday resort, that it was hard to begin to
appreciate the better features, which give it individuality.

Much of our time was spent in Dorset, staying with Anna
Pavord, who could not have been a more generous hostess,

devoting far more time to us than she could really afford and yet giving the impression that she was free as air. Each breakfast (always a good time for me), we sat prolongedly and chatted. Each lunch we took into the garden, bathed in sunshine, whereas normally she would just have snatched something to keep her going, while on the wing.

Things seen: well, at beloved Mapperton, with its hidden, then suddenly revealed formal garden at the bottom of a steep little valley, the floor of this had, since my last visit, been colonized by *Bidens ferulifolia*, self-seeding in the paving cracks. I know that there are seed strains and that they do self-sow, but I would never have imagined that plants could survive the winter as, by their size, it was evident they had, here. There are inferior forms of this bidens around, but the Mapperton one has the double curve in its rays that makes the flower so elegant, while the colouring was sharp yellow and just right against stone walls and paving.

At Kingston Maurward, near Dorchester, where the gardens were still in excellent shape despite the late date, I admired clumps of different kinds of colchicum spaced among a carpet of common dog violet in its purple-leaved form – *Viola riviniana* Purpurea Group, which I am so glad to find is just a strain of our native species and has nothing to do with Labrador, as the epithet *labradorica*, so often given it, seems to indicate.

In the wild, the colchicums that I've seen all flower in a meadow setting, and the green makes a fine background for their otherwise unsupported blossom. In a garden's border setting, I think it is usually nice to provide a background oneself. I can't just remember how you combine them in your piece of woodland. Given more sophisticated surroundings, I like the prostrate *Petunia* 'Purple Wave' as a dramatic background, nearer magenta than purple, for the pinky-mauve-flowered colchicums. For the muscular, white chalices of *Colchicum speciosum* 'Album', I plant a surround of the not-too-vigorous *Helichrysum petiolare* 'Variegatum', in soft-toned green and white. Both these are tender, so that there is no competition when the colchicums' voluminous leaves unfold in spring, the bedding not being added until those leaves are cut away, dead, late in June. But the good-tempered violet could cope with these, I think, provided the colchicums were planted to form clumps rather than a carpet. The carpet would be provided by the violet.

I have a good form of this violet, incidentally, which arose by chance and is a deeper richer shade of violet than usual. It flowers among the as yet naked, but carmine-coloured young stems of *Rosa virginiana*, which forms a suckering colony and which we thin out each winter so as to leave only wands of young shoots. But I can imagine it looking well surrounding bouquets of shiny green young colchicum leaves.

I have never yet succeeded with *Amaryllis belladonna*, whose name alone would make anyone want to grow it. It has never produced more than the odd flower but we saw plenty of successful colonies from Sussex to Cornwall, with dense cohorts of naked purple scapes, crowned by umbels of pink trumpets, usually white within. They develop so quickly and look so exciting in the autumn garden, but are not often well served by a pleasant setting – most often the brick foundations of a south-facing greenhouse wall. The heat that radiates gives the amaryllis a cosy ripening, such as it needs to encourage free flowering, but terracotta shouts at pink. I'm sure you must have discovered a good solution. At Trelissick, near to Truro, it was interplanted at the foot of a low, stone wall, with the hardy fuchsia, 'Chillerton Beauty'. Like many fuchsias, this is freest in autumn and its pink skirt with purple petticoat made an ideal partnership. It isn't tall-growing. But the Cornish climate is wet, and I don't know whether the fuchsia would get sufficient moisture with us.

The bottom of our terrace wall, overlooking the drained upper moat, has always, since before I can remember, been the home of *Iris unguicularis*, which starts flowering, there, in early November and goes on till March. But of recent years, it has done very poorly and I wonder whether the ground is iris-sick. So I plan to try some of the amaryllis bulbs, at present in a pot, there.

Most of these autumn-flowering bulbs start their growing season by flowering and I was interested when Alan Street (who trained with David Ward and has for years been a lynch pin at Avon Bulbs) told me that he always lifts, splits and plants his *I. unguicularis*, for propagation, in the autumn, when they are anyway about to start making new growth.

We visited Keith Wiley at the Fortescue Trust's garden, at Buckland Monachorum, in Devon. I first knew him as a remarkable student when at Wye College and he overlapped Lionel Fortescue, as his gardener, by several years before the latter's death. The original garden was within walls, but Keith has of late extended it very considerably, with interesting new plantings. I suppose their main emphasis is on hardy perennials, such as he sells on the adjoining nursery, whose role is important, but Keith is too versatile a plantsman to neglect shrubs and I was most intrigued by a lime species that was new to me: *Tilia henryana*. It makes a large shrub, and is kept as such by annual stooling. This results in very large leaves, purple when young, and a spread-out flowering season, which was still in progress on our visit. The air was filled with the delicious scent of lime blossom. I should have thought there might be a place for this in an open area of your woodland.

There is a long, straight vista from the far end of this newly developed garden, which was undulating meadow and scrub, back to the house, but the margins of the flanking beds (if one can so designate very extensive plantings in depth) wiggle along their length in uncomfortably tight promontories and recesses, which Pip and I found unbearably fidgety. However, Keith's strong personality does not accept criticism readily. Curves for the sake of having curves are still fashionable. They would be quite appropriate, here – more so than the straight vista – if they were only easier and more natural-seeming.

At Abbotsbury (a twee little olde-worlde town with its beady eye firmly fixed on tourists) in Dorset, we were too late to visit a tithe barn, but on our way back to the car, I spied a large walnut tree, growing in a garden but overhanging a piece of no-man's-land. Pip waded into the bed of nettles underneath it and I told him that a good way to locate fallen walnuts is to shuffle your feet and feel them through your shoe soles. However, his trousers were thin and nettles sting quite readily through cotton. He reached a few nuts by jumping and pulling the branches downwards. I decided to visit the house that clearly owned the tree. Its garden door opened into a fully laid-up tea room. No one there; it was past 6.00pm, but an interior bell brought the owner on the scene. I asked if I might buy some nuts from this tree. He said they'd not yet been gathered; then bethought him that he did have a couple of boxes of them, and proceeded to allocate some to me, refusing to take money for them. Triumphantly, I showed them to Pip, who had stayed in the background as he had one pocket with a suspicious bulge distending it.

Pip can crack nuts between his molars, lucky fellow, and an immediate sampling followed. The last laugh was on me, as my nuts turned out to be the previous year's. I do love fresh walnuts, don't you? I remember them growing very well in East Anglia, when I was stationed there during the war. Perhaps you have a productive specimen. My mother raised one from a nut. It grew quite large and cropped well, but was dangerously near to our neighbours, on our boundary, so it was felled.

To take up some points from your last two letters, Beth, so far unanswered: caryopteris, *Verbena bonariensis* and *Calamintha nepetoides* beneath them – all blue and purple. All very soft and harmonious, but devoid of bite, for my taste! Not a bold flower or leaf or contrast among them. It reminds me of Stephen Lacey's suggestion, in my Exotic Garden, of partnering the *Verbena bonariensis* with *Thalictrum delavayi* and *Origanum laevigatum* 'Hopleys' – again, all mauves and purple and flimsiness.

I don't feel that my nerves need all this soothing. In my case, for instance, I think the red and the strong moon shapes of 'Bishop of Llandaff' dahlias would add excellent spice to these kinds of flowers; or something greeny yellow, like *Patrinia scabiosifolia*, or orange, like *Asclepias tuberosa*.

I agree with you that most grasses look best in a void, surrounded by plants lower than themselves. They can look pleasant enough all grown together, as it may be sensible to do in a nursery, but the uniformity of strap leaves is apt to become numbing, with repetition. All-grass borders are generally evidence of a shortage of original thought. This is often found in institutions, the excuse being that it makes it easy for students to compare differences and similarities. Why is it that the quality of having a good eye for arranging plants in a garden is never taken into consideration when a gardener is appointed?

I was a little surprised to read of your large-fruited *Euonymus alatus*. I didn't know that its fruits were ever large. Usually they are not even numerous, but this seems to be a bumper spindle-berry year. Do you remember the plant you gave me about four years ago, derived from a heavy cropper in, or on the boundary of, your garden? I forget if it was actually a wilding; I imagine not. Anyway, after a prolonged sulk, this year it nearly doubled its size and is full of berry on its second-year wood.

I don't know your white *Agapanthus* 'Albatross', unless it be the same as one given me by Brian Halliwell, when he was Assistant Curator at Kew. He had no name for it but I particularly like it for the flowers' contrasting black anthers, which form specks within the white. I find that suitable partners are not so easily found for agapanthus and I am not that fond of their wealth of lance-leaves. However, I plan, when I have worked up more stock, to use a combination of a late-flowering blue cultivar, 'Loch Hope', I think, with a late-flowering orange crocosmia, 'Star of the East'.

Scent from Spanish broom, *Spartium junceum*, has always been one of its greatest assets, for me. In the south of France, in May, where it grows wild, the scent is quite overwhelming. Mount Etna broom, *Genista aetnensis*, is also good in its quieter way, but the wild broom, *Cytisus scoparius*, of which there are acres and acres in Scotland, has a sour smell that you become suddenly aware of as you drive along, thinking of other matters. *C. x praecox* is similar.

I remember admiring you, years ago, for being able to overwinter and flower *Tropaeolum tricolorum* outside. I tried it but the plants were all killed by frost. Now you write of its swimming among the blue flowers of *Teucrium fruticans*, which sounds so lovely, the red-black-yellow- flowered climber threading its pixie hats among stiff, grey-leaved, pale blue-flowered teucrium. I must try again. All my stock is still bone dry under glass and the tubers must be dealt with. Our mutual friend, Marjorie Hepburn-Scott, in Roxburghshire, had one flowering against a warm wall, when I visited in June. She seemed to have succeeded without trying, but I don't think things happen all that accidentally with her.

It is now evening, and we have had driving rain with gale-force winds for much of the day 26mm (1in) of rain was measured at 10.00am and it has gone on persistently. Every crack and joint in the walls of the Yeoman's Hall, where I sit, and of the bathroom next door, is leaking copiously. This is where the renovations were taking place last winter!

Do you believe in global warming? I find myself sceptical, but if a local pointer has any validity then I must admit that the fact of our Brunswick figs actually ripening a second crop, which we are picking now, is one such. Always, hitherto, this second is overtaken by winter before it can mature. Wasps have gone and blackbirds have lost interest, as also with autumn-fruiting raspberries, so Lloyd is sole beneficiary.

With love, Christo

— ❧ —

Saturday 11 October

My dear Christo,

This morning I sat sipping hot water and lemon, waiting for
the dawn to light up my bedroom as it struggled to push aside a
blanket of heavy grey cloud. I was planning to spend the forecast
wet day writing to you. Later when the post flopped through
the letter-box on to my hall chest, I carried it off to the office, to
sort and see if there was anything exciting for me and there was!
Your handwriting on the familiar brown envelope. Delighted to
see several pages of closely-typed text and, looking forward to
your company for breakfast, I was shocked to read your little
handwritten sheet which had fallen on to my desk. Dear Christo,
I am so sorry you have had this health problem diagnosed. Such
moments are a severe jolt to the system, however much stiff upper
lip we are able to muster, but I know how much you would dislike
me to make a fuss (it would be of no help anyway). As you say
you will live with 'mild Parkinson's' for a long while yet, and
that I am thankful to endorse, remembering an old friend of my
parents, Dora, who had it for many years, and long maintained
an outspoken sense of sharp humour which we all enjoyed – and
sometimes suffered. I feel great sympathy for you, but also great
thankfulness it will not affect your mind. Andrew joins me in
these thoughts, often commenting how remarkable you are to still
be able to create a richer life, for yourself and others, than many
people half your age. I think we have both been blessed (as my
mother would say; fortunate, you might prefer) to have enjoyed
good health, enabling us to carry on as if old age were always
far ahead, but like an old tractor, parts do wear out. Over the
past year or so, I have been made to pause and consider what my
body is trying to tell me, that there are signs of wear and tear, to
slow down a bit. Mercifully I don't yet need spare parts, except
for teeth and spectacles, while the treatment and exercises I have
for my shoulders have made me almost pain-free, much easier
in my movements – but I begin to think twice sometimes about

the number of journeys I make through the house and garden, especially as it always means small staircases to trot up and down.

Andrew's condition slowly deteriorates. He has had two bad patches in recent weeks, involving visits from the doctor, and changes of drugs to help ease his breathing. We now use something called a nebulizer (instead of hot-water inhalants), a machine which I imagine atomizes soothing drugs through a face mask. It's used by asthmatics and anyone with breathing difficulties. We are thankful he does not need a face mask all day, but at intervals. Fortunately he can still find the energy to read for part of the day – and we still enjoy a quiet time together between tea and his early bedtime. From the long sitting-room window he can see across the ponds to a huge stand of white moon daisy, *Leucanthemella serotina*. (It used to be *Chrysanthemum uliginosum* and that's the name I remember.) It looks well with another space-demanding daisy, the lemon-yellow *Helianthus* 'Lemon Queen', both gorgeous now, partnered with tall, flowering columns of Japanese grass, varied forms of miscanthus. In our sitting room, backlit by glass doors on to the terrace, I stand large jugs of these simple flowers, to be able to enjoy them close-to indoors. Earlier I used the clear yellow *Rudbeckia* 'Herbstsonne', with its narrow green central cones (removing much of the foliage to show off the flowers and prevent a heavy, lumpy look), while now we have a bridal-like cascade of the moon daisy, combined with the smaller, white, aster-like flowers of *Boltonia asteroides* var. *latisquama* 'Nana'. I love the effect of these two together in a tall, bell-bottomed jug, so simple and easy to arrange, both lasting well when picked, which is more than can be said for many Michaelmas daisies.

You wondered in your letter how I combined colchicums with other plants. As you suggest, they are naturally mountain-meadow plants, scattered among short grasses and other herbage cropped short by grazing animals. Here I have some in a small area of strimmed turf, together with *Cyclamen hederifolium*, both of which seem to be competing well with the grass roots. Each year

we add more of both to the area, so gradually it is becoming a
pink and white tapestry in autumn, contrasting with the white and
yellow of snowdrops and species narcissus in spring. Elsewhere
they grow through carpets of *Geranium macrorrhizum*, dwarf
periwinkles, *Viola riviniana* Purpurea Group (my ears pricked up
at the sound of your dark-flowered form), and the dwarf,
but spreading geraniums, like forms of *G.* x *cantabrigiense*.
I like the contrast made by the black-leaved, grass-like blades of
Ophiopogon planiscapus 'Nigrescens' growing among them.
All these are flourishing in my Wood Garden, where the overhead
canopy lets in shafts of sunlight to open wide the petals of the
various forms of colchicum, which take your breath away during
September and well into October.

I was amused by your attempts to iron out some of Keith
Wiley's 'fidgety' curves in the Buckland Monachorum garden in
Devon. Sadly I haven't yet seen it. One day I hope to be able to
travel again. I know I need it, to refresh my mind, to be inspired by
other plantings, especially those of the new and upcoming young
plantspeople. But like you I'm not in love with goffered margins,
so awkward to mow round, backing, twisting and turning. I think
it helps to use the mower itself to suggest a comfortable curve, or
as I often do, a hosepipe, to achieve a gentle curve. But *chacun à
son goût*! One must see the situation before criticizing. Generally
I prefer curves created by the plants themselves, especially bold
plants, particularly if they flop on to a paved or gravel walk.

Now I must apologize for last letter's mistake! I referred, as you
suspected, not to *Euonymus alatus*, but to a form of *Euonymus
europaeus*, possibly 'Red Cascade'. The capsules are twice as
large as others, holding bright orange fruits, their weight bowing
some branches to the ground – very handsome. I'm glad the form
I gave you is performing at last. It appeared here as a seedling.
I think euonymus need a period of real heat in summer to fruit
well. Certainly all of mine can be seen from afar along the car
park boundary. Planted in several groups they form a haze of pink

standing out between *Rosa rugosa*, still full of tomato-like hips, the foliage now turning lemon-yellow, while silver birches are changing to amber above them.

On the nursery edge of the Wood Garden I have a young walnut given me by my friend Janet, the potter. Only about four years old, it has doubled in size this summer. I really enjoy a young tree's presence, the leaves huge, healthy and glossy, with plenty of long, strong growth. Old trees never put on such growth or quality of foliage – they don't need to, probably would be detrimental if they did. But I'm in hopes I shall live long enough to have the thrill of finding walnuts under my feet there one day.

Going back to *Euonymus alatus*, we have tried it here with its interesting corky winged bark – but in the Longwood Gardens, Pennsylvania, I was astounded by the effect of domed, twiggy shrubs smothered in autumn colour, a brilliant, fiery carmine-red, every leaf intact, as if sprayed with luminescent paint. Unbelievable! If we continue to have hotter summers it might be worth another try, but sometimes I know when I am beaten.

Possibly because of the warm, dry weather throughout September we seem to have had more than our usual number of overseas visitors, while home-based photographers have also been seeking out new angles. Incidentally, I did watch the programme filmed at Dixter with Carol Klein a few weeks ago, made some notes, but have mislaid them! My main impression was to congratulate the photographer (or producer) who discovered new views and angles of Dixter; but overall on the down side I felt a faint disappointment, largely I think because these programmes try to fit in too much, so we see only tantalizing glimpses of ideas we would love to linger over. The new programme, *Routes Around the World* with Dan Pearson in Japan, I have only just caught up with. Last night he was in Kyoto where I much enjoyed him. He is very photogenic, moves and speaks fluently but not too much, and the gardens were serene. An hour would have passed like a dream – we had half that time.

We see an increasing number of visitors from Japan. (No doubt they either come from you, or continue on their way from here to Dixter.) Among them have been journalists from very expensive-looking Japanese magazines. Recently a young Japanese woman came, representing Japanese television, with a team of English camera, sound and technical men, to make a small piece to put into a film on English styles of gardening. It is, I suppose complimentary to visit English gardens but I think it would be tragic if, in their apparent desire to cultivate Western fashion, including *haute couture*, the Japanese fall flat for English cottage-garden style, or the legendary herbaceous border. Somehow, without the inevitable church tower or gazebo, I don't see how it will fit their architecture or landscape. That's not to say that some of our principles of planting and design could not be adapted – as we have learnt to consider balance, simplicity, unity and harmony, from studying Japanese principles of design.

I was very touched recently to have a letter from a young Japanese student who has been in Britain, working as a trainee gardener for two years. She had visited the garden here on a dull, drizzly day. Almost immediately afterwards she wrote, 'The garden seemed like heaven to me. Mist created calm and peaceful atmosphere. I particularly loved ponds and woodland garden.' Then she delighted me by going on, 'There are two things I need to do. To find a job and study about Japanese garden. You might think it's the other way round but I realized how beautiful and interesting Japanese gardening is after I studied English garden.' Good for her. Hopefully she will blend the best of both.

I was surprised and delighted one morning recently to find Pamela Harper in the garden. Twice we have met in the States, giving talks at the same events, in one case sharing a room in Portland where we had a chance to get to know each other a little. Originally English, she went to the States soon after the war and has, after long and arduous years, deservedly made a reputation as one of America's top garden photographers. She has survived life-threatening illness and financial worry, but now, I was glad to hear, is well, and in a position to do the kind of work she enjoys where and when she feels like it.

This week I had four nations represented for lunch. James van Sweden (one of the United States' best-known landscapers, for whom no area is too large) brought an engaging young Irishman, Dominic Murphy from Dublin (who I am sure we will see more of), together with Yuko Tanabe from Kyushu. Yuko came to us this summer, begging us to give her the chance to dirty her hands, to feel the plants, to have the chance to study plants growing in the garden. She is taking a three-year course at Writtle on landscape design, but was finding computers and blackboard teaching too far removed from the art and craft of gardening. So she came each Wednesday afternoon until the summer holiday, and then after a trip back to Japan, came back to stay as our guest for a few weeks in our caravan overlooking the vegetable garden. Sally had vacated it in early September. I invited Yuko to lunch to meet Jimmy van Sweden. When offering to lend her two of his books one day, she could not believe I had met someone so eminent in his field. Already from her research as a budding landscape designer in Japan she knew of him. Knowing him to be a warm, friendly person (having made several lecture tours with him in the US), I asked if she could spare time from college to come to meet him. She was overwhelmed.

Lunch was on Tuesday this week, a really beautiful, still, sunny day, a blue sky filled with dramatic big cloud banks, most welcome after several grey and windy days, frustrating, without the benefit of a good rain. Jimmy and Dominic arrived mid-morning, and we dived straight into the garden – 'so as not to waste the light'. It was intoxicating for me to share the garden with two such enthusiasts, all of us talking at once much of the time, like an excitable trio from a Verdi opera. By the time we reached the table under the magnolia tree I felt like an uncorked bottle of champagne. It was just as well I had to leave them with a bottle of Andrew's favourite Madeira while I put lunch on the table indoors. (Andrew was too unwell to join us.) Yuko arrived from her classes at 1.30pm, mortified to have kept us waiting, but enchanting in every expression and movement. She is beautiful. Her black hair setting off an oval face, ivory complexion and large, almond-shaped eyes. Add to this her ability to converse, somewhat haltingly at first, with such a wide vocabulary, to discuss Jimmy's books in detail – she was the star guest for us all! How rarely, I commented, do any of us meet anyone who can quote our writing, whose studies and experience allows them to lock new thoughts into the framework of their knowledge. Yuko will continue to come to us once a week. I feel privileged to have had several very promising young students from overseas who have brought new ideas or methods to us, and who will take good memories away from here I hope. Yuko intends one day to study or work in the US, before returning to Japan; already there is an office in Washington, that of J. van Sweden, where she is sure of a warm welcome.

James and Dominic were busy with their cameras. In particular James was excited by a stock bed of *Ligularia* x *palmatiloba*. Bare brown, branching stems held pale-beige, fluffy balls of seed, the low autumn sunlight emphasizing their silky texture. They made an arresting contrast as they stood 2m (6½ft) high behind the long aster border, at its best now in all shades of pink, white and mauve, highlighted with massive stands of *Helianthus* 'Lemon Queen' while the papyrus-like *Helianthus salicifolius* lifts yellow daisies high into the cloud-chasing sky, on 2m (6½ft) plus stems clothed from top to bottom with narrow, willow-shaped leaves.

David and I have plans to add variation to this border, which began just as a stock bed for asters to supply cuttings for the nursery. We have in mind kniphofias and miscanthus, and a solidago new to me, just flowering now in the Wood Garden. It is *Solidago rugosa*; it makes a mesh of branching stems about 1.25m (4ft) tall, holding itself together, creating a delicate, airy effect as its side branches carry long, arched tails encrusted with tiny sharp-lemon daisies, cool against small dark green leaves. (The commonly grown golden rod,

272

Solidago virgaurea, coarse stems and leaves topped with a crowded head of short yellow spikes, I never liked even as a child.)

As usual I cannot end without reference to the weather, which influences our every day. We now have the past year's total rainfall. The winter six months (Oct '96–Apr '97) we had 238mm (9½in), half of that in November. During the summer six months, Apr–Oct '97 we had 269mm (10½in), total 507mm (nearly 20in). (510mm, or just over 20 inches is our average. I still find it easier to visualize inches than millimetres.) But almost 150mm (nearly 6in) fell in June. In August we were thankful to receive 38mm (1½in) but July, August and September saw temperatures reaching 25–30°C (77–86°F) and often plenty of wind with little measurable rain. However, this past week we have had almost 50mm (nearly 2in). That will be very helpful, with re-planting and new grass to be sown to make good repairs before next season.

A pretty sight this week, shared with two of my girls as they were going to the staff rest-room for their coffee break: one of the little black cats, now 17 weeks old, was paddling in a puddle alongside the shed wall. Out she stepped, paused, watching the raindrops falling into the water and delicately stepped in again pawing the water, to find the raindrops, puzzled she could find nothing there. Who says cats detest getting their feet wet? She was obviously having fun, the first time she had seen a decent puddle.

I would very much like to come and see you, Fergus and dear Anne, just for the day, before the frosts come to topple the Exotic Garden, but already there are few free days left before the end of October. I must decide soon. Meanwhile I think often of you, especially in the garden and when I'm cooking; just now it will be quail for supper with broad beans from the freezer, young carrots and potatoes from the garden with a bowlful of strawberry-flavoured grapes *Vitis vinifera* 'Fragola' to finish – they are so good this year, honey-sweet and full of flavour after sun-baked days on a south wall.

Much love, Beth

– ❧ –

Wednesday 29 October

Dear Beth,

I know we write a lot about the weather but it does deeply affect a gardener's life. Up till last night, we'd been having ground frosts, but not enough to kill any plants. Last night, it was really cold and all the tender plants still outside (we'd already made sure of housing those in need) were thoroughly frosted: dahlias, cannas, castor oil, soft salvias, cosmos, annual rudbeckias and many more.

Suddenly, ours being that sort of garden, we find ourselves with a mountain of necessary work, clearing the summer bedding and replanting for next spring. Both the ground and the weather are ideal for this, but poor Fergus is constantly interrupted – often by me, but also on account of his many responsibilities to others, so he gets frustrated. But he remains remarkably patient.

Meantime, the weather remains unbelievably beautiful. When, I wonder, was there last such a sun-drenched October? Even today, I was able to take my coffee and a rug into the orchard, after lunch, and bask (read; snooze) awhile, in perfect comfort. The nights are as beautiful, with a glittering sky. Venus, after an 18-month interval, has reappeared in the evenings. Look for it low in the sunset sky, as it gets dark. Jupiter is then brilliant, in the south, and the two planets will move towards each other in the coming months. I don't know how close they get, but it'll be worth watching.

Pip, who is still with me much of the time, is really interested in all this and will soon get to know the night sky better than I do. He's already so hot on tree recognition, at a distance, that I cannot compete. Currently, he's doing important work, which is a great experience for him, in putting *The Daily Telegraph*-sponsored garden for the next Chelsea Flower Show on to paper – with an axonometric elevation, that shows the garden apparently in 3-D, albeit actually on a 2-D plan. It is so as to present it acceptably to the RHS. Sarah Raven will actually be doing the garden, but Pip is well trained (at Edinburgh University, on the landscape design course) in architectural presentation. Another drawing will show the projected planting.

As I've mentioned before, Sarah is John Raven's daughter. I was lucky enough to have known and been befriended by him. He was a classics tutor at Cambridge, but wild plants were his great love and as well as his *British Mountain Flowers* he wrote a delightful ramble: *A Botanist's Garden*. Sarah has been a practising doctor of medicine, until she gave it up a couple of years ago so as to operate from home on flower arranging for big functions, on running a school for flower arrangers and on writing to promote a more dynamic and showy style of gardening than has been fashionable for many years. She already has one book, *The Cutting Garden*, published by Frances Lincoln, and has another in the pipeline. Lincoln's want *The Bold and Brilliant Garden* as a title. (Cumbersome, I think.) She is really energetic and creative. So is Adam Nicolson, her husband (son of Nigel), who seems to work at his writings non-stop and yet to remain relaxed. He looks exactly like his grandmother, Vita Sackville-West. Theirs is a lovely set-up, if, one wonders, constantly on the verge of penury. Probably that's an illusion. They're only 22km (14 miles) or so from here and deep in the countryside. Much of East Sussex is virtually unspoilt, and heavily wooded.

The brief break that Fergus, Pip and I took in Brittany was great fun. With two of my favourite people for company, it could hardly be otherwise and they are both keen drivers, sharing that equally (I think that each of them would have liked to have done it all). We had smooth Dover–Calais crossings (it's a mere 53 minutes' drive between here and Dover), but it's then a very long haul across the north of France to Brittany. In each direction, that took most of a whole day and the weather was nasty, but the day we spent actually in Brittany was beautiful. Just our luck!

My reason for wanting to go was to meet old Prince Peter Wolkonsky, in his garden, before he died. I'd heard so much about

him as a great character, and at 96, there obviously wasn't time
to waste. We couldn't get into touch with him on the telephone,
but we did with his daughter, who lives near by, at Crech ar Pape
in the Roscoff area, right on the north coast. I knew her and her
husband, Tim Vaughan, when they were both students at Wisley,
quite 20 years ago. Tim was currently in the USA. Isabelle was very
welcoming, but her immediate news was that her father had died,
of a heart attack, the day before.

She gave us a prolonged tour of her own and Timothy's garden,
and this proved to be a star turn. I (we) just wished that you had
been with us. The garden is only seven or eight years old and it
is truly inspired and original, both in its design and its planting.
At first, in the Round Garden, you might be a trifle dismissive.
Trendy, you might think; effective in its way, with box hedging,
a circular central bed of white agapanthus – in seed (and I'm not
crazy about agapanthus foliage). Radiating paths with diamonds
of mown grass (hell to keep neat), set in old street pavis – square
cobbles. A surround of bay laurel hedging, unclipped (but it will
eventually have to be), *Ilex aquifolium* 'Hascombensis', always
a winner, with its small, glossy leaves and upright habit, purple-
leaved *Pittosporum* 'Tom Thumb' in front of a yellow-variegated
Phormium tenax, beds containing bold plantings of the low,
variegated grass, *Hakonechloa macra* 'Aureola', now in flower;
also the pale yellow-variegated *Fuchsia magellanica* 'Sharpitor'.

'This is the red area,' Isabelle told us at the highest point in
the garden (which is on an easy slope), but of course it was well
past red-time. Such as *Crocosmia* 'Lucifer' had been cut down.
The paving was covered with the little red *Verbena peruviana* (also
virtually finished) and you realized that this was still a really private
garden, where such plants won't get trodden on to extinction. Coach
parties do visit by arrangement, from time to time.

An enticing vista led you down the slope and you then
appreciated that the informal plantings within formal outlines
were richly varied. Also that there was a great range of colourful

evergreens, yet they never made you feel closed in or over-evergreened, because interior spaces were kept open and sunny and a large proportion of the shrubs were regularly clipped into yeast-leavened mounds. This has a way of peopling a garden; it felt intimate and there were nice low stone buildings at hand, including the house and a barn that is now more living space. No grass lawns anywhere – such a relief, somehow, because the paving everywhere was beautiful and much colonized by self-sowers.

The vista down which you are beguiled leads into a bigger, enclosed area, a sunken garden with a dry, planted 'pond' at its lowest point. Lovely shapes, and the colour presently dominating (but this varies at different seasons) was yellow – the yellow of large shrubs of *Euryops chrysanthemoides*, highlighted by its own rich green foliage, and the no less intense yellow of *Cassia* (now *Senna*) *corymbosa* – truly huge plants of this exciting leguminous shrub, which is perfectly hardy here – the temperature goes no lower than –3°C (27°F) – and is regularly cut hardback each spring but makes good with tremendous growth, some of it climbing up the walls of the house, in the company of other shrubs.

Grasses are made excellent use of, often as single plants – *Miscanthus sinensis* 'Variegatus', for instance; also a handsome form of common sage, with rather large, grey leaves, *Salvia officinalis* 'Berggarten', together with the yellow-margined *S. o.* 'Icterina', reverting in patches to plain green. That makes a pleasing variation.

Always, you are aware of being close to the sea, and the coast itself is fascinating, with rocky outcrops above flat expanses. Inland, the great crop, as for as long as I can remember, is cauliflower – the famous Roscoff cauliflowers. How the same land manages to produce the same crop decade after decade must be a miracle of inorganic science! A lot of globe artichoke fields, too – our favourite 'Gros Camus de Bretagne'.

Isabelle then took us a few miles to her father's garden (he was in Normandy when he died), though the property is really hers, through her mother, to whom it belonged. Father-in-law and son-in-law were irreconcilably at odds with one another and she'd not visited for a year. Indeed, the gardener, who was mowing, had not heard of the Prince's death. The house is beautiful and beautifully situated in a wooded valley that looks down to an estuary and beyond that, up to Treguier, which has a magnificent gothic cathedral (we visited that). The garden could be marvellous and I would have loved to have seen it through the Prince's eyes, as he clearly loved it dearly, but it is not only seriously neglected; one also feels that its full potential has not been realized and that this could be achieved by Tim and Isabelle.

We stayed the two nights in cheap but clean and hospitable hotels, in family rooms – that typically means one double bed and two singles. We had marvellous fish dinners of five generous courses (I couldn't manage the last two), costing the equivalent of £12. Quite amazing value.

Thursday 30 October

It is now another sunny day, after an even colder night, bringing the rest of the mulberry's leaves down to form a thick carpet, through which you cannot see the lawn grass at all. I should like to let the leaves wither for a few days, making them lighter to handle, before removing them.

I do envy you the wild mushrooms you had in the car park area. When it was warm, after the rains, mid-month, I thought they were bound to appear here. Not so.

October has produced 122mm (nearly 5in) of rain, nearly all of it concentrated in that stormy second week. Now, the ground seems incredibly dry, again, where the bedding is being cleared and replanted. But it works beautifully. I do love autumn and that season has been particularly rewarding of recent years. The pills I'm taking three times a day (I've reduced them to two) make me short of breath and with a pain across my shoulders, as soon as I walk even 100 yards (or metres) and on the level, so I wouldn't enjoy a walk in the woods, where I should love to go and see the colour on the wild service trees and smell the decaying vegetation. I'm seeing my GP the day after tomorrow and some other treatment will have to be devised.

Christo

— ⚜ —

Thursday 30 October

Dear Christo,

Looking through last year's diary, I see that you and Fergus came to lunch this time last year. We had exactly the same beautiful weather we've been having this past week or so, blue skies and golden sunshine to set off all the tones and tints of autumn quickly stealing over the garden now after several night frosts. The lowest so far was last night about −4°C (25°F). This morning the scene from my bedroom window was transformed, everywhere silvered with frost, but it quickly dissolved.

I am glad to see a few more visitors coming to enjoy the garden, while the weather is so inviting. (It might be that schools are having the half-term break, since there have obviously been family groups, sometimes grandparents, parents and children. I like to see that.) It seems such a shame to waste any of the sunshine, when before long we (I) will feel imprisoned beneath a grey blanket of cloud, blotting out the magical light. Just the odd day recently (plus putting back the clocks) was enough to send my spirits plummeting – yet I know nothing has changed radically, just that I have to take a grip of myself, not to be affected by the lack of light.

Earlier this week I was much saddened to have a letter from Bob Seeley. He had begun writing to me, finishing next morning to tell me Rosemary had finally lost her battle with leukaemia and had died during the night. Peace for her, a great loss for Bob. Such a good marriage they made, good for each other, good for their friends. I can still vividly recall the week we spent together

birdwatching in Shetland, with Rosemary opening my eyes to see
birds where previously I could see nothing but rocks and grass. It
is much the same with plants. If you are unfamiliar with a plant,
you can easily look, but your mind will not take it in. Knowing
it especially by name, is like recognizing an old friend. Do you
remember how Rosemary warned us about dive-bombing skuas?
We were walking over short tussocky turf where these birds were
nesting, much to their distress and indignation. I had picked up a
piece of driftwood to hold over my head. You turned up the hood
of your anorak. Suddenly I saw you, walking ahead of me, clipped
over the back of the head by an irate bird. Fortunately no damage
done, but it brought home to me that we were the interlopers.

The weekend of 17–19 October, was probably the last warm
weekend of the year, so warm we could eat outside. Fortunately
Diana came to spend it with us. We spent one morning sorting out
the herbs I had dried during the summer months, putting them into
large paper envelopes where they remain in better condition than
in plastic bags. We store them out of the light, putting just enough
for use in screw-top glass bottles. Then we collected a trolley-load
of pumpkins, squashes and small, ornamental gourds and filled
wide, shallow baskets to stand around the house. One of these
could have become Cinderella's coach. It is very large, beautifully
ribbed to form eleven sections, the top half orange, the lower half
still green, but I suspect it will slowly turn completely orange.
It sits now beside the log basket, on the hearth of my wood-
burning stove.

For some weeks I have meant to tell you of another unusual
decoration which has deceived most visitors who have had lunch
with me. On the wooden table beneath the magnolia tree has stood
a bowl of yellow and orange 'fruits', looking from a distance very
like lemons and tangerines. They are in fact, cucumbers, called
'Crystal Apple'; I trained them up a tripod in the vegetable garden
where they also were decorative. When fit to eat they are pale
creamy-green, crisp to bite into, handy on a picnic. There were

more than we could eat, so they ripened on the vines until I picked
them, all shades of lemon and orange, and piled them into an old
pottery colander (given me years ago by a Mrs Humm who pruned
and picked apples for us on the fruit farm for many years). I like
the look of this old bowl, solid and heavy – and it is useful to have
outside. With good drainage, whatever is put inside doesn't become
waterlogged on the rare occasions we have rain!

On Sunday we woke to find the garden filled with heavy mist,
but not at all cold, curiously warm. After breakfast we hurried
to the Wood Garden to watch the sun draw aside the curtains
of mist between the trees. It was quite breathtaking to stand in
silence, waiting for a shaft of sunlight to suddenly spotlight fairy-
like cobwebs, stretched across the pathways, hanging like lace
bedspreads between tall fern fronds, threaded with glistening drops
of water. Macleaya seed heads were wrapped like spools of yarn,
glistening with crystals, pale against a big evergreen magnolia.
Quickly the mist cleared away, revealing rich autumn colours
against a rare blue sky. (So often our sky is a washy blue, but I
suppose after a month of no measurable rain, the atmosphere
is clear.) *Malus tschonoskii* was at its best. This wild crab from
Russia, shaped much like a Lombardy poplar, turns the brightest
of red and crimson shades. It is easily recognizable this time of year
by its shape and colour. For the rest of the year it makes a good
vertical, whether in summer-green leaf, or bare-branched in winter.
By the pond we found *Crataegus coccinea*, now a mature tree, its
branches bowed with clusters of cherry-sized fruits polished bright
scarlet, glowing in the sunlight. There were still plenty of crimson
hips on *Rosa glauca*, in spite of the blackbirds, skittering around
among dry, fallen leaves, agitated at being interrupted in their
feasting. Wine-coloured leaves on red-stemmed dogwoods were
reflected in the clear, still water.

Early morning is perhaps the best time to see low sunlight
filtering through the flowering grasses. They take several years
to develop character; although some can be effective in the first

year of planting. But the larger grasses, including miscanthus and pampas grasses, need time to produce girth as well as height. Then they become really impressive, with large, silky plumes held high above columns of shimmering ribbon-like foliage. There are so many different ornamental grasses, tall or short, each with distinctive inflorescences, their patterns emphasized by frost crystals melting into dew drops.

This time of year I love the long, black shadows cast across the mown grass walks, interspersed with bright sunlight where droplets of water sparkle here and there like green, blue and golden sequins. Most of the flowers have gone. The pot gardens, so full of life and colour only a few days ago, are cleared away and cuttings having been taken. Large specimens are cut back and stood in the greenhouse to be safe from hard weather. All the agaves have vanished to winter quarters. Once they are all tucked away, I quickly adjust to the arrangements of empty pots, the swept paving, the bare bones, the pared-down look of winter.

There has been a lot of work done to re-fit the old Pratten greenhouse into its new site. Repainted white, inside and out, new staging has been erected with capillary matting on the benches, to cut down watering for Emily who is in charge of the non-hardy plants which overwinter there. David Plummer has made a splendid job fixing bubble plastic over the windows, plus 5cm (2in) thick sheets of polystyrene fixed against the walls, below the staging. A small electric fan heater fitted to a thermostat will be enough to keep this house frost-free, while the time and money we have spent on insulation will save electricity. Emily has been happy as a bird, getting all her plants under cover just before the frosts come. She has had to badger the men to get it all ready for her in time. But they too have had their deadlines. Two big jobs have been in progress, preparing land for sowing grass.

Keith has been itching to sow new grass since September – the ideal time – but it has been too dry to think of it. In the Reservoir Garden the grass had become very poor, mostly annual meadow grass which quickly turns brown with drought. Originally about 20 years ago, the grass there was sown on to a layer of clay, spread over the existing base of gravel soil. By spreading the clay dug out from making the farm reservoir, I hoped to make a more retentive soil over the whole area. On the whole, with additional humus, it has worked well, especially with deep-rooted plants like trees and shrubs. But I felt we needed to make more effort with the grass. Since there are visitors here most days of the year, we could not cut off the entire area. Deciding the lower area nearest the reservoir border was the most needy, we sprayed it off with Round Up (glyphosate), and put in the sub-soiler, 2–2.5m (6½–8ft) deep, pulled behind the tractor to spike up the compacted soil. Next, a spring-tined cultivator was pulled through, to break up the large clods, loosened by the sub-soiler. (We recently bought very cheaply a big agricultural cultivator, which Gerard cut down to about 2–2.5m (6½–8ft), very suitable for work on the nursery stock beds, saving time and effort with hand-digging.) Then to improve both quality and texture of this difficult soil, 25 dumper loads of gravelly soil (saved from re-siting the greenhouse) and home-made compost were spread. Again the sub-soiler was used to help drag this top layer into a greater depth. Finally Keith and Gerard used the small nursery rotavators for the final stir-up before hand-grading and raking to make a good seed bed. Keith put in an auger to measure the depth of improved soil, and I was relieved and delighted after all their hard work to hear we have created a foot of improved soil. We chose a grass mixture suited for hard wear and resistance to drought and look forward to next summer, to see how it performs. As I have said before, your paved areas are a blessing; we always must consider our grass walks. They set off the garden when in good condition, but need a lot of care and attention. Too many feet could wear them out, much as we welcome and need the support of our visitors.

The other area requiring attention was the grass outfield used as our car park. Two years ago Keith and Gerard laid grass pavers, panels of concrete containing open holes for grass to grow through, at the entrance to each long grassy track where cars park on either side. This summer proved to us, despite the drought, that we could prevent grass being churned up by spinning wheels. So now Keith and Gerard, together with a young man called Ben who is here as a student from Odey College, have, with the help of a digging machine, carved out a new track, churned up the bottom, put a layer of sand on which to lay the open 'brickwork', to form two tracks (like the backbone of a fish) down which cars can travel without damaging the grass. This week they have sieved soil to fill in the spaces before sowing the grass. As we look back today along the newly laid track, still bare, we can see the established blocks at the far end indistinguishable from the autumn green mown grass all around. So I look forward to seeing the first tiny blades of grass appearing before very long. The dry weather has helped us to get these jobs done in reasonably good time, but now we badly need rain to germinate the grass seed, to help re-planting around the garden and to relieve trees and hedgerows throughout the district now showing stress.

Friday 31 October

Friday morning, with a letter from you on my table! And such a beautiful month it has been, suddenly collapsing with these quite severe night frosts, but today we still have glorious sunshine. I have just been shopping for the weekend and the girl on the till hoped she would be out in time to get a tan! Walking through the Gravel Garden before putting away the shopping, in spite of overnight frost I picked a small handful of treasures: blue and white forms of *Crocus speciosus*, still opening fresh flowers 7cm (2¾in) across, much larger than the deeper violet-toned *C. medius*. Still undamaged by these early frosts, yellow crocus-like sternbergias have delighted us for weeks now, cheerfully reminiscent of springtime, together with a small troop of snowdrops *Galanthus corcyrensis* (now *G. reginae-olgae* late form) for company. Some of these pretty little snowdrops are almost pure white with only the faintest touch of green on the inner petals. All these flowers now sit open wide on my table in a small blue and white Victorian jug. Before the end of the day David will have lifted and divided some of the clumps of crocuses, while we can still see them, to increase the display in years to come. Obviously we won't move the sternbergias while they are in full leaf.

David is another interested star-gazer. As we drove back recently from Norwich, we watched Venus and Jupiter rising as the light faded behind the flat Norfolk farmland. Jupiter sees me on my way to bed, twinkling through the high dining-room window.

I was interested to hear of your trip to Brittany, but sad to hear you just missed seeing Prince Wolkonsky in his garden in France. When I showed at the RHS Hall, he often came in the evening to look round and have a chat. Some while ago a television programme showed Prince Wolkonsky in his garden. Although in his nineties he appeared completely unconcerned by camera and sound equipment, just chatted naturally and effortlessly about his garden which reflected his taste and character, mellowed by time, no striving for effect – a healthy mixture of love and neglect. I am glad you found his daughter Isabelle, and enjoyed her garden. She came here several times when she was a student, seeking, I think, a little support in her emotional life. I couldn't do much, but admired her openness, hoping she would eventually be able to decide what was best for her. It sounds as if she has achieved that.

I chuckled where you report with relief, 'no grass lawns anywhere!' How sensible when natural paving is to hand, providing the most harmonious building material. And what a difference it makes to have a relatively frost-free garden. Climate and weather mould us as gardeners. No wonder the subject preoccupies us, especially in this country where the weather is so unpredictable. You were lucky to have 122mm (4¾in) of rain in October; we have only had almost 122mm since the beginning of August!

Last evening my good friend and masseuse, Pat, came to sort out my right knee which is being a bit troublesome. It has been so good all summer, literally pain-free, but somehow I must have twisted the knee-cap, now it takes time and patience to get the swelling down. I spoke of you and Pat wondered if you had been recommended massage to help with stiffness. She has a patient with Parkinson's and has helped him considerably over the past couple of years. I'm very sorry to hear you are troubled with breathlessness; sounds as if the medication doesn't altogether suit you. I will ring you soon. Wishing I could jump into the car to drive down to see you. As you will tell from this long spiel, I think of you often.

With love, Beth

—❦—

Thursday 27 November

Dear Beth,

I have just returned from a luncheon given by the Garden Writers' Guild (who they?). I had refused but Frances Lincoln's were keen I should go and so I did, sitting at their table with members of staff and other authors. The Guild seems to be sponsored by a variety of commercial interests connected with horticulture and there was a long list of awards, each sponsored by a different organization. Alan Titchmarsh was announcing the winners and did it extremely well and with his usual assurance. I've known Alan for many years and fame hasn't spoilt him one iota. He's always the same warm person who loves a good laugh.

I was, with *Gardener Cook*, shortlisted for the most inspirational book of the year but pipped at the post by Montagu Don, with a glitzy Conran Octopus book of photographs and the minimum of text. But, at the end, I received the Lifetime Achievement Award 1997, sponsored by Phostrogen (I thought they were in difficulties). I was so surprised that I found I was

286

clapping myself before fully realizing who was the recipient. It carried a very nice stainless-steel trowel and a cheque. It was good to see a lot of friends, though there was little chance of talking to most of them.

The food was good (the Savoy), in contrast to that at Simpson's in the Strand, the previous week, where it was appalling. This was a literary luncheon given by the *Oldie*, and they hold them monthly. A popular event. Three of us each spoke for ten minutes on a recently published book. I (again with *Gardener Cook*) was the last. The other two were John Mortimer and Nigel Nicolson (on his recent autobiography). Those two are really practised after-dinner speakers and did it off the top of their heads, whereas I, who had never done anything of the kind before, had to read a script, which seemed a bit lame, but everyone was very kind.

Nigel said how difficult it was to be the son of two famous parents and thus in their shadow. I see his point and one has often met similar situations, but I couldn't help reflecting that he had benefited from them in being able to milk every drop of their and their friends' fame and notoriety in a best-selling series of books and TV productions.

It was so good, Beth, to have you here for all of 24 hours and I am very glad you organized it. It was like old times. The first time you've been a night away from home since you were last here in March – after which you collapsed! Pip enjoyed driving you home but apparently conversation was so lively that the A12 turning off the M25 was missed, with a considerable addition to the journey. However, he wasn't too late back.

He is currently in Holland, having an interview for temporary work in a landscape architect's office in Arnhem. This being near to Romke and Adriana, he's been staying with them and has extended his visit by a day, so obviously he's having a good time.

Fergus was also invited to the lunch today, but was too conscientious to go, still having a lot of bedding out to get done.

After the first frost – this year at the end of October – we have a mad rush changing over from last summer's garb in anticipation of next spring's display. The weather, of course, hasn't helped, as there's been a lot of rain – most welcome in the long run but on our heavy soil it makes planting extremely sticky. He works off boards – and no matter what the weather is, never complaining. What a man.

All for now, Beth, Christo

– ❧ –

Wednesday 26 November (not sent till Monday 1 Dec) 1997
Dear Christo,

I am relieved to tell you the cold germs of last week have been routed by a few days' rest and possibly by some of my 'magic' herbal potions. Whatever may be the cure, I am feeling enthusiastic again and want to tell you about the party we had here on Friday 14th November to launch our new video, recording the interaction of nursery and garden throughout the year.

Farming Press (Miller Freeman PLC) from Ipswich, who made the video, organized the publicity party and asked us if it could be held here. We said yes, and then the staff put their heads together to decide what to do to transform our L-shaped packing shed into a reception area. Seething with ideas, they wondered whether they should consult Beth, or would she like a surprise? (For our Golden Wedding anniversary four years ago, they had made a total and memorable surprise.) But this time I was glad to be invited to share in the fun. Amazingly perhaps, they decided to illustrate the seasons. After sweeping down the building (even washing the windows), they worked in their normal groups of two or three, each on their own project. A few days before, the garden and nursery had been thoroughly searched during the lunch breaks for inspiration and props. This is what they made of their findings.

For her spring garden Rosie used a silver birch trunk, beautiful in itself, its white coat split vertically to show dark, corky bark, while elsewhere hundreds of fine wrinkles had been formed by the scar tissue where a limb had been cut many years ago. Around its base emerged a little spring garden – bright leaves of *Arum italicum*, pale yellow feverfew, ferns and *Helleborus foetidus* showing flower buds – all providing a setting for cowslips and primroses (dug from Rosie's garden), snowdrops, the skimmed-milk-blue of *Vinca difformis*, a few glacier-blue flowers of *Corydalis flexuosa*, even some pink campion flowers. All was enhanced by bright moss and leaf-mould, while trails of ivy and hazel catkins softened the vertical tree stump.

During the summer months Emily fills our garage roof full of dried flowers of all kinds, so she and Moira had a great time with bunches simply heaped into my big laundry basket or hanging naturally in bunches from the shelf above, together with a big shallow bowl of potpourri, full of colour with bright petals and rosebuds.

Autumn spread low along the top of another bench. Crumpled hessian hid the paraphernalia of packing materials behind, making a good background for branches of yellow birch, flaming scarlet of *Cotinus coggygria*, dark crimson of liquidambar. Berries of pink-fruited sorbus, white snowberry and 'Yellow Hornet' apples hung above a ground layer of fallen leaves, fungi and pine cones.

The interpretation of winter surprised and delighted us all, since it could have been the most difficult. Designed and put together by Lynda, Janet and Ann, they borrowed a black fire grate from Debbie, to make a base, then recreated flames, smoke and ash in a very lively way with 'flames' of red hot pokers (from Janet's garden in Wivenhoe, which is warmer than ours, being next to the tidal water of the River Colne), a glowing heart of *Schizostylis coccinea* and crimson-berried *Crataegus coccinea*, with plums of pampas grass for smoke, *Clematis orientalis* (*C. tibatana vernayi*) seed heads and blue-grey trails of cedar representing fallen ash.

Near by a most life-like robin perched on the handle of an old-fashioned watering can.

And that was not all – Chrissy with Pat to help her filled a dark corner with a pool garden which could have been part of a Chelsea exhibit. A large shallow container filled with water was concealed with moss-covered logs, the crevices filled with ferns, golden sedge and sweet flag, all overhung with silver-leaved willow grass in flower, and bulrushes.

The Beginning, as it was 36 years ago, was taken on by Rosie. A corner site filled with dried seed heads, brambles bearing blackberries, and rosehips, represented the wilderness, while an old Covent Garden basket full of ripe apples, and a handful of wooden labels carrying names of old apple varieties, represented Andrew's fruit orchards. By luck, a handful of huge parasol mushrooms were found to complete this picture, while near by on the wall were photographs I had found showing the site as it was 37 years ago.

David Ward's contribution was a reconstruction of part of one of our Chelsea exhibits, using all contrasting foliage in colour, texture, shapes and forms. This too was illustrated by some colour photographs of the stands he helped me construct at Chelsea. Keith, our technician, contributed by producing our old Chelsea box, complete with all the accoutrement needed for grooming and staging, including our picnic kettle and stove, my apron, gloves and scruffy old trainers!

Debbie welcomed visitors to our shop area with a ceiling-high bouquet of pampas and miscanthus in flower, with white *Aster* 'Monte Cassino' and pink chrysanth, 'Emperor of China' rescued from the frosted border. Last, but not least, she introduced the vegetable garden. Below fruiting fronds of asparagus, rakes, forks and piles of clay pots lay a cornucopia of vegetables: long white radish, carrots, beetroot, turnips and leafy-topped leeks. A very personal touch was my house trug, filled with flowers and vegetables for the house, carried by me almost daily walking back to the house at lunchtime.

Beautiful lively lettering, repeating the free spirit of the exhibits, was designed and painted by Chrissy. Outside, everywhere was mown and swept, even tyre marks raked out of the gravel entrance. A 'friend of friends' had been invited with her staff to provide delicious eats together with tea, coffee, or wine, but I was much too full of excitement to eat any – one glass of wine lasted all afternoon.

One overheard remark, passed on to me, was, 'This makes a change from the hotel lounge decorated with silk flowers.' We felt good. We all enjoyed the party, but the real buzz had come the day before. Although we work all year as a team, it is rare to have the opportunity to leave our daily routines, to share such a novel experience. I was delighted by the amount of cross-fertilization of ideas which went on among my team, who surprised themselves I think by their combined effort. There was a lot of fun too, a large green grasshopper for David's Chelsea, a goldfish for the pool with a life-like wooden duck sheltering among the reeds. As the light faded early on a gloomy November afternoon spotlights appeared where needed – as if by magic.

Poor Christo! Have you nodded off? Forgive me but it has been such a temptation to share our day. Take it a sip at a time, with Fergus and Pip.

Monday 1 December
Two treats this drizzling morning. A letter from you and big-bear-sized bowl of porridge, made overnight in the slow-cooker, with soaked dates and raisins and a touch of crème fraîche. Not a bit traditional I know, should be eaten with salt and standing up, but I sat by the wood-burning stove, relished both and found myself caught up in your book, *Gardener Cook* and found it hard to put down.

Congratulations on the Lifetime Achievement Award. It warms the cockles of the heart to have such recognition, although I find it is the pursuit which gives the sharpest frisson of satisfaction, rather than the end result.

I shall miss writing these letters, and am grateful to our good friend Giles Gordon for tempting me to write by suggesting this novel approach to a book. There has to be an incentive. What next? Who knows?

Love Beth

— ❦ —

Friday 5 December

Dear Beth,

How often have you done any gardening, of late? Myself, none for weeks, now, but this morning was sunny and calm at last and I was tempted out, carefully choosing my weeding area to receive the benefit of the sun's rays, which do, after all, impart warmth even now. The air temperature was only just above freezing and there was a broken skin of ice on the ponds, but the soil was free.

I didn't weed around the *Chusquea culeou*, that noble Chilean bamboo in the front lawn, because I have at last signalled to Fergus that he may dig the whole thing up, next spring, give the ground what I call the Fergus treatment – he is tremendously thorough and will remove lots of sticky clay from lower depths – and replant a large piece. Since seeing how well yours is doing (originally from us), last summer, he has been reminded of how ours should be looking and hasn't left off badgering me (always very nice about it but unstoppable).

So I weeded under the bay tree, where it is never very wet. The bay is so satisfying – a beautiful shape and that rich and cheerful shade of yellowish green that has become more widely applied as bay green. Under it are mostly cyclamen but the area seems to require more frequent weeding than almost any other. There is quite a carpet of dead bay leaves, which don't worry me at this season and they weaken any grass weeds that penetrate.

I always like to give an area like this the personal treatment, from time to time (not every time), as I can see, interpret and

292

decide, as the owner is in a better position to do than anyone else. A weeding job, on your knees so that your eyes are close to the operation, concentrates the attention. We have here a sisyrinchium species with leaves that look important, growing in tufted fans. No one would dream of weeding such a plant out but I know it to be exceeding dull, with tiny bluish flowers that you scarcely notice. New seedlings keep appearing and I shall be extracting them to my last weeding day.

There are crowds of ivy seedlings – the wild *Hedera helix* – which one needs always to be at before they start running and rooting as they go. I have a weak spot for ivy, as I would expect you to. Its foliage is so glossy and rich on mature specimens, of which I allow a number, mostly on ash trees, which have a light, thin crown of foliage; just what suits ivy best. Flowering time, in the autumn, is a festive occasion for many insects; a loud hum issues from a flowering ivy. And then there is the fruit (source of our weeding troubles), which is borne in handsome, domed clusters and adored, when ripening in February, by wood pigeons. These are not daintily built birds and it is laughable to hear them clapping their wings as they attempt to balance on a quite unsuitably weak twig, to reach the berries.

There was a surprising amount of *Oxalis corniculata* var. *atropurpurea* to be weeded out. It is insidious. I don't remember it being a serious nuisance, when I was young, and enjoyed it in steps and paving, as I still do. I was surprised to read in Will Ingwersen's book on alpines that it 'should be avoided like the plague', though he admitted that its bright yellow flowers against purple foliage were pretty. Lately, it has become increasingly aggressive and is a particular nuisance in pots and other containers on the nursery.

An odd weed to find under the bay was a large and healthy seedling of pendulous sedge, *Carex pendula*. Of course, in time it would grow far too coarse and unruly for polite company, which is expected near to one's front entrance, but I have left it for a while, anyway. In its present state, I like it.

Snowdrops are showing through and some crocuses, mainly the autumn-flowering *Crocus speciosus*; I don't see *C. tommasinianus* much, yet, though it'll be out before the end of next month, most likely. I'm giving an illustrated talk in the village, this evening, showing different aspects and areas of Dixter through the year, and there are some lovely crocus pictures – those by the front path taken on 28 February this year.

Your description of your party, with all the staff involved, sounded really good. There'll be no more parties here, yet awhile. In fact Christmas will be an unusually quiet affair. With the builders' trappings all in place and one side of the Great Hall removed, a great deal of cold gets in. They've made a huge partition to keep out the worst of the weather, but we're well aware of it. But there are islands of warmth and I'm writing in one of them.

Sunday 7 December

Pip returned triumphant from Holland, having secured the job he wanted. Five of them were being interviewed the same day. He can stay with Romke and Adriana until he's found lodgings, and will be going at the start of the year. I am so pleased for him. He is in Scotland now, but will be here for Christmas.

My village lecture was incredibly well attended, for a village function. Eighty chairs had been set out but in fact there were 150 in the audience. My last picture was of Fergus, wearing a Turkish cap and with a load of tools over his shoulder, caught on the wing.

Yesterday, we had a tree-planting ceremony on the village green, celebrating the Northiam Hort. Soc.'s 100th anniversary. The parish council, who have the say-so on this piece of land, said that the tree should be an oak. I thought a smaller tree would be more appropriate, as there are houses quite near by. However, an oak it was. Fergus prepared the site and all but completed the tree planting himself before the ceremony. About 60 gathered around, and at noon I wielded the ceremonial spade, saying that

I hoped I shouldn't be shot by the neighbouring property owner whose pretty front garden would be shaded out. The rector had been called in (why?) and read a passage from Isaiah mentioning trees and a couple of prayers, ditto. Then a blessing, and I hope everyone felt better. Afterwards, Fergus was finishing the job and the aforementioned house owner accosted him saying the tree was unsuitable and that she hadn't been consulted. It had nothing to do with him, of course, but I sympathize. Something like a walnut or a thorn would have been far more suitable.

I suppose this'll be my last letter of the year, which means of the series, but it does not mean that we shall stop writing to or telephoning each other. Just that we shall no longer be going public. I don't think that has inhibited us much. The main difference, from a totally private letter, is the extra explanatory matter that is necessary, as, in this letter, 'the autumn-flowering *Crocus speciosus*'. Obviously 'autumn-flowering' would be omitted in a wholly private letter, as we both know this perfectly well. Apart from that, perhaps the odd indiscretion had to be foregone, but nothing much.

Goodbye Beth.

Much love from Christo

—✿—

INDEX

GARDEN CONTACT DETAILS

THE BETH CHATTO GARDENS,
www.bethchatto.co.uk, Elmstead Market,
Colchester, Essex CO7 7DB tel: 01206
822007. Opens 1 March to 31 October,
daily 9am to 5pm (Sundays 10am to 5pm).

GREAT DIXTER,
www.greatdixter.co.uk, Great Dixter,
Northiam, Rye, East Sussex, TN31 6PH
tel: 01797 252878. Opens from March
to October from Tuesday to Sunday and
Bank Holiday Mondays (closed on all other
Mondays) from 11am to 5pm. Please go
online or call the gardens to check opening
times before setting off.

PICTURE CREDITS

The publishers would like to thank Steven
Wooster for all the images of The Beth
Chatto Gardens and Jonathan Buckley for
all the images of Great Dixter and for their
permission to reproduce the photographs in
this book.